EVERYMAN, I will go with thee,

and be thy guide,

In thy most need to go by thy side

JOHN ROBERT SEELEY

Born in London, 10th September 1834. Educated at City of London School and Christ's College, Cambridge; at the former he was chief classical assistant (1859), and in 1863 was appointed Professor of Latin at University College, London. He was Professor of Modern History at Cambridge, 1869–95, and was knighted (K.C.M.G.) in 1894. He died at Cambridge, 13th January 1895.

SIR JOHN R. SEELEY

Ecce Homo

INTRODUCTION BY
JOHN A. T. ROBINSON
M.A., PH.D., D.D.

Dean of Trinity College, University of Cambridge
Assistant Bishop of Southwark
Bishop of Woolwich, 1959–69

DENT: LONDON
EVERYMAN'S LIBRARY
DUTTON: NEW YORK

Introduction © J. M. Dent & Sons Ltd, 1969
All rights reserved
Made in Great Britain
at the
Aldine Press · Letchworth · Herts
for
J. M. DENT & SONS LTD
Aldine House · Bedford Street · London
First included in Everyman's Library 1908
Last reprinted 1970

232
SEE
7002533

NO. 305

SBN: 460 00305 4

INTRODUCTION

THE 1860s, like the 1960s, were a decade of religious ferment. Blow upon blow assailed the complacency of the traditional conservative establishment (though, in notable contrast with the 1960s, our author complained of the Church that 'under the present universal empire of public opinion it is so secure that even those parts of it seem indestructible which deserve to die'!). Scarcely had Bishop Samuel Wilberforce entered the lists in 1860 against Darwin's *Origin of Species* than *Essays and Reviews* let loose from within the Church itself the more insidious menace of biblical criticism. Two years later Bishop Colenso produced his book on the Pentateuch, which touched off a controversy that was to rumble for years. The year 1864 saw the English translation of Renan's *Life of Jesus*, and then in 1865 came *Ecce Homo: A Survey of the Life and Work of Jesus Christ*. It was published anonymously, not out of cowardice but to spare the feelings of the author's father, a pious Evangelical publisher.

It has been called the English Renan, but in fact it is very different. Of the latter's *Life of Jesus*, cruelly styled 'the Gospel in Dresden china', Schweitzer was to write in his famous *Quest of the Historical Jesus* that its portraits 'might have been taken over in a body from the shop window of an ecclesiastical art emporium in the Place St Sulpice'. He quoted a criticism of it that 'It lacks conscience', and added: 'There is a kind of insincerity in the book from beginning to end.' Whatever may be said of *Ecce Homo*, not even its worst enemy could accuse it of lacking conscience or sincerity. It is heavily—we may think over-heavily—endowed with both. Nor, as its subtitle suggests, is it in any true sense a life of Jesus. Nothing is said about his birth, development, death or reported resurrection. In fact it does not really fulfil the promise of its preface which, as prefaces have a habit of doing, attracted some of the critics' fiercest fire. In it the author said he had found himself obliged to reconsider the whole subject from the beginning, and placing himself in imagination at the time when he whom we call Christ bore no such name, but was simply, as St Luke describes him, a young man of promise, popular with those who knew him and appearing to enjoy the Divine favour, to trace his biography from point to point, and accept those conclusions about him, not which church doctors or even apostles have sealed with their authority, but which the facts themselves, critically weighed, appear to warrant.

But there is little or no tracing of Jesus' biography from point to point, and after the opening chapters his life virtually disappears behind his ethical teaching, treated far more moralistically than critically.

The offence of the book, which drew from the reviewers such epithets as 'revolting', 'painful', 'flippantly indecent' and provoked Lord Shaftesbury in an unguarded utterance to pronounce it 'the most pestilential book ever vomited from the jaws of hell', was its unrepentant humanism. But this was not humanism in its modern antichristian sense. It was a profoundly Christian humanism—approaching Christ from the human angle without for one minute denying the validity of the divine. Indeed the last words of the book, deliberately italicized, are '*out of heaven from God*'. There is no denial of the supernatural or the miraculous, and, in an unhappy phrase, the author talks of 'Christ's abstinence from the use of his supernatural power as a device by which he avoided certain inconveniences which would have arisen from the free use of it'. But it is the overmastering effect of a wholly human life shining and convicting in its own power which he sees as the 'moral miracle superinduced upon a physical one'.

It is this 'Enthusiasm of Humanity', the moral force of the spirit of a uniquely true humanity let loose upon the world in Christ, of which his entire book is a passionate—and protracted—advocacy. Ironically what strikes us today is not that he made Christ too human, but that he did not make him human enough. His Christ seems a pasteboard figure, in whose 'mode of thinking, speaking or action' 'no important change took place', and on to whom is loaded the often cloying rhetoric of the highest toned Victorian morality. That this is not simply a modern reaction may be judged from a sympathetic assessment that appeared within two years of publication: *The Credentials of Conscience: A Few Reasons for the Popularity of 'Ecce Homo'*. After saying of the book that he did not understand how its central figure could be 'in all points tempted like as we are', the anonymous critic concludes: 'I think it fails to bring before us "the man Christ Jesus"'—the very aim that the title *Ecce Homo*, 'Behold the Man', professes. And he goes on to advance the thesis that its success stems rather from the psychological needs which it met in middle-class nineteenth-century England: 'Much of the popularity of this book is, I think, owing to the fact that it meets in a most acceptable manner some of the special wants and tendencies of our day'—which he specifies as the demand for Utility, the cry for Authority, the claim for Rationality, the desire for Unity and the demand for Morality.

This, I think, is a percipient recognition. The real achievement of the book lay in the fact that it enabled Christ to come as the answer to the great inarticulate human questions of the 1860s. I recognize the same process at work in the reception of *Honest to God* in the 1960s—and the reviews, both abusive and effusive, have a strange familiarity. The danger is of course that each generation merely sees in Christ the reflection of its own face at the bottom of the well. None of us can avoid this totally, or Jesus would not be the Christ *for us*. The safeguard against such subjectivity must lie in the rigour of our historical criticism. And from this test the author of *Ecce Homo*, who turned out to be John Robert Seeley (subsequently Professor of Modern History at Cambridge University), does not emerge too well.

Seeley began life as a classicist (his first academic work was a commentary on Livy), and it is through classical rather than biblical spectacles that he reads the Gospels. It is partly that his book has the weakness as well as the strength of a layman's writing—trained theologians, like Lightfoot, Hort and Westcott who were later to be his colleagues at Cambridge, could not possibly have written of great New Testament categories like faith, holiness or the Spirit with such fuzziness as he did. But it is largely that the tools were only just becoming available which now enable us to see how uncritical was the historical perspective of one who accepted the canons of historical criticism. ('One of the least "scientific" books ever written on a historical subject', was how G. M. Trevelyan, a later holder of the same chair, described it.) His concept of the Christ who 'announced himself as the Founder and Legislator of a new state', universal in space and time, ignores not only the vital distinction between the Kingdom and the Church, but the entire background of late Jewish apocalyptic whose importance Schweitzer was later to isolate (and distort).

But it would be easy with hindsight simply to be critical. No one, after all, is now going to read Seeley for an introduction to the Gospels, which he constantly and mistakenly refers to as 'biographies'. Yet, after more than a century, his book stands as a milestone in the slow recognition, still not complete, that Jesus of Nazareth, whatever else may need to be said of him, was in every sense a man. Seeley had to fight what he himself called the prevalent feeling towards Christ among religious men of 'an awful fear of his supernatural greatness' and what a supporter called 'the fierce hatred' of the 'sole possessors of infallible truth'.

There are many things we take for granted which it needed courage in Seeley's day to see and to state. One of these, Sir Oliver Lodge, who wrote the introduction to the first Everyman edition, claimed was the inner, spiritual (as opposed to literalistic, miraculous) interpretation of the Temptations in the wilderness, which every sermon now presupposes. But it drew upon Seeley the horror of the reviewers as, still more, did his hint that Christ might have had ordinary (though still very Victorian) feelings about sex. The delicate suggestion that, confronted by the woman taken in adultery, he looked on the ground through embarrassment, provoked the comment from *The Quarterly Review*: 'The coarseness and latitude of the interpretation was never, we believe, exceeded by any comment which was not designed to be profane.' Another anonymous pamphleteer, who complains of the 'indecorous, to to say indecent, mode of writing about our blessed Saviour', is reduced to speechlessness by some apparently innocuous words written in connection with Mary Magdalen: 'It is commonly by love itself that men learn the sacredness of love. Yet, though Christ never entered the realm of sexual love, this sacredness seems to have been felt by him far more deeply than by other men.' 'Comment', he adds, 'on this humanitarian idea is superfluous'!

Poor Seeley. His whole style shows him to have been decorous and even pompous to a degree. (Jesus' words to Zacchaeus that he must dine at his house that day become 'he informed Zacchaeus of his intention to visit

Introduction

him, and signified his pleasure that a banquet should be instantly prepared'!) Yet his book is full of noble and striking phrases (we owe to him 'the royalty of inward happiness'), and I would end with a fine passage, on the tendency of men to build shrines to the prophets they killed, which may stand as a fitting memorial to 'the freedom and the freshness' with which Seeley struck at least one of his contemporaries:

The glory of the original man is this, that he does not take his virtues and his views of things at second hand, but he draws wisdom fresh from nature and from the inspiration within him. To the majority in every age, that is, to the superficial and the feeble, such originality is alarming, perplexing, fatiguing. They unite to crush the innovator. But it may be that by his own energy and by the assistance of his followers he proves too strong for them. Gradually, about the close of his career, or, it may be, after it, they are compelled to withdraw their opposition and to imitate the man whom they had denounced. They are compelled to do that which is most frightful to them, to abandon their routine. And then there occurs to them a thought which brings inexpressible relief. Out of the example of the original man they can make a new routine. They may imitate him in everything except his originality. For one routine is as easy to pace as another. What they dread is the necessity of originating, the fatigue of being really alive.

JOHN A. T. ROBINSON

September 1969

Bibliography

WORKS. *Ecce Homo: A Survey of the Life and Work of Jesus Christ*, 1865; *Life and Times of Stein; or Germany and Prussia in the Napoleonic Age*, 1878; *Natural Religion*, 1882; *The Expansion of England*, 1883; *A Short History of Napoleon the First*, 1886; *Goethe*, 1894; *The Growth of British Policy*, 1895; *Introduction to Political Science*, 1896.

Seeley contributed numerous articles on religious, historical, political and educational subjects to *Macmillan's Magazine* and various learned journals.

BIOGRAPHY. E. A. Abbott, 'Professor Sir John Seeley', *City of London School Magazine*, April 1895; J. W. Hales, 'Professor Sir John Seeley', *Christ's College Magazine*, Lent Term, 1895; J. Venn, 'Some Personal Reminiscences of J. R. Seeley', *The Caian* (Cambridge), IV, 1895; H. A. L. Fisher, 'Sir John Seeley', *Fortnightly Review*, LXVI, 1896; M. Todhunter, 'Sir John Seeley', *Westminster Review*, CXLVI, 1896. *See also* Sir Walter Besant, *Autobiography*, 1902; L. Creighton, *Life and Letters of Mandell Creighton*, 1904; O. Browning, *Memoirs of Sixty Years*, 1910; G. A. Rein, *Sir John Robert Seeley, eine Studie über den Historiker*, 1912; C. A. Bodelsen, *Studies in Mid-Victorian Imperialism*, Copenhagen, 1924; R. H. Murray, *Studies in the English social and political thinkers of the 19th century*, 1929; R. T. Shannon, 'John Robert Seeley and the Idea of a National Church. A Study in Churchmanship, Historiography and Politics', in *Ideas and Institutions of Victorian Britain. Essays in honour of George Kitson Clark*, edited by R. Robson, 1967.

CONTENTS

	PAGE
Introduction by John A. T. Robinson	v

FIRST PART

CHAP.		
I.	THE BAPTIST	1
II.	THE TEMPTATION	7
III.	THE KINGDOM OF GOD	14
IV.	CHRIST'S ROYALTY	24
V.	CHRIST'S CREDENTIALS	33
VI.	CHRIST'S WINNOWING FAN	42
VII.	CONDITIONS OF MEMBERSHIP IN CHRIST'S KINGDOM	55
VIII.	BAPTISM	67
IX.	REFLECTIONS ON THE NATURE OF CHRIST'S SOCIETY	72

SECOND PART

CHRIST'S LEGISLATION

X.	CHRIST'S LEGISLATION COMPARED WITH PHILOSOPHIC SYSTEMS	86
XI.	THE CHRISTIAN REPUBLIC	96
XII.	UNIVERSALITY OF THE CHRISTIAN REPUBLIC	102
XIII.	THE CHRISTIAN A LAW TO HIMSELF	114
XIV.	THE ENTHUSIASM OF HUMANITY	125
XV.	THE LORD'S SUPPER	138
XVI.	POSITIVE MORALITY	144
XVII.	THE LAW OF PHILANTHROPY	152
XVIII.	THE LAW OF EDIFICATION	162
XIX.	THE LAW OF MERCY	181
XX.	THE LAW OF MERCY (*continued*)	194
XXI.	THE LAW OF RESENTMENT	207
XXII.	THE LAW OF FORGIVENESS	225
XXIII.	THE LAW OF FORGIVENESS (*continued*)	241
XXIV.	CONCLUSION	252

'Auctor nominis ejus Christus Tiberio imperitante per procuratorem Pontium Pilatum supplicio affectus erat.'

TACIT. *Ann.* I. 15

PREFACE
TO THE FIRST EDITION

Those who feel dissatisfied with the current conceptions of Christ, if they cannot rest content without a definite opinion, may find it necessary to do what to persons not so dissatisfied it seems audacious and perilous to do. They may be obliged to reconsider the whole subject from the beginning, and placing themselves in imagination at the time when he whom we call Christ bore no such name, but was simply, as St Luke describes him, a young man of promise, popular with those who knew him and appearing to enjoy the Divine favour, to trace his biography from point to point, and accept those conclusions about him, not which church doctors or even apostles have sealed with their authority, but which the facts themselves, critically weighed, appear to warrant.

This is what the present writer undertook to do for the satisfaction of his own mind, and because, after reading a good many books on Christ, he felt still constrained to confess that there was no historical character whose motives, objects and feelings remained so incomprehensible to him. The inquiry which proved serviceable to himself may chance to be useful to others.

What is now published is a fragment. No theological questions whatever are here discussed. Christ, as the creator of modern theology and religion, will make the subject of another volume, which, however, the author does not hope to publish for some time to come. In the meanwhile he has endeavoured to furnish an answer to the question: What was Christ's object in founding the Society which is called by his name, and how is it adapted to attain that object?

ECCE HOMO

FIRST PART

CHAPTER I

THE BAPTIST

THE CHRISTIAN CHURCH sprang from a movement which was not begun by Christ. When he appeared upon the scene the first wave of this movement had already passed over the surface of the Jewish nation. He found their hearts recently stirred by thoughts and hopes which prepared them to listen to his words. It is indeed true that not Judæa only but the whole Roman Empire was in a condition singularly favourable to the reception of a doctrine and an organisation such as that of the Christian Church. The drama of ancient society had been played out; the ancient city life, with the traditions and morality belonging to it, was obsolete; a vast empire, built upon the ruins of so many nationalities and upon the disgrace of so many national gods, demanded new usages and new objects of worship; a vast peace, where war between neighbouring cities had been the accustomed condition of life and the only recognised teacher of virtue, called for a new morality. There was a clear stage, as it afterwards appeared, for a Universal Church. But Palestine was not only ready to receive such an innovation, but prepared, even before the predestined Founder appeared, to make more or less abortive essays towards it. At the moment of his almost unobserved entrance, the whole nation were intent upon the career of one who was attempting in an imperfect manner that which Christ afterwards fully accomplished.

It was the glory of John the Baptist to have successfully revived the function of the prophet. For several centuries the function had remained in abeyance. It had become a remote, though it was still a fondly-cherished, tradition that there had been a time when the nation had received guidance from commissioned representatives of its invisible King. We possess still the utterances of many of these prophets, and when we consider the age in which they were delivered, we can clearly perceive that no more precious treasure was ever bestowed upon a nation than these oracles of God which were committed to the Jews. They unite in what was then the most effective way all that is highest in poetry and most fundamental in political science with what is most practical in philosophy and most inspiring in religion. But prophecy was one of those gifts which, like poetry or high art, are particularly apt to die out under change of times. Several centuries had succeeded each other which were all alike incapable of producing it. When John the Baptist appeared, not the oldest man in Palestine could remember to have spoken even in his earliest childhood with any man who had seen a prophet. The ancient scrolls remained, as amongst ourselves those Gothic cathedrals remain, of which we may produce more or less faithful imitations, but to the number of which we shall never add another. In these circumstances it was an occurrence of the first magnitude, more important far than war or revolution, when a new prophet actually appeared. John the Baptist defied all the opposition of those *scribes*, who in the long silence of the prophetic inspiration had become the teachers of the nation, and who resisted him with the conservatism of lawyers united to the bigotry of priests. He made his way back to the hidden fountains; and received at last that national acknowledgment which silenced even these professional jealousies, that irresistible voice of the people in which the Jew was accustomed to hear the voice of God. Armed with the prophetic authority, he undertook a singular enterprise, of which probably most of those who witnessed it died without suspecting the importance, but which we can see to have been the foundation of the Universal Church.

The Baptist

There may have been many who listened with awe to his prophetic summons, and presented themselves as candidates for his baptism in implicit faith that the ordinance was divine, who nevertheless in after years asked themselves what purpose it had served. It was a solemn scene doubtless, when crowds from every part of Palestine gathered by the side of Jordan, and there renewed, as it were, the covenant made between their ancestor and Jehovah. It seemed the beginning of a new age, the restoration of the ancient theocracy, the final close of that dismal period in which the race had lost its peculiarity, had taken a varnish of Greek manners, and had contributed nothing but a few dull chapters of profane history, filled with the usual chaos of faction fights, usurpations, royal crimes, and outbreaks, blind and brave, of patriotism and the love of liberty. But many of those who witnessed the scene and shared in the enthusiasm which it awakened must have remembered it in later days as having inspired hopes which had not been realised. It must have seemed to many that the theocracy had not in fact been restored, that the old routine had been interrupted only for a moment, that the baptised nation had speedily contracted new pollution, and that no deliverance had been wrought from the "wrath to come." And they may have asked in doubt, Is God so little parsimonious of His noblest gift, as to waste upon a doomed generation that which He did not vouchsafe to many nobler generations that had preceded them, and to send a second and far greater Elijah to prophesy in vain?

But if there were such persons, they were ignorant of one important fact. John the Baptist was like the Emperor Nerva. In his career it was given him to do two things—to inaugurate a new régime, and also to nominate a successor who was far greater than himself. And by this successor his work was taken up, developed, completed, and made permanent; so that, however John may have seemed to his own generation to have lived in vain, and those scenes on the banks of Jordan to have been the delusive promise of a future that was never to be, at the distance of near two thousand years he appears not less but far greater than he appeared to his contemporaries, and all that his baptism promised to do appears utterly insignificant compared with what it has actually done.

The Baptist addressed all who came to him in the same stern tone of authority. Young and old gathered round him, and among them must have been many whom he had known in earlier life, and some to whom he had been taught to look up to with humility and respect. But in his capacity of prophet he made no distinction. All alike he exhorted to repentance; all alike he found courage to baptise. In a single case, however, his confidence failed him. There appeared among the candidates a young man of nearly his own age, who was related to his family. We must suppose that he had had personal intercourse with Christ before; for though one of our authorities represents John as saying that he knew him not except by the supernatural sign that pointed him out at his baptism, yet we must interpret this as meaning only that he did not before know him for his successor. For it appears that before the appearance of the sign John had addressed Christ with expressions of reverence, and had declared himself unfit to baptise him. After this meeting we are told that on several occasions he pointed out Christ as the hope of the nation, as destined to develop the work he himself had begun into something far more memorable, and as so greatly superior to himself, that, to repeat his emphatic words, he was not worthy to untie his shoe.

Now, before we enter into an examination of Christ's own public career, it will be interesting to consider what definite qualities this contemporary and sagacious observer remarked in him, and exactly what he expected him to do. The Baptist's opinion of Christ's character then is summed up for us in the title he gave him—the Lamb of God taking away the sins of the world. There seems to be in the last part of this description an allusion to the usages of the Jewish sacrificial system, and in order to explain it fully it would be necessary to anticipate much that will come more conveniently later in this treatise. But when we remember that the Baptist's mind was doubtless full of imagery drawn from the Old Testament,

The Baptist

and that the conception of a lamb of God makes the subject of one of the most striking of the Psalms, we shall perceive what he meant to convey by this phrase. The Psalmist describes himself as one of Jehovah's flock, safe under His care, absolved from all anxieties by the sense of His protection, and gaining from this confidence of safety the leisure to enjoy without satiety all the simple pleasures which make up life, the freshness of the meadow, the coolness of the stream. It is the most complete picture of happiness that ever was or can be drawn. It represents that state of mind for which all alike sigh, and the want of which makes life a failure to most; it represents that *Heaven* which is everywhere if we could but enter it, and yet almost nowhere because so few of us can. The two or three who win it may be called victors in life's conflict; to them belongs the *regnum et diadema tutum*. They may pass obscure lives in humble dwellings, or like Fra Angelico in a narrow monastic cell, but they are vexed with no flap of unclean wings about the ceiling. From some such humble dwelling Christ came to receive the prophet's baptism. The Baptist was no lamb of God. He was a wrestler with life, one to whom peace of mind does not come easily, but only after a long struggle. His restlessness had driven him into the desert, where he had contended for years with thoughts he could not master, and from whence he had uttered his startling alarum to the nation. He was among the dogs rather than among the lambs of the Shepherd. He recognised the superiority of him whose confidence had never been disturbed, whose steadfast peace no agitations of life had ever ruffled. He did obeisance to the royalty of inward happiness.

One who was to earn the name of Saviour of mankind had need of this gift more than of any other. He who was to reconcile God and man needed to be first at peace himself. The door of heaven, so to speak, can be opened only from within. Such then was the impression of Christ's character which the Baptist formed. What now did he expect him to do?

He said that Christ bore a fan in his hand, with which

he would winnow the nation, gathering the good around him, separating and rejecting the bad. We shall find occasion soon to speak of this more particularly; at present let us remark that it shows us what course the Baptist imagined that the movement he had commenced would take. He had renewed the old theocratic covenant with the nation. But not all the nation was fit to remain in such a covenant. A sifting was necessary; from the approaching downfall of the Jewish nationality, from the wrath to come, an election should be rescued who should perpetuate the covenant. It is superfluous to remark how just this anticipation was, and how precisely it describes Christ's work, which consisted in collecting all the better spirits of the nation, and bringing them under that revised covenant which we call Christianity, and which survived and diffused itself after the fall of the Temple.

Further, Christ was to baptise with a holy spirit and with fire. John felt his own baptism to have something cold and negative about it. It was a renouncing of definite bad practices. The soldier bound himself to refrain from violence, the tax-gatherer from extortion. But more than this was wanting. It was necessary that an enthusiasm should be kindled. The phrase " baptise with fire " seems at first sight to contain a mixture of metaphors. Baptism means cleansing, and fire means warmth. How can warmth cleanse? The answer is that *moral* warmth does cleanse. No heart is pure that is not passionate; no virtue is safe that is not enthusiastic. And such an enthusiastic virtue Christ was to introduce. The whole of the present volume will be a comment on this text.

CHAPTER II

THE TEMPTATION

LET us delay a few more moments on the threshold of our subject, while we consider an incident which is said to have occurred just before Christ entered upon the work of his life.

Signs miraculous or considered miraculous are said to have attested the greatness of Christ's mission at the moment of his baptism. There settled on his head a dove, in which the Baptist saw a visible incarnation of that Holy Spirit with which he declared that Christ should baptise. A sound was heard in the sky which was interpreted as the voice of God Himself, acknowledging His beloved Son. In the agitation of mind caused by his baptism, by the Baptist's designation of him as the future prophet, and by these signs, Christ retired into the wilderness; and there in solitude, and after a mental struggle such as John perhaps had undergone before he appeared as the prophet of the nation, matured that plan of action which we see him executing with the firmest assurance and consistency from the moment of his return to society. A particular account, also involving some miraculous circumstances, of the temptations with which he contended successfully in the wilderness, is given in our biographies.

Miracles are, in themselves, extremely improbable things, and cannot be admitted unless supported by a great concurrence of evidence. For some of the Evangelical miracles there is a concurrence of evidence which, when fairly considered, is very great indeed; for example, for the Resurrection, for the appearance of Christ to St. Paul, for the general fact that Christ was a miraculous healer of disease. The evidence by which these facts are supported cannot be tolerably accounted for by any hypothesis except that of their being true. And if they are once admitted, the antecedent improbability of many miracles less strongly attested is much diminished. Nevertheless nothing is more natural than that exaggerations and even inventions should be mixed in our biographies with genuine facts. Now the miracles of the baptism are not among those which are attested by strong external evidence. There is nothing necessarily miraculous in the appearance of the dove, and a peal of thunder might be shaped into intelligible words by the excited imagination of men accustomed to consider thunder as the voice of God. Of the incidents of the temptation it is to be remarked that they are not described to us by eye-witnesses; they may have been communicated to his followers by Christ himself, the best of witnesses, but we have no positive assurance that they were so communicated.

On the other hand, a retirement of Christ into the desert, and a remarkable mental struggle at the beginning of his career, are incidents extremely probable in themselves; and the account of the temptation, from whatever source derived, has a very striking internal consistency, a certain inimitable probability of improbability, if the expression may be allowed. That popular imagination which gives birth to rumours and then believes them, is not generally capable of great or sublime or well-sustained efforts.

Wunderthätige Bilder sind meist nur schlechte Gemälde.

The popular imagination is fertile and tenacious, but not very powerful or profound. Christ in the wilderness was a subject upon which the imagination would very readily work, but at the same time far too great a subject for it to work upon successfully; we should expect strange stories to be told of his adventures in such a solitude, but we should also expect the stories to be very childish. Now the story of Christ's temptation is as unique as Christ's character. It is such a temptation as was never experienced by anyone else, yet just such a

The Temptation

temptation as Christ, and Christ in those peculiar circumstances, might be expected to experience. And further, this appropriateness of all the circumstances hardly seems to be perceived by the Evangelists themselves who narrate them. Their narrative is not like a poem, though it affords the materials for a poem; it is rather a dry chronicle.

Let us consider the situation. We are to fix in our minds Christ's peculiar character, as it has been gathered from the Baptist's description of him. His character then was such that he was compared to a lamb, a lamb of God. He was without ambition, and he had a peculiar, unrivalled simplicity of devout confidence in God. Such is the person to whom it is now announced by a great prophet that he has been called to a most peculiar, a pre-eminent career. But this does not fully describe the situation; a most important circumstance has yet to be mentioned. From the time of his temptation Christ appeared as a worker of miracles. We are expressly told by St. John that he had wrought none before, but all our authorities concur in representing him as possessing and using the gift after this time. We are to conceive him therefore as becoming now for the first time conscious of miraculous powers. Now none of our biographies point this out, and yet it is visibly the key to the whole narration. What is called Christ's temptation is the excitement of his mind which was caused by the nascent consciousness of supernatural power.

He finds himself in a barren region without food. The tumult of his mind has hitherto kept him unconscious of his bodily wants, but the overwhelming reaction of lassitude now comes on. And with the hunger comes the temptation, " Son of God, into whose service all natural forces have been given, command that these stones become bread." The possession of special power, and nothing else, constitutes the temptation here; it is the greatest with which virtue can be assailed. By it the virtuous man is removed from ordinary rules, from the safe course which has been marked by the footsteps of countless good men before him, and has to make, as it were, a new morality for himself. In difficult circumstances few men can wield extraordinary power long without positively committing crime. But here we see the good man placed in a position utterly strange, deprived of the stay of all precedent or example, gifted with power not only extraordinary but supernatural and unlimited, and thrown for his morality entirely upon the instinct of virtue within him. Philosophers had imagined some such situation, and had presented it under the fable of the ring of Gyges, but with them the only question was whether distinctions of right and wrong would not vanish altogether in such circumstances. The question by which Christ's mind was perplexed was far different; it was what newer and stricter obligations are involved in the possession of new powers.

A strange, and yet, given the exceptional circumstances, a most natural and necessary temptation. Still more unique, and yet at the same time natural, is Christ's resistance to it. Unique by its elevation, and natural by its appropriateness to his character. He is awe-struck rather than elated by his new gifts; he declines to use for his own convenience what he regards as a sacred deposit committed to him for the good of others. In his extreme need he prefers to suffer rather than to help himself from resources which he conceives placed in his hands in trust for the kingdom of God. Did ever inventor or poet dare to picture to himself a self-denial like this? But, on the other hand, what course could so exactly suit the character of Christ as the Baptist painted it? What answer could more exquisitely become the Lamb of God than that quotation—" Man doth not live by bread only, but by every word that proceeds out of the mouth of God "? Is it not substantially the same as that which the Psalmist uses in the very psalm in which he pictures himself as one of God's lambs, " He prepareth for me a table in the wilderness "?

Then follows a temptation, which again is extremely appropriate, because it is founded upon this very confidence of Divine protection. A new temptation arises by reaction out of the triumph of faith: " Throw thyself down, for it is written, He shall give His angels charge over thee, and in their hands they shall bear thee up." To no other person but Christ could such a temptation occur; to him, we may boldly say, such a temptation *must*, at some time, have occurred. And if in the Son of God there was filial reverence as well as filial confidence, it must have been resisted, as it is recorded to have been resisted, " Thou shalt not tempt the Lord thy God."

The third temptation is somewhat less easy to understand, but its appropriateness to the character and condition of Christ, and its utter inappropriateness to every other character and condition, are quite as clear. A vision of universal monarchy rose before him. What suggested such thoughts to the son of a carpenter? What but the same new sense of supernatural power which tempted him to turn stones into bread, and to throw himself into the arms of ministering angels? This, together with the Baptist's predictions, and those Messianic predictions of the ancient prophets, on which we can imagine that he had been intensely brooding, might naturally suggest such an imagination. He pictured himself enthroned in Jerusalem as Messiah, and the gold of Arabia offered in tribute to him. But, says the narrative, *the devil said to Him, If thou wilt fall down and worship me, all shall be thine.* This, at least, it may be thought, was not a temptation likely to overcome the Lamb of God. One remarkable for simplicity of character, one who was struggling with the fresh conviction that he was himself that Messiah, that beloved Son of God, whose glorious reign wise men had been permitted to foresee from a distance of centuries; was he, in the moment of his first enthusiasm, and fresh in the possession of sacred prerogatives of power, which he feared to use in self-defence even against famine, likely to do homage to a spirit of evil for that which he must have believed to be surely his by gift of God? We should remember that the report of these temptations, if trustworthy, must have come to us through Christ himself, and that it may probably contain the facts mixed with his comments upon them. We are perhaps to understand that he was tempted to do something which on reflection appeared to him equivalent to an act of homage to the evil spirit. What then could this be? It will explain much that follows in Christ's life, and render the whole story very complete and consistent, if we suppose that what he was tempted to do was to employ force in the establishment of his Messianic kingdom. On this hypothesis, the third temptation arises from the same source as the others; the mental struggle is still caused by the question how to use the supernatural power. Nothing more natural than that it should occur to Christ that this power was expressly given to him for the purpose of establishing, in defiance of all resistance, his everlasting kingdom. He must have heard from his instructors that the Messiah was to put all enemies under his feet, and to crush all opposition by irresistible God-given might. This certainly was the general expectation; this appeared legibly written in the prophetical books. And, in the sequel, it was because Christ refused to use his supernatural power in this way that his countrymen rejected him. It was not that they expected a king, and that he appeared only as a teacher; on the contrary, he systematically described himself as a king. The stumbling-block was this, that, professing to be a king, he declined to use the weapons of force and compulsion that belong to kings. And as this caused so much surprise to his countrymen, it is natural that he should himself have undergone a struggle before he determined thus to run counter to the traditional theory of the Messiah and to all the prejudices of the nation. The tempter, we may suppose, approached him with the whisper, " Gird thee with thy sword upon thy thigh; ride on, and thy right hand shall teach thee terrible things."

If this was the temptation, then again how characteristic of the Lamb of God was the resistance to it, and at the same time how incomparably great the self-restraint involved in that resistance! One who believes himself born for universal monarchy, and capable by his rule of giving happiness to the world, is entrusted with powers which seem to afford the ready means of attaining that supremacy. By the overwhelming force of visible miracle

The Temptation

it is possible for him to establish an absolute dominion, and to give to the race the laws which may make it happy. But he deliberately determines to adopt another course, to found his empire upon the consent and not the fears of mankind, to trust himself with his royal claims and his terrible purity and superiority defenceless among mankind, and, however bitterly their envy may persecute him, to use his supernatural powers only in doing them good. This he actually did, and evidently in pursuance of a fixed plan; he persevered in this course, although politically, so to speak, it was fatal to his position, and though it bewildered his most attached followers; but by doing so he raised himself to a throne on which he has been seated for nigh two thousand years, and gained an authority over men greater far than they have allowed to any legislator, greater than prophecy had ever attributed to the Messiah himself.

As the time of his retirement in the wilderness was the season in which we may suppose the plan of his subsequent career was formed, and the only season in which he betrayed any hesitation or mental perplexity, it is natural to suppose that he formed this particular determination at this time; and, if so, the narrative gains completeness and consistency by the hypothesis that the act of homage to the evil spirit to which Christ was tempted, was the founding his Messianic kingdom upon force.

Such then is the story of Christ's temptation. It rests, indeed, on no very strong external evidence, and there may be exaggeration in its details; but in its substance it can scarcely be other than true—first, because it is so much stranger than fiction, and next because in its strangeness it is so nicely adapted to the character of Christ as we already know it, and still more as it will unfold itself to us in the course of this investigation.

CHAPTER III

THE KINGDOM OF GOD

It is the object of the present treatise to exhibit Christ's career in outline. No other career ever had so much unity; no other biography is so simple, or can so well afford to dispense with details. Men in general take up scheme after scheme, as circumstances suggest one or another, and therefore most biographies are compelled to pass from one subject to another, and to enter into a multitude of minute questions, to divide the life carefully into periods by chronological landmarks accurately determined, to trace the gradual development of character and ripening or change of opinions. But Christ formed one plan and executed it: no important change took place in his mode of thinking, speaking, or acting; at least the evidence before us does not enable us to trace any such change. It is possible, indeed, for students of his life to find details which they may occupy themselves with discussing; they may map out the chronology of it, and devise methods of harmonising the different accounts; but such details are of little importance compared with the one grand question, what was Christ's plan, and throw scarcely any light upon that question. What was Christ's plan, is the main question which will be investigated in the present treatise, and that vision of universal monarchy which we have just been considering affords an appropriate introduction to it.

In discussing that vision we were obliged to anticipate. Let us now enquire, as a new question, what course Christ adopted when he mingled once more with his fellow-countrymen after his seclusion in the wilderness, and when he entered upon his public career? John's message to the nation had been, as we have seen, " The kingdom

The Kingdom of God

of God is at hand." Now this proclamation Christ took up from his lips and carried everywhere. For a while the two prophets worked simultaneously, though, as it seems, separately, and the preaching of the one was an echo of that of the other. Our first object, then, must be to ascertain what it was which they anticipated under the name of the kingdom of God. And to ascertain this we should not look onward to that which actually took place, but placing ourselves in imagination among their audience, consider what meaning a Jew would be likely to attach to the proclamation they delivered. The conception of a kingdom of God was no new one, but familiar to every Jew. Every Jew looked back to the time when Jehovah was regarded as the King of Israel. The title had belonged to Jehovah in a very peculiar sense; it had not been transferred to Him from the visible earthly king as in many other countries, but appropriated to Him so exclusively that for a long time no human king had been appointed, and that when at last the people demanded to be ruled by kings like the nations around them, the demand was treated by the most ardent worshippers of Jehovah as high treason against Him. And though a dynasty was actually founded, yet the belief in the true royalty of Jehovah was not destroyed or weakened, only modified by the change. Every nation of originality has its favourite principles, its political intuitions, to which it clings with fondness. One nation admires free speech and liberty, another the equality of all citizens; just in the same manner the Jews attached themselves to the principle of the Sovereignty of God, and believed the happiness of the nation to depend upon its free acknowledgment of this principle. But in the time of Christ all true Jews were depressed with the feeling that the theocracy was in a great degree a thing of the past, that they were in a new age with new things about them, that Greek and Roman principles and ways of thinking were in the ascendant, and that the face of the Invisible King no longer shone full upon them. This feeling had become so deep and habitual, that at a much earlier time the sect of the Pharisees had been formed to preserve the peculiarity of the nation from the inroad of foreign thought, and whatever ancient Jewish feeling remained had gathered itself into this sect as into a last citadel. In these circumstances the cry, " The kingdom of God is at hand," could not be mistaken. It meant that the theocracy was to be restored, that the nation was called to commence a new era by falling back upon its first principles.

In making this proclamation John and Christ did not assume any new character. They revived the obsolete function of the prophet, and did for their generation what a Samuel and an Elijah had done for theirs. As every great nation has its favourite political principles, so it has its peculiar type of statesmen. The nation which strives after individual liberty produces statesmen whose principal qualities are personal independence, moral courage, and a certain skill in quarrelling by rule. The pursuit of equality produces men of commanding will, who are able to crush aristocratical insolence, and by ruling the country themselves to prevent the citizens from tyrannising over each other. In like manner the peculiar political genius of the Jews produced a peculiar type of statesman. The man who rose to eminence in that commonwealth was the man who had a stronger sense than others of the presence, power, and justice of the Invisible King, and his great function was to awaken the same sense in others by eloquent words and decided acts. The Jewish statesman was the prophet, and his business was to redeliver to each successive generation, in the language likely to prove most convincing and persuasive to it, a proclamation of which the meaning always was, " The kingdom of God is at hand." The occasion of such proclamation might be peculiar and determine it to a peculiar form, but one general description of the Jewish prophet will apply to all of them, including John and Christ — viz. that he is one who, foreseeing the approach of great national calamities and attributing them to the nation's disloyalty to their Invisible King, devotes himself to the task of averting them by a reformation of manners and an emphatic republication of the Mosaic Law. All the Jewish prophets answer this description, whether the calamity they foresee be a plague

The Kingdom of God

of locusts, an Assyrian invasion, a Babylonish captivity, or a Roman conquest with the abomination of desolation standing in the holy place.

So far all prophets must of necessity resemble each other, but there are other matters in which it is equally necessary that they should differ. All prophets proclaim one eternal principle, and so far are alike; but as it is their duty to apply the principle to the special conditions of their age, they must needs differ as much as those conditions differ. As the prophet whose prophecy is new in substance is no prophet but a deceiver, so the prophet whose prophecy is old in form is no prophet but a plagiarist. And thus if the revived theocracy of Christ had been simply and merely the theocracy of Moses or David, his countrymen would have had as good a right to deny his prophetic mission as if he had preached no theocracy at all. To express the same thing in the language of our own time, the destinies of a nation cannot be safely trusted to a politician who does not recognise the difference between the present and the past, and who hopes to restore the precise institutions under which the nation had prospered centuries before. It is therefore most important to enquire under what form Christ proposed to revive the theocracy.

We have remarked that the ancient theocracy had passed through two principal stages. In the first the sense of Jehovah's sovereignty had been so absorbing that it had been thought impious to give the name of king to any human being. It is true that in this stage the notion of a human representative of Jehovah had been familiar to the nation. In their dangers and difficulties, when the sighs of the people were heard in heaven, the hand of Jehovah had seemed to them as mighty, and His arm as visibly outstretched, when He sent rescue through a legislator or judge in whom His wisdom dwelt, as when He divided the sea by immediate power. God's presence in men had been recognised as fully as His presence in nature. "When the people come to *me* to enquire of *God*," is a phrase used by Moses. But it had been held impossible to predict beforehand in what man God's presence would manifest itself. The divine inspiration which made a man capable of ruling had been considered to resemble that which made a man a prophet, or makes in these days a poet or inspired artist. And it was thought that to give a man the title of a king for life, and to transfer it regularly to his descendants without demanding proofs that the divine wisdom remained and descended with equal regularity, was equivalent to depriving Jehovah of His power of choosing His own ministers.

For a long time, therefore, a system of hero-worship prevailed. Whenever the need of a central government was strongly felt, it was committed to the man who appeared ablest and wisest. At length, however, the wish of the people for a government that might be permanent, that might hold definite prerogatives and be transferred according to a fixed rule, grew clamorous. Prophecy protested solemnly, but at last yielded, and an hereditary monarchy was founded. From this time forward until the Babylonish captivity Judæa was under the government of Jehovah represented by a king of the house of David. This new constitution had all the advantages which we know to attach to hereditary monarchy. The nation gained from it a tranquillity and security which were not interrupted, as before, at the death of each ruler, and the national pride and patriotism were fostered by the splendour and antiquity of its royal house. But the spirit of prophecy, which had at first protested against the change, continued to be somewhat perplexed by the new institution. The king, it reasoned, if he was not then a usurper of Jehovah's right, what was he? Could the country have two kings, and could loyalty to the one be reconciled with loyalty to the other? From this perplexity it found an escape by picturing the earthly king as standing in a peculiar relation to the heavenly. If the inspired hero or legislator of early times had been a favoured servant of Jehovah, the king must needs be more. He who, not on some special occasion but always, represented Jehovah, he who reflected not only His wisdom or justice but His very majesty and royalty in the presence of His subjects, the assessor of Jehovah's throne, the man that was the fellow of the Lord of Hosts, deserved to be called not His servant but His Son. But the more the dignity of a Jewish king appeared unutterable, the more unworthy of it did almost every individual king appear. The ancient judge had been all that he professed to be. His special endowment might be of a mean order, but it was undeniable. No one questioned the stoutness of Samson's sinews. But the king, of whom so much more was expected, might happen and did sometimes happen to have much less. The spirit of prophecy consoled itself for these failures by painting upon the future such a king as might satisfy all the conditions its enthusiasm demanded, and might deserve to sit by Jehovah's right hand and judge the chosen people.

These were the two forms which the ancient theocracy had assumed. Now under which form did Christ propose to revive it? The vision of universal monarchy which he saw in the desert suggests the answer. He conceived the theocracy restored as it had been in the time of David, with a visible monarch at its head, and that monarch himself.

We are concerned at present simply with the fact that Christ laid claim to the royal title, and not with the question what special powers he claimed under that title. The fact itself cannot be denied without rejecting all the evidence before us. His biographers regard him as king by hereditary right, and attach great importance to the proofs of his lineal descent from David. It does not appear, and it is not easy to believe, that he shared this feeling. But if not, it was because he believed his royalty to rest on a higher right. He could not derive honour from David because he held himself far greater than David. He was not king by a title derived from his ancestor, but by the same title as his ancestor. David had owed his sovereignty to that heroic will and wisdom in which the prophet Samuel had recognised a divine right to rule. The same title had Christ in a yet higher degree, and it had been recognised and proclaimed with equal solemnity by the greatest prophetic authority of the age. The prophetic designation which had fallen upon him had perhaps revealed to himself for the first time his own royal qualities, and the mental struggles which followed, if they had led him to a peculiar view of the kind of sovereignty to which he was destined, had left upon his mind a most absolute and serene conviction of his royal rights. During his whole public life he is distinguished from the other prominent characters of Jewish history by his unbounded personal pretensions. He calls himself habitually king and master, he claims expressly the character of that divine Messiah for which the ancient prophets had directed the nation to look.

So far, then, it appears that Christ proposed to revive the theocracy in the form which it had worn in the age of David and Solomon. A hero-king was to represent to the nation their Jehovah, and to rule in the indefeasible right of natural superiority. But was the new monarchy to be a copy of the old? A thousand years had passed since the age of David. A new world had come into being. The cities through which Christ walked, the Jerusalem at which he kept the annual feasts, were filled with men compared with whom the contemporaries of David might be called barbarous — men whose characters had been moulded during many centuries by law, by trade and foreign intercourse, by wealth and art, by literature and prophecy. Was it possible that the old heroic monarchy could be revived in the midst of a complicated and intellectual civilisation?

This difficulty does not seem to have occurred to Christ's contemporaries. The religious Jews were looking for the appearance of one who should be neither more nor less than David had been. They expected, it seems, to see once more a warrior-king, judging in the gate of Jerusalem, or surrounded by his mighty men, or carrying his victorious arms into the neighbouring countries, or receiving submissive embassies from Rome and Seleucia, and in the meantime holding awful communication with Jehovah, administering His law and singing His praise. It was natural enough that such vague fancies should fill the minds of ordinary men. It was as impossible for them to conceive the true Christ, to imagine what he

The Kingdom of God

would do or how he would do it, as it was impossible for them to fill his place. Meanwhile the Christ himself, meditating upon his mission in the desert, saw difficulties such as other men had no suspicion of. He saw that he must lead a life altogether different from that of David, that the pictures drawn by the prophets of an ideal Jewish king were coloured by the manners of the times in which they had lived; that those pictures bore indeed a certain resemblance to the truth, but that the work before him was far more complicated and more delicate than the wisest prophet had suspected.

It was in this way that the quarrel began between the Jews and their divine Messiah. Their heads were full of the languid dreams of commentators, the impracticable pedantries of men who live in the past. He was grappling with the facts of his age in the strength of an inspiration to which no truth was hidden and no enterprise impossible. Accordingly he appeared before them, as it were, under a disguise. He confounded their calculations, and professing to be the king they expected, he did none of the things which they expected the king to do. He revived the theocracy, and the monarchy, but in a form not only unlike the system of David but utterly new and unprecedented.

It is not uncommon to describe the Jews as having simply made the mistake of confounding a figurative expression with a literal one. It is said that when Christ called himself a king he was speaking figuratively, and that by " king " he meant, as some say, God, as others, a wise man and teacher of morality, but that the Jews persisted in understanding the expression literally. Such interpreters do not see that they attribute to intelligent men a mistake worthy of children or savages. We do not find in history whole nations misled, bloody catastrophes and revolutions produced, by verbal mistakes that could be explained in a moment. Again, they attribute to Christ conduct which is quite unaccountable. A wise man may at times dilate upon the authority which his wisdom gives him, and in doing so may compare himself to a king; but if he saw that his words were so grossly misapprehended that he was in danger of involving himself and others in political difficulties, he would certainly withdraw or explain the metaphor. But it is evident that Christ clung firmly to the title, and attached great importance to it. This appears in the most signal manner on the occasion of his last entry into Jerusalem. He entered in a public triumph preceded by those who hailed him as son of David, and when requested by those who thought the populace guilty of this very misconception of mistaking a wise man for a king to silence their enthusiastic cries, he pointedly refused. Again, it is clear that this assumption of royalty was the ground of his execution. The inscription which was put upon His cross ran, This is Jesus, *the King of the Jews*. He had himself provoked this accusation of rebellion against the Roman government; he must have known that the language he used would be interpreted so. Was there then nothing substantial in the royalty he claimed? Did he die for a metaphor?

It will soon become necessary to consider at leisure in what sense Christ understood His own royalty. At present it is enough to remark that, though he understood it in a very peculiar sense, and though he abdicated many of the functions of a sovereign, he yet regarded it as a royalty not less substantial, and far more dignified, than that of his ancestor David. We may go one step farther before entering into the details, and note the exact ground of the quarrel which the Jews had with him. He understood the work of the Messiah in one sense, and they in another, but what was the point of irreconcilable difference? They laid information against him before the Roman government as a dangerous character; their real complaint against him was precisely this, that he was *not* dangerous. Pilate executed him on the ground that his kingdom was of this world; the Jews procured his execution precisely because it was not. In other words, they could not forgive him for claiming royalty and at the same time rejecting the use of physical force. His royal pretensions were not in themselves distasteful to them; backed by a military force, and favoured by success,

The Kingdom of God

those pretensions would have been enthusiastically received. His tranquil life, passed in teaching and healing the sick, could not in itself excite their hatred. An eloquent teacher, gathering disciples round him in Jerusalem and offering a new and devout interpretation of the Mosaic law, might have aroused a little spite, but not the cry of " Crucify him!" They did not object to the king, they did not object to the philosopher; but they objected to the king in the garb of the philosopher. They were offended at what they thought the degradation of their great ideal. A king who neither had not cared to have a court or an army; a king who could not enforce a command; a king who preached and lectured like a scribe, yet in his weakness and insignificance could not forget his dignity, had his royal title often in his mouth, and lectured with an authority that no scribe assumed—these violent contrasts, this disappointment of their theories, this homely parody of their hopes, inspired them with an irritation, and at last a malignant disgust, which it is not hard to understand.

That they were wrong we are all ready to admit. But what Christ really meant to do, and in what new form he proposed to revive the ancient monarchy, is not so clear as the error of his adversaries. It is this which we proceed to consider.

CHAPTER IV

CHRIST'S ROYALTY

From the perplexity in which the Jews were involved by the contrast between Christ's royal pretensions and the homely tenor of his life, they sometimes endeavoured to deliver themselves by applying practical tests. They laid matters before him of which it might seem the duty of a king to take cognisance. By this means they discovered that he considered several of the ordinary functions of a king not to lie within his province. For example, they showed him some of the tribute-money, and asked him whether they ought to pay it. It was an obvious but at the same time a very effective way of sifting his monarchical claims. In the times of David the Jews had imposed tribute on the surrounding nations; it was a thing scarcely conceivable that in the age of the Messiah they should pay tribute to the foreigner. If Christ were a commissioned and worthy successor of the national hero, it seemed certain that he would be fired with indignation at the thought of so deep a national degradation. Strange to say, he appeared little interested in the question, and coldly bade them not be ashamed to pay back into Cæsar's treasury the coins that came from Cæsar's mint. If there be one function more than another which seems proper to a king, it is that of maintaining and asserting the independence of his realm; yet this function Christ peremptorily declined to undertake.

The ancient kings of Judah had been judges. Accordingly the Jews invited Christ more than once to undertake the office of a judge. We read of a civil action concerning an inheritance which was submitted to him, and of a criminal case of adultery in which he was asked to pronounce judgment. In both cases he declined the

Christ's Royalty

office, and in one of them with an express declaration that he had received no commission to exercise judicial functions.

The ancient kings of Judah had commanded the armies of the nation. It has been already remarked that Christ refrained in the most decided manner from undertaking this function. He expressly told Pilate that his kingdom was one the members of which did not fight, and, consistently with this principle, he forbade his follower Peter to take up arms even in order to save him from arrest.

What functions then *did* Christ undertake? We feel baffled at the beginning of our investigation, and can enter into the perplexity of the Jews, for those which we have enumerated are the principal functions of the ancient monarchy. All of them Christ declined, and yet continued to speak of himself as king, and that with such consistency and clearness that those who were nearest to his person understood him most literally, and quarrelled for places and dignities under him. Our perplexity arises from this: that whereas Christ announced the restoration of the Davidic monarchy, and presented himself to the nation as their king, yet, when we compare the position he assumed with that of an ancient Jewish king, we fail to find any point of resemblance.

But the truth is, as it appears after a little consideration, that in this rough comparison we have not sufficiently remembered the very peculiar view taken by the Jews—perhaps originally by other ancient nations—of royalty. It is possible, though it cannot be proved, that other nations, such as the Greeks, gave the name of king, in the first instance, to the god of the particular tribe, and afterwards transferred it to the human being who was supposed to be sprung from him, or beloved and inspired by him. But that among the Jews the notion of royalty was derived from that of divinity, seems clear. Human kings were appointed late in Palestine, but from a much earlier time the twelve tribes had lived under a monarchy. Their national Divinity had been their king. He had been believed to march at the head of their armies, and to bestow victory, to punish wrong-doing, and to heal differences when the tribes were at peace. The human king who was afterwards appointed was king but in a secondary sense, as the deputy of the Invisible King, and the inspired depositary of His will. Now it is important to remark that the human king represented the Divine King in certain matters only, and not in others. In the habitual acts of administration the king officiated, but there were some acts which Jehovah had done for the nation once for all, in which, as they were not to be repeated, none of the house of David could represent Him. Yet these acts were far greater than those which were regularly repeated, and displayed much more magnificently the royalty of Jehovah.

These acts were two—the calling of the nation, and the institution of its laws.

It was believed, in the first place, that the nation owed its separate existence to Jehovah's election of Abraham. The origin of other nations is lost in antiquity, but we can still trace the movements of the primitive shepherd who separated himself from his Chaldæan countrymen in obedience to an irresistible divine impulse, and lived a wandering life among his flocks and herds, ennobled by his unborn descendants as other men are by their dead ancestors, rich, as it were by a reversed inheritance from the ages after him, and actually bearing in his body Moses and David and Christ. His life was passed in mysterious communion with the Sovereign Will which had isolated him in the present and given him for compensation a home in the future.

This then was the first work which the Invisible King did for his subjects. He created the nation over which He was to reign. And the Jews in after times loved to speak of Him as the God of Abraham, Isaac, and Jacob, the God, that is, who had watched over the growth of a family into a nation, who had sealed that family for Himself and chosen the nation.

But this had been done once for all. The king of the house of David might represent to the people their Invisible King at the head of an army, or on the judgment-seat, but he could not represent to them the Founder of their commonwealth, the God who had been, as it were, their dwelling-place in all generations.

The covenant between Abraham and his invisible Guide had been simple. No condition but isolation and the sign of it, circumcision, had been imposed upon the first Hebrew; he received and obeyed occasional monitions, and he was blessed with a continually increasing prosperity. But the family grew into a nation, and then the covenant was enlarged. He who had called the nation now did for it the second work of a king and gave it a law. No longer special commands imposed on special persons, but general laws binding on every Israelite at all times alike, laws regulating the behaviour of every Israelite towards his brother Israelite and towards the Invisible King, laws which turned a wandering tribe of the desert into a nation worthy of the settled seat, the mountain fastness girdled with plain and cornfield and protected by Jordan and the sea, with which at the same time their Patron endowed them. In this work of legislation He was represented by Moses, of whom it therefore is written that " he was *king* in Jeshurun." This too was a work done once for all. No king of the house of David ever represented the Invisible King in His capacity of legislator. To study the divine law diligently and administer it faithfully was the highest praise to which a David or Hezekiah could aspire.

Thus the kings of the house of David were representatives of the Invisible King in certain matters only. The greatest works which can be done for a nation by its shepherd were quite beyond their scope and province.

We may now perceive how Christ might abdicate all the functions they had undertaken, and yet remain a king in a much higher sense than they, and in what respect the conception of the Messiah formed by the Jews of Christ's time might differ from that which Christ himself formed of him. It was the fatal mistake of the most influential body in the nation, that mixed body which is called the Scribes and Pharisees, to regard the Mosaic law as final and unalterable. They fell into the besetting sin of lawyers in all ages. Assuming therefore that nothing remained for the Messiah to do in legislation, they were driven to suppose that he too, like the ancient kings, would be but an imperfect representative of the Supreme King. And so they were driven to conceive him as occupied with administration or conquest, and, had their dream been realised, the Christ would have appeared in history far inferior to Moses.

On the other hand, Christ fixed his thoughts solely on the greater and more fundamental works of a heroic royalty. He respected the Mosaic legislation not less than his contemporaries, but he deliberately proposed to himself to supersede it by a new one promulgated on his own authority. He undertook the part rather of a second Moses than of a second David, and though he declined to take cognisance of special legal cases that were submitted to him, we never find him refusing to deliver judgment upon a general point of law. But he went still deeper, and undertook a work yet more radical than that of Moses. Not only did he boldly announce that the work done on Sinai was to be done over again by himself, but even the earlier and primary work of the Invisible King done in Ur of the Chaldees, the Call which had brought the nation into existence, he declared himself commissioned to repeat. In that proclamation, " the kingdom of heaven is at hand," we have hitherto seen only a restoration of the ancient theocracy, but a closer consideration will show us that the restoration was no mere resumption of the old system at the point at which it had been left off and in the original form, but a recommencement of the whole history from the beginning; not a revival of the old covenant but a new covenant, a new election, a new legislation, a new community. In the early time there came a voice to Abraham which said, " Get thee out of thy kindred, and from thy country, and from thy father's house, into a land of which I shall tell thee: and I will make of thee a great nation, and in thee shall all families of the earth be blessed." And now there was heard throughout Palestine a voice proclaiming, " There is no man that hath given up father, or mother, or house, or children, or lands, for my sake and the gospel's, but he

Christ's Royalty

shall receive an hundredfold more in this present life, and in the world to come life everlasting." The two calls resemble each other in sound; in substance and meaning they are exactly parallel. The object of both was to create a new society which should stand in a peculiar relation to God, and which should have a legislation different from and higher than that which springs up in secular states. And from both such a society sprang, from the first the ancient Jewish theocracy, from the second the Christian Church.

It is not now so hard to understand Christ's royal pretensions. He declined, it is true, to command armies, or preside in law courts, but higher works such as imply equal control over the wills of men, the very works for which the nation chiefly hymned their Jehovah, he undertook in His name to do. He undertook to be the Father of an everlasting state, and the Legislator of a worldwide society.

But this is not yet all. Christ was more than a new Moses and a new Abraham. For completeness we must here touch on a mysterious subject, of which the full discussion must be reserved for another place. Since the time of the Mosaic legislation a revolution had happened in the minds of men, which, though it is little considered because it happened gradually, is surely the greatest which the human mind has ever experienced. Man had in the interval come to consider or suspect himself to be *immortal*. It is surprising that the early Jews, in whom the sense of God was so strong, and who were familiar with the conception of an Eternal Being, should yet have been behind rather than before other nations in suspecting the immortality of the soul. The Greek did not even in the earliest times believe death to be annihilation, though he thought it was fatal to all joy and vigour; but the early Jews, the Legislator himself and most of the Psalmists, limit their hopes and fears to the present life, and compare man to the beasts that perish. How strange a revolution of thought when the area of human hopes and fortunes suddenly extended itself without limit! Then first man must have felt himself great. Then first, too, human relations gained a solidity and permanence which they had never before seemed to have; then the great and wise of a remote past started into life again; then the remote future moved nearer and became vivid like the present. This revolution had in a great measure taken place before the time of Christ. The suspicion of immortality appears in the later prophets, that suspicion which Christ himself was to develop into a glorious confidence.

This extension of the term of human life had a prodigious effect upon morality. We have spoken of Jehovah as legislating for the Jews. But a law is nothing unless it is enforced. Now in what way did Jehovah enforce the law He had given? In the first place by commissioned judges appointed from the people and inspired by Him with the necessary wisdom. But many crimes pass undetected by the judge, or his wisdom fails him and the wrong person is punished, or he takes a bribe and perverts justice. In these cases, then, what did Jehovah do? How did He enforce His law? Did He suffer the guilty man to escape, or had He other ministers of justice beside the judge and the king? It was supposed that in such cases He called in the powers of nature against the transgressor, destroyed his vines with hailstones and his mulberry-trees with the frost, or abandoned his flocks and herds to the Bedouins of the desert. But this theory was found to be unsatisfactory. Life is a short term. The transgressor has but to tide over a few years, and he is in the haven beside the just man, where the God of the living cannot touch him. And the Jew, watching the ways of Jehovah, could not but observe that this often happened. He was troubled to see over and over again prosperous villany carried to an honoured grave in the fullness of years and the satiety of enjoyment. Another conjecture was hazarded. It was said the bad man prospers sometimes, but he has no children, or at least his house soon dies out. Among Jews and Gentiles alike this theory found favour for a time—

> οὐδέ τι μιν παῖδες ποτὶ γούνασι παππάζουσιν
> ἐλθόντ' ἐκ πολεμοῖο καὶ αἰνῆς δηϊότητος.

Christ's Royalty

But again facts were too stubborn to be resisted, and the Psalmist is obliged to admit that here too the wicked prosper—" They have children at their desire, and leave the rest of their substance to their babes."

In these circumstances morality must have preserved but a precarious existence. Good and evil were almost on equal terms. The good man had sacrifices to make and trials to undergo, but little reward to expect. The bad man had the obvious gains of his villany, without any very serious danger of punishment. In these circumstances, also, the Kingship of Jehovah Himself must have wanted majesty. Profoundly as some Jews felt His greatness, the common feeling towards Him must have been one of far less awe than that which we feel for the Almighty God. For He seemed to have little power either to help His friends or punish His enemies. Human life being essentially short, He could but lengthen or shorten it a little. And the little power He had He seemed not to use.

The Jehovah, therefore, whom Christ came to represent, at a time when the immortality of the soul was a doctrine extensively received or favoured, was practically a much more powerful and awful King than He who had spoken by Moses, and His relation to His subjects was far more intimate. In the earlier time He had enforced His law mainly through the civil magistrate; His other judgments were exceptional and rare. But now the office of the civil magistrate retreated into the background, and Jehovah was conceived rather as holding His assize in that mysterious region which had recently become visible to men on the other side of death, as a distant land becomes visible on the other side of a river or strait,—the region which a Jew might compare to the Holy Land itself, the residence of Jehovah, parted from the desert and the unconsecrated earth by the stream of Jordan.

When Christ, therefore, declined the office of civil judge, it does not follow that he declined all judicial functions. Of the judgments of Jehovah we see that those pronounced by the magistrate formed now but a small part. And in declining these he took all the others, the diviner judgments, into his own hand. We cannot here delay upon this subject, but the fact appears upon the surface of our biographies that Christ, however carefully abstaining from the function of the civil magistrate, was yet continually engaged in passing judgment upon men. Some he assured of the forgiveness of their sins, upon others he pronounced a severe sentence. But in all cases he did so in a style which plainly showed, so as sometimes to startle by its boldness those who heard, that he considered the ultimate and highest decision upon men's deeds, that decision to which all the unjustly condemned at human tribunals appeal, and which weighs not the deed only, but motives, and temptations, and ignorances, and all the complex conditions of the deed—that he considered, in short, heaven and hell to be in his hand.

We conclude, then, that Christ in describing himself as a king, and at the same time as king of the Kingdom of God — in other words, as a king representing the Majesty of the Invisible King of a theocracy—claimed the character first of Founder, next of Legislator, thirdly, in a certain high and peculiar sense, of Judge, of a new divine society.

CHAPTER V

CHRIST'S CREDENTIALS

In defining as above the position which Christ assumed, we have not entered into controvertible matter. We have not rested upon single passages, nor drawn upon the fourth Gospel. To deny that Christ did undertake to found and to legislate for a new theocratic society, and that he did claim the office of Judge of mankind, is indeed possible, but only to those who altogether deny the credibility of the extant biographies of Christ. If those biographies be admitted to be generally trustworthy, then Christ undertook to be what we have described; if not, then of course this, but also every other, account of him falls to the ground.

When we contemplate this scheme as a whole, and glance at the execution and results of it, three things strike us with astonishment. First, its prodigious originality, if the expression may be used. What other man has had the courage or elevation of mind to say, " I will build up a state by the mere force of my will, without help from the kings of the world, without taking advantage of any of the secondary causes which unite men together—unity of interest or speech, or blood-relationship. I will make laws for my state which shall never be repealed, and I will defy all the powers of destruction that are at work in the world to destroy what I build "?

Secondly, we are astonished at the calm confidence with which the scheme was carried out. The reason why statesmen can seldom work on this vast scale is that it commonly requires a whole lifetime to gain that ascendency over their fellow-men which such schemes presuppose. Some of the leading organisers of the world have said, " I will work my way to supreme power, and then I will execute great plans." But Christ overleaped the first stage altogether. He did not work his way to royalty, but simply said to all men, " I am your king." He did not struggle forward to a position in which he could found a new state, but simply founded it.

Thirdly, we are astonished at the prodigious success of the scheme. It is not more certain that Christ presented himself to men as the founder, legislator, and judge of a divine society than it is certain that men have accepted him in these characters, that the divine society has been founded, that it has lasted nearly two thousand years, that it has extended over a large and the most highly civilised portion of the earth's surface, and that it continues full of vigour at the present day.

Between the astonishing design and its astonishing success there intervenes an astonishing instrumentality—that of miracles. It will be thought by some that in asserting miracles to have been actually wrought by Christ we go beyond what the evidence, perhaps beyond what any possible evidence, is able to sustain. Waiving then for the present the question whether miracles were actually wrought, we may state a fact which is fully capable of being established by ordinary evidence, and which is actually established by evidence as ample as any historical fact whatever—the fact, namely, that Christ *professed* to work miracles. We may go further, and assert with confidence that Christ was believed by his followers really to work miracles, and that it was mainly on this account that they conceded to him the pre-eminent dignity and authority which he claimed. The accounts we have of these miracles may be exaggerated; it is possible that in some special cases stories have been related which have no foundation whatever; but, on the whole, miracles play so important a part in Christ's scheme that any theory which would represent them as due entirely to the imagination of his followers or of a later age destroys the credibility of the documents not partially but wholly, and leaves Christ a personage as mythical as Hercules. Now the present treatise aims to show that the Christ of the Gospels is not mythical, by showing that the character

Christ's Credentials

those biographies portray is in all its large features strikingly consistent, and at the same time so peculiar as to be altogether beyond the reach of invention both by individual genius and still more by what is called the "consciousness of an age." Now if the character depicted in the Gospels is in the main real and historical, they must be generally trustworthy, and, if so, the responsibility of miracles is fixed on Christ. In this case the reality of the miracles themselves depends in a great degree on the opinion we form of Christ's veracity, and this opinion must arise gradually from the careful examination of his whole life. For our present purpose, which is to investigate the plan which Christ formed and the way in which he executed it, it matters nothing whether the miracles were real or imaginary; in either case, being believed to be real, they had the same effect. Provisionally therefore we may speak of them as real.

Assuming then that Christ performed genuine miracles, we have before us the explanation of the ascendency which he was able to exert. Yet it is important to consider in what precise manner men were affected by this supernatural power. By itself, supernatural power would not have procured for Christ the kind of ascendency he wanted, but exactly that ascendency which he so decidedly rejected. We have seen him in the wilderness, as it appeared, declining an empire founded on compulsion; and, if this be conjectural, at least there is no doubt that it was by declining to use compulsion that he offended his countrymen. Nor can we have any doubt that, his object being what we have ascertained it to be, he was right in resting as little as possible upon force. A leader of armies, a tyrant, may want physical force and may desire the means of crushing opposition; but a wise legislator would desire that the citizens should receive his laws rather because they felt the value of them than from terror; and a judge, such as Christ professed to be, would prefer to influence the conscience and arouse the sense of shame rather than to work upon the fear of punishment. Supernatural power was not invariably connected in the minds of the ancients with God and goodness; it was supposed to be in the gift of evil spirits as well as good; it was regarded with horror in as many cases as with reverence. And, indeed, when wielded by Christ, the first impression which it produced upon those who witnessed it was one of alarm and distress. Men were not so much disposed to admire or adore as to escape precipitately from the presence of one so formidable. The Gadarenes prayed Christ to depart out of their coasts. Even Peter made the same petition, and that at a time when he knew too much of his Master utterly to misapprehend his character and purpose.

It appears, then, that these supernatural powers freely used were calculated to hinder Christ's plan almost as much as to further it. The sense of being in the hands of a Divine Teacher is in itself elevating and beneficial, but the close proximity of an overwhelming force crushes freedom and reason. Had Christ used supernatural power without restraint, as his countrymen seemed to expect of him and as ancient prophecy seemed to justify them in expecting, when it spoke of the Messiah ruling the nations with a rod of iron and breaking them in pieces like a potter's vessel, we cannot imagine that any redemption would have been wrought for man. The power would have neutralised instead of seconding the wisdom and goodness which wielded it. So long as it was present it would have fettered and frozen the faculties of those on whom it worked, so that the legislation which it was used to introduce would have been placed on the same footing as the commands of a tyrant, and, on the other hand, as soon as it was removed, the legislation and it would have passed into oblivion together.

We have anticipated in a former chapter the means by which Christ avoided this result. He imposed upon himself a strict restraint in the use of his supernatural powers. He adopted the principle that he was not sent to destroy men's lives but to save them, and rigidly abstained in practice from inflicting any kind of damage or harm. In this course he persevered so steadily that it became generally understood. Every one knew that this *king*, whose royal pretensions were so prominent, had

Christ's Credentials

an absolutely unlimited patience, and that he would endure the keenest criticism, the bitterest and most malignant personal attacks. Men's mouths were opened to discuss his claims and character with entire freedom; so far from regarding him with that excessive fear which might have prevented them from receiving his doctrine intelligently, they learnt gradually to treat him, even while they acknowledged his extraordinary power, with a reckless animosity which they would have been afraid to show towards an ordinary enemy. With curious inconsistency they openly charged him with being leagued with the devil; in other words, they acknowledged that he was capable of boundless mischief, and yet they were so little afraid of him that they were ready to provoke him to use his whole power against themselves. The truth was, that they believed him to be disarmed by his own deliberate resolution, and they judged rightly. He punished their malice only by verbal reproofs, and they gradually gathered courage to attack the life of one whose miraculous powers they did not question.

Meantime, while this magnanimous self-restraint saved him from false friends and mercenary or servile flatterers, and saved the kingdom he founded from the corruption of self-interest and worldliness, it gave him a power over the good such as nothing else could have given. For the noblest and most amiable thing that can be seen is power mixed with gentleness, the reposing, self-restraining attitude of strength. These are " the fine strains of honour," these are " the graces of the gods "—

> To tear with thunder the wide cheeks o' the air,
> And yet to charge the sulphur with a bolt
> That shall but rive an oak.

And while he did no mischief under any provocation, his power flowed in acts of beneficence on every side. Men could approach near to him, could eat and drink with him, could listen to his talk, and ask him questions, and they found him not accessible only, but warm-hearted, and not occupied so much with his own plans that he could not attend to a case of distress or mental perplexity. They found him full of sympathy and appreciation, dropping words of praise, ejaculations of admiration, tears. He surrounded himself with those who had tasted of his bounty, sick people whom he had cured, lepers whose death-in-life, demoniacs whose hell-in-life, he had terminated with a single powerful word. Among these came loving hearts who thanked him for friends and relatives rescued for them out of the jaws of premature death, and others whom he had saved, by a power which did not seem different, from vice and degradation.

This temperance in the use of supernatural power is the masterpiece of Christ. It is a moral miracle superinduced upon a physical one. This repose in greatness makes him surely the most sublime image ever offered to the human imagination. And it is precisely this trait which gave him his immense and immediate ascendency over men. If the question be put—Why was Christ so successful? Why did men gather round him at his call, form themselves into a new society according to his wish, and accept him with unbounded devotion as their legislator and judge? some will answer, " Because of the miracles which attested his divine character"; others, " Because of the intrinsic beauty and divinity of the great law of love which he propounded." But miracles, as we have seen, have not by themselves this persuasive power. That a man possesses a strange power which I cannot understand is no reason why I should receive his words as divine oracles of truth. The powerful man is not of necessity also wise; his power may terrify, but not convince. On the other hand, the law of love, however divine, was but a precept. Undoubtedly it deserved that men should accept it for its intrinsic worth, but men are not commonly so eager to receive the words of wise men nor so unbounded in their gratitude to them. It was neither for his miracles nor for the beauty of his doctrine that Christ was worshipped. Nor was it for his winning personal character, nor for the persecutions he endured, nor for his martyrdom. It was for the inimitable unity which all these things made when taken together. In other words, it was for this, that he whose power and greatness as shown in his miracles were overwhelming

Christ's Credentials 39

denied himself the use of his power, treated it as a slight thing, walked among men as though he were one of them, relieved them in distress, taught them to love each other, bore with undisturbed patience a perpetual hailstorm of calumny; and when his enemies grew fiercer, continued still to endure their attacks in silence, until, petrified and bewildered with astonishment, men saw him arrested and put to death with torture, refusing steadfastly to use in his own behalf the power he conceived he held for the benefit of others. It was the combination of greatness and self-sacrifice which won their hearts, the mighty powers held under a mighty control, the unspeakable condescension, the *Cross* of *Christ*.

By this, and by nothing else, the enthusiasm of a Paul was kindled. The statement rests on no hypothesis or conjecture; his Epistles bear testimony to it throughout. The trait in Christ which filled his whole mind was his condescension. The charm of that condescension lay in its being voluntary. The cross of Christ, of which Paul so often speaks as the only thing he found worth glorying in, as that in comparison with which everything in the world was as *dung*, was the voluntary submission to death of one who had the power to escape death; this he says in express words. And what Paul constantly repeats in impassioned language, the other apostles echo. Christ's voluntary surrender of power is their favourite subject, the humiliation implied in his whole life and crowned by his death. This sacrifice, which they regard as made for *them*, demands in their opinion to be requited by an absolute devotion on their part to Christ. Beyond controversy such was their feeling, and this feeling was the ground of that obedience to Christ and acceptance of his legislation which made the success of his scheme. If we suppose that Christ really performed no miracles, and that those which are attributed to him were the product of self-deception mixed in some proportion or other with imposture, then no doubt the faith of St. Paul and St. John was an empty chimera, a mere misconception; but it is none the less true that those apparent miracles were essential to Christ's success, and that had he not pretended to perform them, the Christian Church would never have been founded, and the name of Jesus of Nazareth would be known at this day only to the curious in Jewish antiquities.

We have represented Christ's abstinence from the use of his supernatural power as a device by which he avoided certain inconveniences which would have arisen from the free use of it. It is true that had he not practised this abstinence, his legislation could not have gained the worthy and intelligent acceptance it did gain; and by adopting this contrivance he triumphantly attained the object he proposed to himself. Still it was no mere measure of prudence or policy. Christ himself probably never thought of it as a contrivance or device; to him such self-restraint no doubt appeared simply required by duty, an essential part of fidelity to the commission he bore. And when we have investigated the character of Christ's legislation, we shall find that the great self-denial of his life, besides being a means of introducing his legislation, was the greatest of all illustrations of the spirit of that legislation. The kind of life he prescribed to his followers he exemplified in his own person in the most striking way, by dedicating all his extraordinary powers to beneficent uses only, and deliberately placing himself for all purposes of hostility and self-defence on a level with the weakest.

To sum up the results of this chapter. We began by remarking that an astonishing plan met with an astonishing success, and we raised the question to what instrumentality that success was due. Christ announced himself as the Founder and Legislator of a new Society, and as the Supreme Judge of men. Now by what means did he procure that these immense pretensions should be allowed? He might have done it by sheer power; he might have adopted persuasion, and pointed out the merits of the scheme and of the legislation he proposed to introduce. But he adopted a third plan, which had the effect not merely of securing obedience, but of exciting enthusiasm and devotion. He laid men under an immense *obligation*. He convinced them that he was a person of

Christ's Credentials

altogether transcendent greatness, one who needed nothing at their hands, one whom it was impossible to benefit by conferring riches, or fame, or dominion upon him, and that, being so great, he had devoted himself of mere benevolence to their good. He showed them that for their sakes he lived a hard and laborious life, and exposed himself to the utmost malice of powerful men. They saw him hungry, though they believed him able to turn stones into bread; they saw his royal pretensions spurned, though they believed that he could in a moment take into his hand all the kingdoms of the world and the glory of them; they saw his life in danger; they saw him at last expire in agonies, though they believed that, had he so willed it, no danger could harm him, and that had he thrown himself from the topmost pinnacle of the temple he would have been softly received in the arms of ministering angels. Witnessing his sufferings, and convinced by the miracles they saw him work that they were voluntarily endured, men's hearts were touched, and pity for weakness blending strangely with wondering admiration of unlimited power, an agitation of gratitude, sympathy, and astonishment, such as nothing else could ever excite, sprang up in them, and when, turning from his deeds to his words, they found this very self-denial which had guided his own life prescribed as the principle which should guide theirs, gratitude broke forth in joyful obedience, self-denial produced self-denial, and the Law and Law-Giver together were enshrined in their inmost hearts for inseparable veneration.

CHAPTER VI

CHRIST'S WINNOWING FAN

The first step in our investigation is now taken. We have considered the Christian Church in its idea, that is to say, as it existed in the mind of its founder and before it was realised. Our task will now become more historical and will deal with the actual establishment of the new Theocracy; but we shall endeavour to keep the idea always in view and sedulously to avoid all such details as may have the effect of obscuring it.

The founder's plan was simply this, to renew in a form adapted to the new time that divine Society of which the Old Testament contains the history. The essential features of that ancient Theocracy were: (1) the divine Call and Election of Abraham; (2) the divine legislation given to the nation through Moses; (3) the personal relation and responsibility of every individual member of the Theocracy to its invisible King. As the new Theocracy was to be the counterpart of the old, it was to be expected that these three features would be reflected in it. Accordingly we have found Christ undertaking to issue a Call to men such as was given to Abraham, to deliver a Legislation such as Israel had received from Moses, and to occupy a personal relation of Judge and Master to every man such as in the earlier Theocracy had been occupied by Jehovah Himself without representative.

Such was the plan. In proceeding to consider the execution of it, these three essential features will afford the means of a convenient arrangement, and the correspondence of the new Theocracy to the old in respect of them will afford a constant instructive illustration. Our investigation divides itself from this point into three parts. We shall treat in order the Call, the Legislation,

Christ's Winnowing Fan 43

and the Divine Royalty of Christ, and in proceeding now to consider the Call we shall ask the question, In what respect did the Call issued by Christ differ from that which came to Abraham?

The Call then which the first Christians received differed from that received by Abraham, in the first place, in this respect, that it did not separate them from civil society. Abraham was commanded to isolate himself, abandoning his family and his native country. The life he adopted was one which was possible in his age and country. All external authority whatsoever he threw off; his actions were controlled by no power except that invisible one which had decreed his isolation. In his case the problem of the connection between Church and State was solved in the most simple manner, namely, by the abolition of the State. There was but one Society, of which God was king, the patriarch being His deputy. What intercourse he occasionally had with the world outside his own pastoral encampment was not like the intercourse of one citizen with another, but consisted of formal negotiations or wars such as are transacted between states. Now the early Christians, it is true, compare themselves with Abraham in this respect. They call themselves strangers and pilgrims upon the earth, wanderers without a country for the present, but expecting one on the other side of death. Applied to them, however, these expressions are not literally true but metaphorical, and mean only that the secular states of which they were members did not excite their interest or their patriotism so strongly as the divine Society into which Christ had called them. All of them were members of some secular state as well as of the Christian Church; a complex system of obligations lay upon all of them already when the new Christian obligations were imposed, and their activity was confined by a multitude of prohibitions.

In this respect the Christian commonwealth was not only unlike the camp of Abraham but unlike the ancient theocracy at every period of its history. For the political organisation of the Israelites sprang up, as it were, in the bosom of the ecclesiastical one, and was never regarded as distinct from it. The ancient Hebrew never regarded himself as living under two laws, one human and the other divine. To him all law alike was divine, whether it punished theft or denounced death against idolatry. He believed both tables of the law to have been written with the finger of God. When he went before the civil tribunals it was " to enquire of God." But the Christian regarded the civil power of his time as external altogether to the divine society, and though he might be ready to recognise it as in some sense a divine ordinance and as having a right to his obedience, yet on the other hand it knew nothing of that other commonwealth to which he professed to belong, had no respect for its laws, and would barely tolerate its existence.

The divine Society had therefore to make its choice between declaring open war against the secular societies in the midst of which it was established, or refraining from all such acts as those societies would not allow. Following his principle of abstaining from force, Christ adopted the latter course. Now one principal thing no secular government would tolerate, namely, judicial tribunals and a penal administration independent of its own. We arrive therefore at the first distinguishing characteristic of the Society into which Christ called men. It was a Society whose rules were enforced by no punishments. The ancient Israelite who practised idolatry was stoned to death, but the Christian who sacrificed to the genius of Cæsar could suffer nothing but exclusion from the Society, and this in times of persecution was in its immediate effects of the nature rather of a reward than of a punishment. At first it may seem that a society could exert no strong effect upon mankind which contained no power of compulsion or punishment. But we are to remember what was said above of the judicial power of Jehovah under the old theocracy. That judicial power was exerted through the civil law courts, it is true, but also in another way. Jehovah was considered as judging in heaven as well as in the law court, and as punishing by providential visitations and by mysterious pains inflicted on the dead as well as by the hands of the executioners of civil justice. Now in relinquishing the ordinary and administrative punishments, Christ retained for his Society the supernatural ones. And, so long as faith in the truth of his words continued lively among his followers, the state he founded was not distinguished among the states of the world by laxity of obedience in its members; rather have these supernatural terrors and hopes, intimately blended with other motives of which a time will come to speak, excited in the Christian Church a more serious and enthusiastic loyalty than any secular commonwealth has known.

We have learnt then thus much of the nature of Christ's Call. When he went everywhere proclaiming the kingdom of God and summoning men to enrol themselves as members of it, he did not command them to abandon the national societies in which they were already enrolled. The Jew did not cease to be a Jew nor to yield obedience to Jewish and Roman authority, when he became a Christian; nor did he even cease to take an interest in national affairs. Particular Christians might do so and might merge all patriotic feelings in their devotion to the divine Society, but Christ himself never ceased to feel keenly as a patriot. What the Jew did on becoming a Christian was to enter into a new relation which was additional to those relations in which he stood already. Besides the authorities which he acknowledged before, he now acknowledged the authority of Christ; the law of Christ became binding upon him as well as the law of his country; and besides standing in awe of the civil judge and of the punishments he might inflict, he now stood in awe of Christ, whom he regarded as representing the supreme judicial majesty of Jehovah in the invisible world.

Such then was the nature of Christ's Call. We go on to consider who were the objects of it. Here again the Call of Abraham suggests by contrast a peculiarity in that uttered by Christ. In the former case one man only was called, in the latter all men whatsoever. The earlier Call was rigidly exclusive, the latter infinitely comprehensive.

This comprehensiveness may take us by surprise when

we consider the Baptist's anticipations of Christ's work. The baptism of John seems to have been absolutely comprehensive; all those who came John accepted. But he said in reference to Christ, " There stands one among you . . . whose *fan* is in his hand, and he will thoroughly purge his floor, and gather his wheat into the garner, but the chaff he will burn with unquenchable fire." It seems evident that the Baptist meant to warn those whom he had baptised without distinction or condition, that Christ's work would be more thorough and searching than his, and that he would apply a test of some kind, by which the insincere would be detected and separated from the good. It was the Baptist's belief that a divine judgment was impending over the nation, and he seems to predict that Christ would make a selection of the sounder members of the nation who would then be rescued from the catastrophe, while the others would be left to their fate. This prediction assuredly suggests to us a course of action different from that which Christ pursued. We do not at first sight discern the fan in his hand. We do not find him, as we might expect, discriminating the good from the bad, and honouring the former only with his call, but on the contrary we find him summoning all in the same words and with the same urgency. Nevertheless on a closer examination it will appear that Christ did perform this work of discrimination, and that in a very remarkable manner, and that no expressions could be more strikingly just than those in which the Baptist described it.

The difficulty of determining whether a man is or is not good has now become a commonplace of moralists and satirists. It is almost impossible to discover any test which is satisfactory, and the test which is actually applied by society is known to be unsatisfactory in the extreme. The good man of society is simply the man who keeps to the prescribed routine of what is commonly considered to be duty; the bad man he who deserts it. In order to arrive at this view men start from a proposition which is true, but they make the mistake of assuming the converse proposition to be true. It is true that the good

Christ's Winnowing Fan

man does good deeds, but it is not necessarily true that he who does good deeds is a good man. Selfish prudence dictates a virtuous course of action almost as imperatively as virtue itself; on the other hand, bad deeds may be caused by bad teaching, bad example or the pressure of necessity, not less than by a vicious disposition. And Christ showed throughout his life a remarkably strong conviction of this. He found society in Palestine in an especial degree wedded to the conventional standard. He found one class regarded with the most excessive reverence for their minute observance of proprieties, while those who sinned fell under a pitiless excommunication. But the winnowings of this social fan did not satisfy him. He was persuaded that it winnowed away much that was valuable, and he occupied himself with rescuing the outcasts who had been thus hastily rejected; much, on the other hand, which society stored up in its garner he vehemently pronounced to be chaff. What standard then did he substitute in the place of this conventional one which he repudiated? The society which he formed was recruited from all classes; no one was repelled on account of his past life; publicans and prostitutes were freely admitted into it, and men of blameless lives and bred in Pharisaic sanctity learned in Christ's circle to hold intercourse with those whose company they would earlier have avoided as contaminating. As we have seen, no one was excluded who did but choose to enter. Christ compared himself to a king who kept open house and surrounded his dinner-table with beggars from the highway. And yet in those who became members of the society, certain common qualities might be observed, and it will be generally admitted that they formed on the whole the sounder part of the nation. Doubtless there were traitors and unworthy members among them; Christ early remarked and illustrated by a striking allegory the impossibility of perfectly sifting the seed sown in the Gospel-field. Doubtless, also, the fan in special cases winnowed out some wheat, and there remained to the end in the Pharisaic party good men that were incurably mistaken. But on the whole a winnowing was accomplished; and almost all the genuine worth and virtue of the nation was gathered into the Christian Church; what remained without was perversity and prejudice, ignorance of the time, ignorance of the truth, that mass of fierce infatuation which was burnt up in the flames which consumed the temple or shared the fall of the Antichrist Barcochebah.

Some discriminating influence then was clearly at work, nor is it very difficult to discern its nature. Christ did not go out of his way to choose his followers; the Call itself sifted them; the Call itself was the fan he bore in his hand. For, though in form the same, it was in practical power very different from that Call which John had issued. Both John and Christ proclaimed the advent of a new divine Society, but John only proclaimed it as near, while Christ exhibited it as present, and laid upon those who desired to become members of it the practical obligations and burdens which were involved in membership. To obey John's call was easy, it involved nothing beyond submission to a ceremony; and when the prophet had acquired a certain amount of credit, no doubt it became the *fashion* to receive baptism from him. This being so, he may well have felt that his work was but skin deep; his prophetic appeals to the conscience had created a mighty stir but no real conviction, no division between the good and bad, no national repentance. Idle people resorted to his preaching for a new sensation, frivolous people sought excitement in his baptism. With that honest humility so characteristic of him he confessed, not precisely his failure, but the essentially imperfect and preliminary nature of his work. No Messiah, no prophet am I, he said. He said, I am a *voice*, a cry faintly heard in the distance; I command nothing; I exact nothing; I do but bid you be ready.

But after Aaron the eloquent speaker, there came the new Moses, the Founder and Legislator. To listen to him was no amusement for an idle hour; his preaching formed no convenient resort for light-minded people. His tone was not more serious than John's, and it was somewhat less vehement, but it was far more imperious and exacting. John was contented with hearers; when he had delivered

Christ's Winnowing Fan

his admonitions he relaxed his hold, and it was free to those who had listened to subside into the easy tranquillity which his eloquence had disturbed while it lasted. But Christ demanded *followers*, recruits for the great work he had in hand, settlers for the new city that was to be founded, subjects for the king he announced himself to be. Those who listened to him must be prepared to change all their prospects, and to adopt a new mode of life. The new mode of life was indeed not necessarily a hard one. Christ did not impose ascetic exercises upon his followers. He was an indulgent master, and for a considerable time those who enrolled themselves in the new Theocracy had no reason to dread any serious persecution from Jew or Roman. But he forewarned them that times would change in this respect, and in the meanwhile the devotion of a life to a new discipline, even though not a severe one, demands at least a certain power of self-devotion which many do not possess; and Christ's discipline was in fact harder to human nature than it seemed, for it demanded a certain moral originality and strenuousness of self-regeneration which men find in the long run more burdensome than the severest physical endurances and austerities. Clearly, therefore, Christ's Call imposed upon men the necessity of making a great resolution, of sacrificing a good deal. On the other hand, what did it offer? What equivalent could be expected by those who made the sacrifice? Perhaps those who gathered early about the Messiah might expect places and dignities in his kingdom, to sit on thrones judging the tribes of Israel. This was undoubtedly the current belief, and it may have led many to attach themselves to Christ from motives purely mercenary. But in a little time such adventurers must have remarked that in Christ's language which would strike them with a sudden chill. They must have felt their hopes gliding away beneath their feet as they listened. The sacrifices they had made were unquestionable; many had left their homes and adopted a wandering life with their master; they had joined a suspected sect, they were partisans of an extreme movement, they had placed themselves in opposition to the orthodoxy of the country. The risk they ran was certain, but the rewards they had expected in the coming kingdom of the Messiah were less certain. It would seem to them that Christ explained his promises away. The royalty which he professed to bear himself was to vulgar apprehensions a mock royalty. It had no substance of power or wealth; yet he continued to call it royalty. They would soon begin to suspect that the subordinate dignities in the new kingdom were of the same insubstantial character. And many of them would hear with bitter disappointment, and some with furious hatred, exhortations to humility, to contentment with a lowly place, from the lips of him whom they had expected to make their fortunes. In this way the interested and mercenary would fall off from him. The Call, which had acted as a test upon some directly by requiring from them an effort which they were not prepared to make, would winnow away others more gradually as soon as it was understood to offer no prospects which could tempt a worldly mind.

In this way, without excluding any, Christ suffered the unworthy to exclude themselves. He kept them aloof by offering them nothing which they could find attractive. And all those who found Christ's Call attractive were such as were worthy to receive it. Some made up their minds without hesitation. The worldly, the preoccupied turned away with peremptory contempt; a few of rare devotion closed with the Call at once. But the greater number were placed by it in a state of painful suspense and hesitation which lasted a long time. First, to understand distinctly what it was which was proposed to them; next, to make up their minds as to the character of him who made such novel proposals, and advanced pretensions so unbounded; all this cost them much perplexity. But when so much was done, and they had decided favourably to the Prophet and his Theocracy, then came the greater difficulty, that of resolving to embark in an enterprise so unprecedented even at the beck of one whom they acknowledged to hold a divine commission. To break with prejudice and with convention, to enter upon a great and free life, is not done until some doubts have been mastered

Christ's Winnowing Fan

and some coward hesitations silenced. In the midst of men who were in one stage or other of this mental conflict, Christ moved. His words spread around him a perpetual ferment, an ever-seething effervescence. Anxious broodings, waxing or waning convictions, resolutions slowly shaping themselves, a great travail of hearts, went on about him. An appeal had been made to what was noblest in each; each had been summoned to shake off routine and convention; some were gathering strength to accomplish the feat, some abandoning the attempt in despair. According to the issue of the conflict each man's worthiness would appear. This then was the winnowing which Christ did among men. The Call itself was in his hand as a fan.

Of this effect produced by his words he was fully conscious. He watched it with constant interest, and of his recorded sayings a large proportion are illustrative descriptions of the different effect of the Call upon different characters. At one time he described the ferment it produced and its gradual diffusion through the community by comparing the kingdom of heaven to leaven which a woman hides in three measures of meal until the whole is leavened. At another time he compares the Call (the Word) to seed sown in different sorts of ground, but bearing a prosperous crop in one sort only. To one class he found it was like a treasure hidden in a field, which not to lose a man sells all his property and buys the field; to another class it is an invitation which they decline with civil excuses. Thus it shows each man in his genuine character, and, on the whole, those who accept the Call and abide by it are worthy of it. Yet to this rule there are a good many exceptions. When the seed has been sown in the best ground, tares will spring up with the wheat; thrown in, as it were, by some spiteful neighbour. And when the winnowing has thus failed through mishap, we must not interfere further, says Christ; he will have no artificial winnowing by mere presumptuous private judgment of each other.

These are specimens of Christ's reflections upon the working of his proclamation. They offer nothing which need surprise us. Such a winnowing of men as he accomplished is not unique in kind. Every high-minded leader who gathers followers round him for any great purpose, when he calls to self-sacrifice and has no worldly rewards to offer, does something similar. He too in his degree winnows men. And therefore in tracing the history of many other movements which have agitated large numbers, we are often reminded of those parables of Christ that begin, " The kingdom of heaven is like—." If those parables are read together, they present an almost complete account of the ferment produced in a large and various society by a great principle presented to it impressively and practically. In all such cases each individual that comes within the influence may be said to pass an ordeal, and some characters come out from it vindicated that before were suspected to be worthless, and others are unmasked that had before imposed upon the world. But now what is the quality that carries a man through the ordeal? Can we find a name for it? It is, no doubt, neither more nor less than moral worth or goodness; but this is no reason why a more precise name should not be given to this particular aspect of goodness. For, in fact, all the good qualities to which we give names, as justice, temperance, courage, etc., are not so much parts of goodness as aspects of it, and no man can have any one of them without having in a degree all the others. What then shall we call goodness when it shows itself conquering convention, and unselfishly ranging itself on the right side in those crises when good and evil are most visibly opposed to each other?

The first Christians had manifestly occasion for such a word, and one came into use which may be said to have become a permanent addition to the moral vocabulary of the world. This word was *faith*. It was not altogether new; it might be found in the writings of the prophets; but it had never before seemed so important or so expressive of the essential worth of a man. When he rejected the test of correct conduct which society uses, Christ substituted the test of faith. It is to be understood that this is not strictly a Christian virtue; it is the

Christ's Winnowing Fan

virtue required of one who wishes to become a Christian. So much a man must bring with him; without it he is not worthy of the kingdom of God. To those who lack faith Christ will not be Legislator or King. He does not, indeed, dismiss them, but he suffers them to abandon a society which soon ceases to have any attraction for them. Such, then, is the new test, and it will be found the only one which could answer Christ's purpose of excluding all hollow disciples and including all, however rude and vicious, who were capable of better things. Every other good quality which we may wish to make the test of a man implies either too little or too much for this purpose.

Justice is often but a form of pedantry, mercy mere easiness of temper, courage a mere firmness of physical constitution; but if these virtues are genuine, then they indicate not goodness merely but goodness considerably developed. A man may be potentially just or merciful, yet from defect of training he may be actually neither. We want a test which shall admit all who have it in them to be good whether their good qualities be trained or no. Such a test is found in faith. He who, when goodness is impressively put before him, exhibits an instinctive loyalty to it, starts forward to take its side, trusts himself to it, such a man has faith, and the root of the matter is in such a man. He may have habits of vice, but the loyal and faithful instinct in him will place him above many that practise virtue. He may be rude in thought and character, but he will unconsciously gravitate towards what is right. Other virtues can scarcely thrive without a fine natural organisation and a happy training. But the most neglected and ungifted of men may make a beginning with faith. Other virtues want civilisation, a certain amount of knowledge, a few books; but in half-brutal countenances faith will light up a glimmer of nobleness. The savage, who can do little else, can wonder and worship and enthusiastically obey. He who cannot know what is right can know that some one else knows, he who has no law may still have a master, he who is incapable of justice may be capable of fidelity, he who understands little may have his sins forgiven because he loves much.

Let us sum up the points of difference which we have discovered between the Old Theocracy and the New. The Old Theocracy was utterly independent of all political organisations. It was therefore able to create a political organisation of its own. The laws of the Theocracy were enforced by temporal punishments, as indeed at a time when the immortality of the soul was not recognised they could be enforced by no other. The New Theocracy was set up in the midst of a political organisation highly civilised and exacting. It was therefore as completely devoid of any system of temporal punishments as the Old had been devoid of any other system. But, on the other hand, its members believed themselves to live under the eye of a Judge whose tribunal was in heaven and into whose hands they were to fall at death. Again, the Old Theocracy selected a single family out of the mass of mankind, while the New gathered out of mankind, by a summons which though absolutely comprehensive was yet not likely to be obeyed but by a certain class, all such as possessed any natural loyalty to goodness, enthusiasm enough to join a great cause, and devotion enough to sacrifice something to it.

CHAPTER VII

CONDITIONS OF MEMBERSHIP IN CHRIST'S KINGDOM

The question now arises, What was involved in obeying Christ's summons? When the crowd of faithful and loyal hearts gathered round him, struck with admiration of the wisdom that was so condescending and the power that was so beneficent, when, without throwing off the yoke of citizenship in earthly states, they accepted the burdens of citizenship in the New Jerusalem, and without ceasing to be amenable to Jewish and Roman judges, became responsible for all their deeds and even for all their thoughts to Christ, what was the extent of the new obligation which they incurred? How did a Christian differ from another man?

Ever since the Church was founded up to the present time this question, What makes a man a Christian? has been an all-important practical question. The answers given to it in the present day differ widely with the tolerance of those who give them, but they are generally the same in kind. They consist in specifying certain doctrines about God and Christ which a Christian must needs believe. One will say, He is no Christian who does not believe that the death of Christ effected a permanent change in the relations between man and God. Another will say, He is no Christian who does not believe in the Divinity of Christ. A third will say, It is necessary to believe in the Resurrection. Whether or no these beliefs, any or all of them, be necessary to the character of a Christian now, we may assert with absolute confidence that they were not required of the first followers of Christ, and further, that most of them had never occurred to their minds. Nothing could suggest to them the Resurrection of Christ until he began darkly to prophesy of it to his most intimate disciples; and when he did so they listened, we are told, with bewilderment and incredulity. So far from regarding the cross of Christ as the basis of a reconciliation between God and man, they would have listened with horror to the suggestion that their Master was destined to such a death. The Divinity of his person might indeed occur to some of those who witnessed his miraculous works, but it was certainly not generally received in the society, for we find Christ pronouncing a solemn blessing upon Peter for being the first to arrive at the conclusion that he was the Messiah. It appears, then, that so long as their Master was with them the creed of the first Christians was of the most unformed and elementary character. To the ordinary belief of their age and country they added nothing except certain vague conceptions of the greatness of the new Prophet, whom the less advanced regarded as likely before long to establish a new royal dynasty at Jerusalem, while others of greater penetration regarded him as a new Moses and a divinely commissioned reformer of the law. It is clear, then, that those who consider an elaborate creed essential to the Christian character must pronounce Christ's first disciples utterly unworthy to bear the name of Christians. But to this such persons may answer that the first disciples were indeed only Christians in a very imperfect sense, and that before the Resurrection it could not be otherwise. That event increased the number of dogmas which Christians are required to receive; before it happened their creed was necessarily meagre, but since it has happened a Christian is not worthy of the name if he does not believe much more than any of Christ's first followers.

This view is plausible and agrees at first sight with the conclusions at which we have already arrived. Christ, we have said, announced himself as the Founder and Legislator of a new state, and summoned men before him in that capacity. He did not invite them as friends, nor even as pupils, but summoned them as subjects. It was natural that when they first gathered round him, and even for some time afterwards, they should differ from other men in nothing but the loyalty which had

Membership in Christ's Kingdom 57

led them to obey the call. They understood that they had been summoned in order to receive laws, but those laws could not be promulgated all at once. In the meantime, while they were expecting the institutions that had been promised to them, though Christians in will they could not be called Christians in the full sense of the word. Though out of them the Christian Church was to spring, yet they might well be as unlike the Christian Church as the acorn is unlike the oak, or as the crew of the Mayflower was unlike the States of New England. But after the Church had received its Founder's laws—laws which, like the Decalogue, contained not merely practical rules of life but declarations concerning the nature of God and man's relation to Him, then Christianity may have begun to mean no mere fidelity or loyalty to Christ's person, but the practical obedience to his rules of life, and the unquestioning acceptance of his theological teaching.

In a sense it is true that Christianity does mean this. Christ demanded as much and was assuredly not satisfied with less. In the same way every state demands of its citizens perfect patriotism and perfect obedience to the laws. Yet perfect patriotism and obedience is scarcely found in any citizen of any state; but the state, though it demands so much, does not exclude the citizen who renders less. It is one thing to be an imperfect citizen, and another to be excluded from citizenship altogether. In like manner it is one thing to be an imperfect Christian, and another to be utterly unworthy of the name. And it will be found on further examination that the Christian Church is content with a much more imperfect obedience to its law than any secular states. It does not, indeed, promulgate laws without expecting them to be observed; it constantly maintains a standard by which every Christian is to try himself; nevertheless whereas every secular state enacts and obtains from its members an almost perfect obedience to its laws, the laws of the Divine State are fully observed by scarcely any one, and the most that can be said even of Christians that rise decidedly above the average is that they do not forget them, and that by slow degrees they arrive at a general conformity with them. The reason of this will appear when we treat in detail of Christ's legislation. It will then become clear that Christ's legislation is of a nature infinitely more complex in its exactions upon every individual than any secular code, and that accordingly a complete observance of it is infinitely difficult. For this reason it is a matter of universal consent among Christians that no man is to suffer exclusion from their society for any breach of Christ's laws that is not of a flagrant and outrageous kind. Though it is common to hear a man pronounced no Christian for not believing in what is called the Atonement, yet no such excommunication is passed upon men in whom some very unchristian vices, such as selfishness or reckless party-spirit, are plainly visible. The reason of our tolerance in the latter case is that we all acknowledge the immense difficulty of overcoming a vice when it has become confirmed, and we charitably give the man who has visibly not overcome his vices credit at least for struggling against them.

This is quite right; only we ought to be just as tolerant of an imperfect creed as we are of an imperfect practice. Everything which can be urged in excuse for the latter may also be pleaded for the former. If the way to Christian action is beset by corrupt habits and misleading passions, the path to Christian truth is overgrown with prejudices and strewn with fallen theories and rotting systems which hide it from our view. It is quite as hard to think rightly as it is to act rightly, or even to feel rightly. And as all allow that an error is a less culpable thing than a crime or a vicious passion, it is monstrous that it should be more severely punished; it is monstrous that Christ who was called the friend of publicans and sinners, should be represented as the pitiless enemy of bewildered seekers of truth. How could men have been guilty of such an inconsistency? By speaking of what they do not understand. Men, in general, do not understand or appreciate the difficulty of finding truth. All men must act, and therefore all men learn in some degree how difficult it is to act rightly. The consequence is that

Membership in Christ's Kingdom

all men can make excuse for those who fail to act rightly. But all men are not compelled to make an independent search for truth, and those who voluntarily undertake to do so are always few. They ought, indeed, to find pity and charity when they fail, for their undertaking is full of hazard, and in the course of it they are too apt to leave friends and companions behind them, and when they succeed they bring back glorious spoils for those who remained at home criticising them. But they cannot expect such charity, for the hazards and difficulties of the undertaking are known to themselves alone. To the world at large it seems quite easy to find truth and inexcusable to miss it. And no wonder! For by finding truth they mean only learning by rote the maxims current around them.

Present to an ordinary man the maxim, " Love your enemies "; you may hear him sigh as he answers that the saying is divine, but he fears he shall never practise it. The reason is that he has an enemy and fully understands what it is to love him, and also what it is to hate him. Present to the same man the saying, " The Word was made flesh," and what will he answer? If he answered the truth he would say that he did not understand it; but he would not be quite an ordinary man if he could recognise his own ignorance so plainly. He will answer that he *believes* it, by which he means that as the words make no impression whatever upon his mind, so they excite no opposition in it. Present the same two texts to a thinker. It is not impossible that the first may seem to him no hard saying; he may have no enemies, or his thoughtful habits may have brought his passions under control. But the second will overwhelm him with difficulty. For he knows what it asserts; he may have been accustomed to regard the λόγος as the technicality of an extinct philosophy, and may be staggered to find it thus imported into history and made the groundwork of what aspires to be a permanent theology. It is at this point, then, that the thinker will sigh, and you will hear him murmur that it is a great saying, but he fears he shall never believe it.

Thus Christian belief is fully as hard a thing as Christian practice. It is intrinsically as hard, and those who do not perceive the difficulty of it understand it just so much less than those who do. Christ's first followers, as we have seen, were far from possessing the full Christian belief. Not till long after his departure did they arrive at those conclusions which are now regarded as constituting Christian theology. In their position, we have admitted, this was almost inevitable. The great events upon which that theology rests, had either not happened, or not been maturely considered. These difficulties have been removed; but have not other difficulties taken their place? Two may be mentioned which beset the modern enquirer into Christianity, and often make his theology as imperfect and confused as that of the crowd of disciples who gathered round Christ.

1. To the first Christians the capital facts of Christ's life were future and therefore obscure; to the moderns they gather an almost equal obscurity from being long past. The immensity of distance from which we contemplate them raises many obstacles to belief. Before the theology can be inferred from the facts they must be well authenticated. Those who witnessed them or talked with those who had witnessed them were relieved from all trouble on this head. But in these days many fail in the preliminary undertaking. Complicated questions of evidence perplex them: they are assailed with doubts of the possibility of transmitting from age to age a trustworthy account of any long series of incidents, especially a series including miracles. Suppose this difficulty surmounted, still the same remoteness of the life of Christ creates much difficulty in ascertaining the meaning of the words he used, and the exact nature of the doctrines he taught. For those words and those doctrines have been subjected to the ingenuity of many generations of commentators. Spoken originally to men of the ancient world, they have received a succession of medieval and modern glosses, and if we put these aside and study the text for ourselves, our own training, the education and habits of the nineteenth century, disqualify us in a considerable degree for

Membership in Christ's Kingdom

entering into its meaning. Only a well-trained historical imagination, active and yet calm, is competent so to revive the circumstances of place and time in which the words were delivered as to draw from them, at a distance of eighteen hundred years, a meaning tolerably like that which they conveyed to those who heard them.

2. Christ's first followers had a sympathy with him, and his mode of teaching had an adaptation to them, which arose from the fact of the Master and disciples being contemporaries and fellow-countrymen. It is common to say of political constitutions that they must grow and cannot be made. Now the constitution which Christ gave to mankind has been found capable of being transplanted into almost every soil, but, notwithstanding, it is native to Palestine, and must have been embraced by those to whom it was first given with an ease and readiness which the Western nations cannot emulate. Christ's constitution was not a new invention, but a crowning development of that which had existed in Palestine since the race of Israel had lived there. For centuries the Jews had been accustomed to receive truth by authoritative proclamation from the mouth of a prophet. How the truth came to the prophet he himself knew not; the only account he could give of the matter was that it was put into his mouth by the Invisible King of the Theocracy, and that he knew it to be truth. And those who listened put the proclamation to no rigid test. They watched the prophet to see if he were honest, and if his proclamation shook their hearts and stirred their blood and seemed to bring them into the presence of the Invisible King, they then felt sure of its truth and safe in following it. Now of these prophets Christ was distinctly one, the greatest of all. He had the same intuitive certainty, for which he gave no reason, yet which no one could attribute to mere self-confidence, the same tone of unbounded authority assumed in the name of God, the same power of subduing the heart and arousing the conscience. Therefore those who heard him found something familiar in his style. It reminded them of all that they were most accustomed to venerate, of Moses,

Isaiah, Ezra, and they seemed to fall into their natural places when they sat at his feet and treasured up his words as oracles of truth.

Now this mode of communicating and receiving truth is not indeed repugnant to the Western nations. From the time of Pythagoras and Heraclitus to the time of Carlyle and Mazzini, men have arisen at intervals in the West who have seemed to themselves to discover truth, not so much by a process of reasoning as by an intense gaze, and who have announced their conclusions in the voice of a herald, using the name of God and giving no reason. And in the Western world these men have always met with a certain acceptance; they have generally succeeded in gathering round them followers of respectable character and understanding; and so fully is the possibility of such a prophetic discovery of truth recognised, that the Jewish prophets themselves have been received throughout the West with profound veneration. Still the respect for authority in knowledge is far less in the West than in the East. This is plain when we consider that the Jewish prophets seem to have been accepted by the whole nation, and that when thus accepted it was considered presumption to deny anything that they said. On the other hand, no one in the West ever reaches such an eminence as to have no detractors, and we are all bold enough to doubt what is said even by those whom we reverence most. The reason of this is that in the West a *method* has been laid down which places the gifted man and the ungifted in some degree on a level. It is still, no doubt, the gifted man in general who discovers truth, but when the discovery is made the ungifted man can test it and judge of it. Whereas it would appear that where the processes of thought have never been analysed and reduced to method, there is no means of discovering the error of a gifted man, except through the emphatic contradiction of one who has won the reputation of being more gifted.

It follows from this that when Christian theology passed into the Gentile world, when it diffused itself from the Mosaic East into the Socratic West, it must have encountered

Membership in Christ's Kingdom

a new difficulty. The Jew who listened to Christ had been educated to rest in authority. He had believed in all that Moses had taught, in all that Isaiah had taught, and as soon as he was convinced that Christ was greater than Moses and Isaiah, he submitted with the same deference to his authority, and accepted all that Christ taught. When the life of Christ was put before the Greek, it affected him to a certain extent as it had done the Jew. He was seized with admiration and reverence. He regarded him as a divine man, and placed him first by the side of Orpheus and Pythagoras, and in the end above both. But this veneration did not imply the same absolute devotion of the intellect which it had invoked in the case of the Jew. For the Greek had other methods of arriving at truth besides imbibing it directly from the lips of wise men. He had a logic in which he had great confidence, and which had already led him to certain definite conclusions. If these conclusions should be at war with those authoritatively announced by Christ? Here was a difficulty at the very beginning, and in the course of time this difficulty has increased. The scientific methods laid down at first in Greece have been improved, and applied with such success that their credit is greatly risen. Men may still be disposed to believe in Christ's infallible wisdom, but their minds are now accustomed to work with great freedom upon all subjects, to have more respect for reasoning than for authority, and almost to deny knowledge to be knowledge when it rests only upon hearsay, and is not verified to the mind itself by demonstration, or at least probable evidence. Accustomed to test and weigh everything, and trained in the practice of suspending the judgment, they become not so much unwilling as positively unable to receive a proposition merely because it is authoritatively delivered.

Such are some of the difficulties of Christian belief. We conclude that though it is always easy for thoughtless men to be orthodox, yet to grasp with any strong practical apprehension the theology of Christ is a thing as hard as to practise his moral law. Yet if he meant anything by his constant denunciation of hypocrites, there is nothing which he would have visited with sterner censure than that short cut to belief which many persons take when, overwhelmed with the difficulties which beset their minds, and afraid of damnation, they suddenly resolve to strive no longer, but, giving their minds a holiday, to rest content with saying that they believe and acting as if they did. A melancholy end of Christianity indeed! Can there be such a disfranchised pauper class among the citizens of the New Jerusalem?

But when it is once acknowledged that to attain a full and firm belief in Christ's theology is hard, then it follows at once that a man may be a Christian without it. It has been shown that the first of all requirements made from the earliest Christians was faith, a loyal and free confidence in Christ. This was what made the difference between them and the careless crowd or the hostile Pharisee—that to them Christ was a beloved Master and friend. But this faith, if they had it but as a grain of mustard-seed, must have assured them that it was not in his character to exact of them what it was beyond their power to render, and to expect them at once to grasp truths which it might well take them all their lives to learn. And did he as a matter of fact do so? Do we find him frequently examining his followers in their creed, and rejecting one as a sceptic and another as an infidel? Sceptics they were all, so long as he was among them, a society of doubters, attaining to faith only at intervals and then falling back again into uncertainty. And from their Master they received reproofs for this, but reproofs tenderly expressed, not dry threats nor cold dismission. Assuredly those who represent Christ as presenting to man an abstruse theology, and saying to them peremptorily, " Believe or be damned," have the coarsest conception of the Saviour of the world. He will reject, he tells us, those who refuse to clothe the naked or tend the sick, those whose lamps have gone out, those who have buried their talents, not those whose minds are poorly furnished with theological knowledge. Incredulity and uncertainty, as long as it seemed honest, he always treated with kind consideration; and so disposed was he to the largest tolerance that on one occasion he refused to condemn one who, showing some respect for his character, yet disobeyed his first and most peremptory law—namely, that which commanded all persons to follow and attach themselves to him. And on this occasion he uttered words which breathe that contempt for forms and that respect for what is substantial which is the unfailing mark of a commanding spirit—" he that is not against us is on our part."

To what conclusion, then, are we led by these reflections upon the question of this chapter—the question, namely, what was involved in accepting Christ's call. Those who gathered round him did in the first place contract an obligation of personal loyalty to him. On the ground of this loyalty he proceeded to form them into a society, and to promulgate an elaborate legislation, comprising and intimately connected with certain declarations, authoritatively delivered, concerning the nature of God, the relation of man to him, and the invisible world. In doing so he assumed the part of a Moses. Now the legislation of Moses had been absolutely binding upon the whole community. Disobedience to his laws had been punished by the civil judge, and so had every act which implied a conception of the Divine Nature different from that which he had prescribed. The new Moses, we have seen, had no civil judges to enforce his legislation, but he represented his unfaithful servants as being liable to prosecution before the tribunals of the invisible world. He described those tribunals as passing capital sentences upon some criminals, and dismissing them, as he expressed it, into " the outer darkness "—that is, beyond the pomœrium of that sacred city which is lighted by the glory of God. These are the traitors to the Theocracy who have broken its essential obligations. Who then are they? And what are these essential obligations?

Under the Mosaic law, as under all secular codes, certain definite acts were regarded as unpardonable. Moses punished the dishonouring of parents and idolatry with death, i.e. absolute exclusion. Now in this respect the new Moses is infinitely more tolerant. There are no specific acts which are unpardonable to the Christian. No amount of disobedience which can be named, no amount of disbelief or ignorance of doctrine, is sufficient to deprive a man of the name of Christian. For it is held in the Christian Church that the man most stained with crime, and even most unsuccessful in breaking himself of criminal habits, and in the same manner the man whose speculative notions are most erroneous or despairing, may yet possess that rudiment of goodness which Christ called faith. But, on another side, the new Moses is infinitely more exacting than the old. For the most blameless observance of the whole law is not enough to save the Christian from exclusion, unless it has actually sprung from genuine goodness. It may spring from natural caution or long-sighted selfishness, and in the heart of the strict moralist there may be no spark of faith. For such a moralist Christ has no mercy. And so it became a maxim in the Christian Church that faith justifies a man without the deeds of the law.

Faith was described above as no proper Christian virtue, but as that which was required of a man before he became a Christian. This virtue was to be taken by Christ and trained by his legislation and theology into something far riper and higher. But if the training should through untoward circumstances almost entirely fail, and faith remain a scarcely developed principle, bearing fruit but seldom and fitfully in action—*never* is inconceivable—still in the Christian view it is life to the soul, and the faithful soul, however undeveloped, is at home within the illuminated circle, and not in the outer darkness.

CHAPTER VIII

BAPTISM

We have before us the new Moses surrounded by those who are waiting to receive from his lips the institutions of a new Theocracy. They have been gathered out of the nation; they form the elect part of it. But no constraint has been used in enlisting some and rejecting others. Those are here in whose hearts there is something which answers to such a trumpet-call as that which John and Christ had caused to resound through the land. Those whose lives are sunk in routine, and no longer capable of aspiring or willing or believing, are not here. But among the followers of the Legislator there is but one common quality. All, except a very few adventurers who have joined him under a mistake and will soon withdraw, have some degree of what he calls faith. All look up to him, trust in him, are prepared to obey him and to sacrifice something for him. He requires no more. This is a valid title to citizenship in the Theocracy. But in habits and character they differ as much as the individuals in any other crowd. Some are sunk in vice, others lead blameless lives; some have cultivated minds, others are rude peasants; some offer to Jehovah prayers conceived in the style of Hebrew psalmists and prophets, others worship some monstrous idol of the terrified imagination or passionless abstraction of philosophy. It is the object of the society into which this motley crowd are now gathered gradually to elevate each member of it, to cure him of vice, to soften his rudeness, to deliver him from the dominion of superstitious fears or intellectual conceits. But this is the point towards which the society tends, not that with which it begins. The progress of each citizen towards this perfection will bear proportion to his natural organisation, to the force with which the influences of the society are brought to bear upon him, and to the stage of enlightenment from which he starts. With some it will be rapid, with others so slow as to be almost imperceptible. But the first propelling power, the indispensable condition of progress, is the personal relation of loyal vassalage of the citizen to the Prince of the Theocracy.

The test of this loyalty lay, as we have seen, in the mere fact that a man was prepared to attach himself to Christ's person and obey his commands, though by doing so some risk and some sacrifice was incurred. Christ, however, did not retain everyone who accepted the Call about his person; some he dismissed to their homes, laying upon them no burdensome commands. It was necessary therefore that some mark should be devised by which the follower of Christ might be distinguished, and by consenting to bear which he might give proof of his loyalty. Some initiatory rite was necessary, some public formality, in which the new volunteer might take, as it were, the military oath and confess his chief before men. If such a ceremony could be devised, which should at the same time indicate that the new votary had taken upon himself not merely a new service but an entirely new mode of life, it would be so much the better. Now there was already in use among the Jews the rite of baptism. It was undergone by those who became proselytes to Judaism. Such proselytes signified by submitting to it that they passed out of their secular life into the dedicated life of citizens in a Theocracy. The water in which they were bathed washed away from them the whole unhallowed and unprofitable past; they rose out of it new men into a new world, and felt as though death were behind them and they had been born again into a higher state. No ceremony could be better adapted to Christ's purpose than this. It was already in use, and had acquired a meaning and associations which were universally understood. By calling upon all alike, Jews as well as Gentiles, to submit to it, Christ would intimate that he did not merely revive the old Theocracy but instituted a

Baptism

new one, so that the children of Abraham themselves, members of a theocracy from their birth, had a past to wash away and a new life to begin, not less than the unsanctified Gentile. And at the same time, being publicly performed, it would serve as well as any other rite to test the loyalty of the new recruit and his readiness to be known by his Master's name.

This ceremony, then, Christ adopted, and he made it absolutely binding upon all his followers to submit to it. In the fourth Gospel there is a story which illustrates in the most striking manner the importance which Christ attached to baptism. A man of advanced years and influential position, named Nicodemus, visited Christ, we are told, in secret, and entered into conversation with him. He began by an explicit avowal of belief in Christ's divine mission. What he would have gone on to say we may conjecture from these two facts, namely, that he believed in Christ, and that nevertheless he visited him secretly. It appears that he hoped to comply with Christ's demand of personal homage and submission, but to be excused from making a public avowal of it. And when we consider the high position of Nicodemus, it is natural to suppose that he hoped to receive such a special exemption in consideration of the services he had it in his power to render. He could push the movement among the influential classes; he could cautiously dispose the Pharisaic sect to a coalition with Christ on the ground of their common national and theocratic feeling; he might become a useful friend in the metropolis, and might fight against the prejudice which a provincial and Galilæan party could not but excite. These advantages Christ would secure by allowing Nicodemus to become a secret member of his Theocracy, and by excusing him, until a better opportunity should present itself, from publicly undergoing the rite of baptism. On the other hand, by insisting upon this he would at once destroy all the influence of Nicodemus with the authorities of Jerusalem, and with it all his power of becoming a nursing-father to the infant Church. When we consider the great contempt which Christ constantly expressed for forms and ceremonies, and in particular for those " washings " which were usual among the Pharisees, we are prepared to find him readily acceding to the request of Nicodemus. Instead of which he shut the petitioner's mouth by an abrupt declaration that there was no way into the Theocracy but through baptism. The kingdom of God, he insisted, though it had no locality and no separation from the secular states of mankind, though it had no law-courts, no lictors and no fasces, was yet a true state. Men were not to make a light thing of entering it, to give their names to the Founder at a secret interview, and immediately return to their accustomed places of resort and take up the routine of secular life where it had been left. Those who would enrol themselves among the citizens of it were to understand that they began their life anew, as truly as if they had been born again. And lest the Divine Society, in its contempt for material boundaries and for the distinctness which is given by unity of place, should lose its distinctness altogether and degenerate into a theory or a sentiment or a devout imagination, the initiatory rite of baptism, with its publicity and formality, was pronounced as indispensable to membership as that spiritual inspiration which is membership itself.

Baptism being thus indispensable, we may be surprised to find it so seldom mentioned in the accounts of Christ's life. We do not read, for example, of the baptism of his principal disciples. But it is to be remembered that the rite of baptism, though used by Christ, was not introduced by him, and that he recognised the Theocracy as having begun to exist in a rudimentary form before his own public appearance. The work of John was merged in that of Christ as a river in the sea, but Christ regards those who had received John's baptism as being already members of the Theocracy. Since the time of John, he says, the kingdom of heaven suffereth violence, and the violent take it by force. Now Christ's first followers were likely to be drawn from John's circle; partly because John himself directed his followers to Christ, partly because those who were affected by the eloquence of the one prophet were naturally formed to fall under the influence of the other.

Baptism

That the fact actually was so is attested by our biographies, which distinctly speak of Christ as finding his earliest disciples in the neighbourhood and among the followers of the Baptist. This being the case, we may presume that the bulk of the first Christians received baptism from John, and found themselves already enrolled in a Society, the objects of which neither they nor perhaps the Baptist himself clearly understood, before they had ever seen the face of Christ. The Acts of the Apostles affords many proofs that the first Christians regarded John's disciples as members of the Church, but imperfectly instructed.

CHAPTER IX

REFLECTIONS ON THE NATURE OF CHRIST'S SOCIETY

Of the three parts into which our investigation is divided, Christ's Call, his Legislation, and his Divine Royalty or relation to Jehovah, the first is now completed. We have considered the nature of the Call, its difference from that which was given to Abraham, the means which were taken to procure a body of men such as might suitably form the foundation of a new and unique Commonwealth, and the nature of the obligations they incurred in accepting the Call: ἓν μὲν τόδ ἤδη τῶν τριῶν παλαισμάτων.

But before we proceed to consider Christ's Legislation, it will be well to linger awhile and reflect on what we have learnt. Having ascertained so far what Christ undertook to do and did, it will be well to compare it with other similar schemes and to form some opinion upon the success it was likely to meet with.

Let us ask ourselves what was the ultimate object of Christ's scheme. When the Divine Society was established and organised, what did he expect it to accomplish? To the question we may suppose he would have answered, The object of the Divine Society is that God's will may be done on earth as it is done in heaven. In the language of our own day, its object was the improvement of morality. Now this is no strange or unusual object. Many schemes have been proposed for curing human nature of its vices and helping it to right thought and right action. We have now before us the outline of Christ's scheme, and are in a condition to compare it with some others that have had the same object, and by so doing to discover in what its peculiarity consists. Now there is one large class of such schemes with which mankind have occupied themselves diligently for many

Nature of Christ's Society 73

centuries, and which for the purpose of comparison with Christianity may be treated as a single scheme. Ever since the time of Socrates philosophy has occupied itself with the same problem; it has been one of the principal boasts of philosophy that it teaches virtue and weeds vice out of the mind. At the present day those who reject Christianity commonly represent that in advanced civilisation it gives place naturally to moral philosophy. Their belief is that the true and only method of making men good is by philosophy; and that the good influence of Christianity in past ages has been due to the truths of moral philosophy which are blended in it with superstitions which the world in its progress is leaving behind.

Of course there have been a multitude of systems of moral philosophy, which have differed from each other in a considerable degree, but they have all resembled each other in being philosophy. For the present purpose their differences are not important; the important thing is that there have been two conspicuous attempts to improve mankind morally—the one by moral philosophy, the other by means of the Christian Church. Now, as nothing assists conception so much as comparison, and it is hardly possible to understand anything properly without putting it by the side of something else, we may expect to gain some insight into Christ's method of curing human nature by comparing it with that of the philosophers.

At the first glance the two methods may seem to bear a strong resemblance, and we may suspect that the difference between them is superficial, and not more than is readily accounted for by the difference between manners and modes of thought in Greece and Palestine. It may seem to us that Socrates and Christ were in fact occupied in the same way; certainly both lived in the midst of admiring disciples, whose minds and characters were formed by their words; both discussed moral questions, the one with methodical reasoning as a Greek addressing Greeks, the other with the authoritative tone and earnestness of a Jew. There may seem here at first sight a substantial resemblance and a superficial difference. But if we make a more careful comparison, we shall find that precisely the contrary is true, and that the difference is really radical, while the resemblance is accidental. It is true that Socrates, like Christ, formed a sort of society, and that the successors of Socrates formed societies, which lasted several centuries, the Academy, the Porch, the Garden. But these philosophical societies merely existed for convenience. No necessary tie bound the members of them together. As the teacher had but one tongue and but one lifetime, it was obviously better that he should take his pupils in large numbers, or, as it were, in classes, rather than teach every individual separately, and therefore before the invention of the printing-press a philosopher usually gathered a society round him. Doubtless, when this had been done, a certain *esprit de corps* sprang up among such societies, and they did, in special cases, approximate in some degree to churches. But that this was accidental, and not in the original design, appears from the fact that since the great diffusion of books, philosophers have almost ceased to form societies, and content themselves, for the most part, with producing conviction in the minds of isolated students by published writings. If Socrates were to appear at the present day he would hardly bear that resemblance to Christ which he bore at Athens. He would form no society.

Now it was not from accident or for convenience that Christ formed a society. Nor were his followers merely united by the common desire to hear him speak, and afterwards by the friendly feelings that grew out of intimacy. We have seen already, and shall see yet more clearly in the sequel, that to organise a society, and to bind the members of it together by the closest ties, were the business of his life. For this reason it was that he called men away from their homes, imposed upon some a wandering life, upon others the sacrifice of their property, and endeavoured by all means to divorce them from their former connection in order that they might find a new home in the Church. For this reason he instituted a solemn initiation, and for this reason refused absolutely to give to anyone a dispensation from it. For

Nature of Christ's Society 75

this reason too, as we shall see, he established a common feast, which was through all ages to remind Christians of their indissoluble union. Thus although the term disciples or learners is applied in our biographies to the followers of Christ, yet we should not suffer this phrase to remind us of a philosophical school. Learners they might be, but they loved better to speak of themselves as subjects or even " slaves " of Jesus Christ, and to each other he exhorted them to be as brothers.

Thus the resemblance between Christ and the ancient philosophers vanishes on examination. He was the founder of a society to which for a time he found it useful to give instruction; they gave instruction to pupils who found it convenient to form themselves into a society for the sake of receiving it. Hence it was that while they assumed a name derived from the wisdom they possessed and communicated, and were called philosophers, he took his title from the community he founded and ruled, and called himself King. But as the obvious resemblance between Christ and such a philosopher as Socrates vanishes on examination, so we shall find that the obvious difference between them — namely, that the one used reasoning and the other authority—appears upon examination to be radical and fundamental. It was the perpetual object of Socrates as much as possible to sink his own personality. He wished his arguments to have all the weight they might deserve, and his authority to count for nothing. Those who have considered the meaning of his famous irony know that it was not by any means what such a writer as Cicero supposes, a humorous device to make his conversation more racy and the confutation of his adversaries more unexpected and decisive. He professed to know nothing because he wished to exalt his method at his own expense. He wanted to give men not truths but a power of arriving at truths, and therefore what he found it most necessary to avoid was the tendency of his hearers to adopt his conclusions out of mere admiration for his wisdom and love for his person rather than rational conviction. By his determined and consistent abstinence from all dogmatic assertion he gradually trained men to believe in a method which, if only carefully used, discovered truth or verified it as surely, within certain limitations, in the hands of an ordinary man as in those of a sage. Deservedly he gained the greatest personal admiration, but his highest claim to it was the trouble he took to avoid it, and the tenacity with which he laboured to set the tranquil and methodical operations of the intellect in the search of truth above the blind impulses of feeling and personal admiration.

Now in all this we find Christ at the very opposite extreme. As with Socrates argument is everything and personal authority nothing, so with Christ personal authority is all in all and argument altogether unemployed. As Socrates is never tired of depreciating himself and dissembling his own superiority to those with whom he converses, so Christ perpetually and consistently exalts himself. As Socrates firmly denies what all admit, and explains away what the oracle had announced, viz. his own superior wisdom, so Christ steadfastly asserts what many were not prepared to admit, viz. his own absolute superiority to all men and his natural title to universal royalty. The same contrast appears in the requirements they made of their followers. Socrates cared nothing what those whom he conversed with thought of him; he would bear any amount of rudeness from them; but he cared very much about the subject of discussion and about obtaining a triumph for his method. On the other hand, the one thing which Christ required was a certain personal attachment to himself, a fidelity or loyalty; and so long as they manifested this, he was in no haste to deliver their minds from speculative error.

We may be sure that so marked a contrast does not arise merely from the difference between a Semitic and European mind. The truth is that as the resemblance between the earliest Christian Church and a philosophical school is delusive, so is the resemblance between Christ himself and any Greek philosopher. Christ had a totally different object and used totally different means from Socrates. The resemblance is, no doubt, at first sight striking. Both were teachers, both were prodigiously

Nature of Christ's Society

influential, both suffered martyrdom. But if we examine these points of resemblance we shall see that martyrdom was, as it were, an accident of the life of Socrates, and teaching in a great degree an accident of Christ's, and that their influence upon men has been of a totally different kind — that of Socrates being an intellectual influence upon thought, that of Christ a personal influence upon feeling. What real student of Socrates concerns himself with his martyrdom? It is an impressive page of history, but the importance of Socrates to men has no concern with it. Had he died in his bed he would still have been the creator of science. On the other hand, if we isolate Christ's teaching from his life we may come to the conclusion that it contains little that could not be found elsewhere, and found accompanied with reasoning and explanation. Those who fix their eyes on the Sermon on the Mount, or rather on the naked propositions which it contains, and disregard Christ's life, his cross, and his resurrection, commit the same mistake in studying Christianity that the student of Socratic philosophy would commit if he studied only the dramatic story of his death. Both Socrates and Christ uttered remarkable thoughts and lived remarkable lives. But Socrates holds his place in history by his thoughts and not by his life, Christ by his life and not by his thoughts.

It follows that it is a mistake to regard Christianity as a rudimentary or imperfect moral philosophy. Philosophy is one thing, and Christianity quite another. And the difference between them lies here—that philosophy hopes to cure the vices of human nature by working upon the head, and Christianity by educating the heart. The philosopher works upon the man in isolation, though he may for convenience assemble his pupils in classes. He also abstains carefully from biassing his feelings by any personal motives and abjures the very principle of authority, making it his object to render his pupil his own master, to put him in possession of a rule by which he may guide his actions, and to relieve him from dependence upon any external guardianship. Christianity abhors isolation; it gathers men into a society and binds them in the closest manner, first to each other, and next to Christ himself, whom it represents as claiming their enthusiastic devotion on the ground of gratitude, and as exhibiting to them by a transcendent example, and also incidentally by teaching, but rather rhetorical than scientific teaching, the life they should lead.

Christianity, then, and moral philosophy are totally different things, and yet profess to have the same object, namely, the moral improvement of mankind. This being the case, as it is probable that they are not precisely equally adapted to attain the object, it would seem to follow that one of the two is unnecessary. But on consideration we shall find that each has its function, and that philosophy undertakes quite another sort of moral improvement than Christianity. The difference may be shortly expressed thus:—Both endeavour to lead men to do what is right, but philosophy undertakes to explain what it is right to do, while Christianity undertakes to make men disposed to do it. Wrong actions spring from two causes—bad moral dispositions, and intellectual misapprehensions. Good men do wrong perpetually, because they have not the mental training and skill which may enable them to discern the right course in given circumstances. They have good impulses, but they misconceive the facts before them, and miscalculate the effect of actions. Their intentions are right, but they take wrong means of carrying them out. There may be a conflict of good impulses, and in such cases one at least must remain unindulged. Duty, in short, as it represents itself to us, is a very complicated matter. To do it with certainty a man must not be good merely but wise. He must have reflected deeply on human affairs and on social laws; he must have reduced the confusion of good feelings which exists at starting in the well-disposed mind to order and clearness. This, then, is what philosophy undertakes to help him to do.

But suppose the good feelings wanting at the outset. What will it avail in such a case that philosophy should point out the right course? When the man whose impulses

Nature of Christ's Society

are bad has plainly understood by the aid of philosophy which is the right course and which the wrong, what will he do? Clearly he will take the wrong. Some additional machinery is wanted which may evoke the good impulses, cherish them, and make them masters of the bad ones. If this is not done, what avails it to give a man the knowledge of what is right? It will but help him to avoid it. We have heard of a fruit which gave the knowledge of good, but it was " knowledge of good bought dear by knowing ill."

Now this machinery is what Christ undertakes to supply. Philosophers had drawn their pupils from the élite of humanity; but Christ finds his material among the worst and meanest, for he does not propose merely to make the good better but the bad good. And what is his machinery? He says the first step towards good dispositions is for a man to form a strong personal attachment. Let him first be drawn out of himself. Next let the object of that attachment be a person of striking and conspicuous goodness. To worship such a person will be the best exercise in virtue that he can have. Let him vow obedience in life and death to such a person; let him mix and live with others who have made the same vow. He will have ever before his eyes an ideal of what he may himself become. His heart will be stirred by new feelings, a new world will be gradually revealed to him, and, more than this, a new self within his old self will make its presence felt, and a change will pass over him which he will feel it most appropriate to call a new birth. This is Christ's scheme stated in its most naked form; we shall have abundant opportunities in the sequel of expounding it more fully. But if philosophy undertakes to solve the same problem, what is its method? By what means does it hope to awaken good impulses in hearts that were before enslaved to bad ones? By eloquent exhortation perhaps, or by the examples of life led philosophically. Nay, whatever effect these instruments may have, they are instruments of the same kind as those of Christianity. Example is a personal influence, and impassioned eloquence works upon the feelings. If we are to exchange Christianity for these, it must be because the philosophers can put before us an example more elevated than that of Christ, and eloquence more impressive than that of the Sermon on the Mount. Philosophy, as such, works by reasoning, by enlightening the mind, by exposing miscalculations and revealing things as they are. Now by what process of this kind can the bad man be turned into the good? Where is the demonstration that will make the selfish man prefer another's interest to his own? Your dialectic may force him to acknowledge the right action, but where is the dialectic that shall force him to do it? Where is the logical dilemma that can make a knave honest?

The truth is that philosophy has no instruments that it can use for this purpose. There exists no other such instrument but that personal one of which Christ availed himself. And this personal influence it is the natural operation of philosophy in some degree to counteract. So far from creating good impulses, philosophy does something towards paralysing and destroying them. For perpetual and absorbing mental activity blunts in some degree those feelings in which the life of virtue resides; at the same time it creates a habit of solitude, and solitude is the death of all but the strongest virtue. But the philosopher may answer to this that the more important part of moral improvement is that which explains to us what it is right to do, and that good impulses are provided by nature with tolerable impartiality to all. We may think that good impulses do not require to be artificially provided, or that they cannot be provided in any great degree by any machinery. Well! it is a question of fact. His own experience must decide it for each person. Assuredly there are vast moral differences in the people we meet, and we are able for the most part to refer those differences to some cause or other. Let the Christian principle be compared in its results with the philosophical one; that is, let the virtue which has arisen from contact and personal ties with the good be compared with that which is the unaided fruit of solitary reflection. Who is the philosophic good man? He is one who has considered all the objects and consequences of human action; he has, in the first place, per-

Nature of Christ's Society

ceived that there is in him a principle of sympathy, the due development of which demands that he should habitually consider the advantage of others; he has been led by reflection to perceive that the advantage of one individual may often involve the injury of several; he has thence concluded that it is necessary to lay down systematic rules for his actions lest he should be led into such miscalculations, and he has in this reasonable and gradual manner arrived at a system of morality. This is the philosophic good man. Do we find the result satisfactory? Do we not find in him a languid, melancholic, dull and hard temperament of virtue? He does right perhaps, but without warmth or promptitude. And no wonder! The principle of sympathy was feeble in him at the beginning for want of contact with those who might have called it into play, and it has been made feebler still by hard brain-work and solitude. He startles us at times by sudden immoralities into which he is betrayed by ingenuity unchecked by healthy feeling. His virtue has intermissions and fits of lassitude; he becomes guilty of small transgressions for which he hopes to compensate by works of easy supererogation. Virtue thus exhibited does not excite in the beholder those " strange yearnings " of devotion of which Plato spoke. No one loves such a man; people feel for him an esteem mixed with pity. On the other hand, who is the good man that we admire and love? How do men become for the most part " pure, generous, and humane "? By personal, not by logical influences. They have been reared by parents who had these qualities, they have lived in a society which had a high tone, they have been accustomed to see just acts done, to hear gentle words spoken, and the justness and the gentleness have passed into their hearts and slowly moulded their habits, and made their moral discernment clear; they remember commands and prohibitions which it is a pleasure to obey for the sake of those who gave them; often they think of those who may be dead and say, " How would this action appear to him? Would he approve that word, or disapprove it? " To such no baseness appears a small baseness because its consequences may be small, nor does the yoke of law seem burdensome although it is ever on their necks, nor do they dream of covering a sin by an atoning act of virtue. Often in solitude they blush when some impure fancy sails across the clear heaven of their minds, because they are never alone, because the absent Examples, the Authorities they still revere, rule not their actions only but their inmost hearts; because their conscience is indeed awake and alive, representing all the nobleness with which they stand in sympathy, and reporting their most hidden indecorum before a public opinion of the absent and the dead.

Of these two influences—that of Reason and that of Living Example—which would a wise reformer reinforce? Christ chose the last. He gathered all men into a common relation to himself, and demanded that each should set him on the pedestal of his heart, giving a lower place to all other objects of worship, to father and mother, to husband or wife. In him should the loyalty of all hearts centre, he should be their pattern, their Authority, and Judge. Of him and his service should no man be ashamed, but to those who acknowledged it morality should be an easy yoke, and the law of right as spontaneous as the law of life; sufferings should be easy to bear, and the loss of worldly friends repaired by a new home in the bosom of the Christian kingdom; finally, in death itself their sleep should be sweet upon whose tombstone it could be written " Obdormivit in Christo."

We have insisted upon the effect of personal influence in creating virtuous impulses. We have described Christ's Theocracy as a great attempt to set all the virtue of the world upon this basis, and to give it a visible centre or fountain. But we have used generalities. It is advisable, before quitting the subject, to give a single example of the magical passing of virtue out of the virtuous man into the hearts of those with whom he comes in contact. A remarkable story which appears in St. John's biography, though it is apparently an interpolation in that place, may serve this purpose, and will at the same

Nature of Christ's Society 83

time illustrate the difference between scholastic or scientific and living or instinctive virtue. Some of the leading religious men of Jerusalem had detected a woman in adultery. It occurred to them that the case afforded a good opportunity of making an experiment upon Christ. They might use it to discover how he regarded the Mosaic law. That he was heterodox on the subject of that law they had reason to believe, for he had openly quoted some Mosaic maxims and declared them at least incomplete, substituting for them new rules of his own, which at least in some cases appeared to abrogate the old. It might be possible, they thought, by means of this woman to satisfy at once themselves and the people of his heterodoxy. They brought the woman before him, quoted the law of Moses on the subject of adultery, and asked Christ directly whether he agreed with the lawgiver. They asked for his judgment.

A judgment he gave them, but quite different, both in matter and manner, from what they had expected. In thinking of the " case " they had forgotten the woman, they had forgotten even the deed. What became of the criminal appeared to them wholly unimportant; towards her crime or her character they had no feeling whatever, not even hatred, still less pity or sympathetic shame. If they had been asked about her, they might probably have answered, with Mephistopheles, " She is not the first "; nor would they have thought their answer fiendish, only practical and business-like. Perhaps they might on reflection have admitted that their frame of mind was not strictly moral, not quite what it should be, that it would have been better if, besides considering the legal and religious questions involved, they could have found leisure for some shame at the scandal and some hatred for the sinner. But they would have argued that such strict propriety is not possible in this world, that we have too much on our hands to think of these niceties, that the man who makes leisure for such refinements will find his work in arrears at the end of the day, and probably also that he is doing injustice to his family and those dependent on him.

This they might fluently and plausibly have urged. But the judgment of Christ was upon them, making all things seem new, and shining like the lightning from the one end of heaven to the other. He was standing, it would seem, in the centre of a circle, when the crime was narrated, how the adultery had been detected *in the very act*. The shame of the deed itself, and the brazen hardness of the prosecutors, the legality that had no justice and did not even pretend to have mercy, the religious malice that could make its advantage out of the fall and ruin and ignominious death of a fellow-creature—all this was eagerly and rudely thrust before his mind at once. The effect upon him was such as might have been produced upon many since, but perhaps upon scarcely any man that ever lived before. He was seized with an intolerable sense of shame. He could not meet the eye of the crowd, or of the accusers, and perhaps at that moment least of all of the woman. Standing as he did in the midst of an eager multitude that did not in the least appreciate his feelings, he could not escape. In his burning embarrassment and confusion he stooped down so as to hide his face, and began writing with his finger on the ground. His tormentors continued their clamour, until he raised his head for a moment and said, " He that is without sin among you let him first cast a stone at her," and then instantly returned to his former attitude. They had a glimpse perhaps of the glowing blush upon his face, and awoke suddenly with astonishment to a new sense of their condition and their conduct. The older men naturally felt it first and slunk away; the younger followed their example. The crowd dissolved and left Christ alone with the woman. Not till then could he bear to stand upright; and when he had lifted himself up, consistently with his principle, he dismissed the woman, as having no commission to interfere with the office of the civil judge.

But the mighty power of living purity had done its work. He had refused to judge a woman, but he had judged a whole crowd. He had awakened the slumbering conscience in many hardened hearts, given them a

Nature of Christ's Society

new delicacy, a new ideal, a new view and reading of the Mosaic law.

And yet this crowd was either indifferent or bitterly hostile to him. Let us imagine the correcting, elevating influence of his presence upon those who, so far from being indifferent, were bound to him by the ties which bind a soldier to his superior officer, a clansman to his chief, a subject to a king ruling by Divine right, aye, and by ties far closer. The ancient philosophers were accustomed to enquire about virtue, whether it can be taught. Yes! it can be taught, and in this way. But if this way be abandoned, and moral philosophy be set up to do that which in the nature of things philosophy can never do, the effect will appear in a certain slow deterioration of manners which it would be hard to describe had it not been described already in well-known words: " Sophistry and calculation " will take the place of " chivalry." There will be no more " generous loyalty," no more " proud submission," no more " dignified obedience." A stain will no more be felt like a wound, and our hardened and coarsened manners will lose the " sensibility of principle and the chastity of honour."

PART SECOND

CHRIST'S LEGISLATION

CHAPTER X

CHRIST'S LEGISLATION COMPARED WITH PHILOSOPHIC SYSTEMS

We have thus traced the rise of a monarchy, the purest and the most ideal that has ever existed among men. The most ideal, for in this monarchy alone the obedience of the subject was in no case reluctant or mercenary, but grounded upon a genuine conviction of the immeasurable superiority in goodness, wisdom, and power of the ruler. Such a superiority is always supposed to exist in a king, and to constitute the ground of his authority; but this is in most cases a fiction which deceives no one, and only sustains itself in bombastic titles and hollow liturgies of court etiquette. Where, however, the king has risen in disturbed times from a private station, and has won his sceptre by merit, the theory is no mere constitutional fiction. Such a king is, to many of his subjects, the true master he claims to be to all; there are many who obey him from a voluntary loyalty, who do in their hearts worship his superiority, and who find their freedom in accepting his yoke. But even in this case there are many whose submission is reluctant and sullen, or else mercenary and hypocritical. There is always at least a minority whose subjection is secured by force. In Christ's monarchy no force was used, though all power was at command; the obedience of his servants became in the end, though not till after his departure, absolutely unqualified, even when it involved the sacrifice of life; and

Christ's Legislation

it was obtained from them by no other means than the natural influence of a natural superiority.

This monarchy was essentially despotic, and might, in spite of the goodness of the sovereign, have had some mischievous consequences, if he had remained too long among his subjects, and if his dictation had descended too much into particulars. But he shunned the details of administration, and assumed only the higher functions of a heroic monarch—those of organisation and legislation. And when these were sufficiently discharged, when his whole mind and will had expressed itself in precept and signed itself for ever in transcendent deeds, he withdrew to a secret post of observation, from whence he visited his people for the future only in refreshing inspirations and great acts of providential justice.

The time has now come for examining the legislation which Christ gave to his Society. It has an important point of likeness and at the same time of unlikeness to the legislation which it superseded. The legislation which Jehovah gave to the Jews was always regarded by them not merely as a rule for their own actions, but as a reflection and revelation of the character of their Invisible King. The faithful Jew in obeying Jehovah became like Him. This inspiring reflection gave life and moral vigour to the Mosaic system. But that system laboured at the same time under the disadvantage that Jehovah was known to His subjects *only* through His law. Only in prohibition and penalty was He revealed, only in thunder could His voice be heard. Now the law of Christ was in like manner a reflection of the mind of the lawgiver; but the new Jehovah made his character known not by his code merely, but by a life led in the sight of men, by " going in and out " among the people. The effect of this novelty was incalculable. It was a moral emancipation; it was freedom succeeding slavery. The experience of daily life may explain this to us. It is a slavish toil to learn any art by text-books merely, without the assistance of a tutor; the written rule is of little use, is scarcely intelligible, until we have seen it reduced to practice by one who can practise it easily and make its justice apparent. The ease and readiness of the master are infectious; the pupil, as he looks on, conceives a new hope, a new self-reliance; he seems already to touch the goal which before appeared removed to a hopeless distance. It is a slavery when soldiers are driven against the enemy by the despotic command of a leader who does not share the danger, but the service becomes free and glorious when the general rides to the front. Such was the revival of spirit which the Jew experienced when he took the oath to Christ, and which he described by saying that he was no longer under the law but under grace. He had gained a tutor instead of a text-book, a leader instead of a master, and when he learned what to do, he learned at the same time how to do it, and received encouragement in attempting it. And the law which Christ gave was not only illustrated, but infinitely enlarged by his deeds. For every deed was itself a precedent to be followed, and therefore to discuss the legislation of Christ is to discuss his character: for it may be justly said that Christ himself is the Christian law.

We must therefore be careful not to consider Christ's maxims apart from the deeds which were intended to illustrate them. There have been few teachers whose words will less bear to be divorced from their context of occasion and circumstance. But we find in our biographies the report of a long discourse, which, as far as we know, was suggested by no special incidents, and which seems to have been intended as a general exposition of the laws of the new kingdom. This discourse is commonly called the Sermon on the Mount; it is recognised by all as the fundamental document of Christian morality, and by some it is regarded as constituting Christ's principal claim upon the homage of the world. Naturally therefore it first attracts the attention of those who wish to consider him in his character of legislator or moralist.

The style of the Sermon on the Mount is neither purely philosophical nor purely practical. It refers throughout to first principles, but it does not state them in an abstract form; on the other hand, it enters into special cases and detail, but never so far as to lose sight of

Christ's Legislation

first principles. It is equally unlike the early national codes, which simply formularised without method existing customs, and the early moral treatises such as those of Plato and Aristotle, which are purely scientific. Of Jewish writings it resembles most the book of Deuteronomy, in which the Mosaic law was recapitulated in such a manner as to make the principles on which it was founded apparent; of Gentile writings it may be compared with those of Epictetus, Aurelius, and Seneca, in which we see a scientific morality brought to bear upon the struggles and details of actual life. It uses all the philosophical machinery of generalisation and distinction, but its object is not philosophical but practical—that is, not truth but good.

As then this discourse has a philosophic unity, let us try to discover what that unity is. As it propounds to us a scheme of life founded upon a principle, let us try to state the principle. The work of all legislators, reformers, and philosophers is in one respect alike; it is in all cases a protest against a kind of life which, notwithstanding, might seem to have its attractions, which, at any rate, suggests itself very naturally to men, and is not abandoned without reluctance. All reformers call on men to reduce their lives to a rule different from that of immediate self-interest, to live according to a permanent principle and not, as the poet says, " at random." Against the dominion of appetite all the teachers of mankind are at one: all agree in repudiating the doctrine of the savage:

> I bow to ne'er a god except myself,
> And to my Belly, first of deities.
> To eat and drink your daily food and drink,
> This is the creed of sober-minded people,
> And not to fret yourself. But those who make
> Laws, and sophisticate the life of man,
> I bid them pack.

In the time of Christ, when Socrates had been in his grave four hundred years, it was hardly necessary for a philosopher to inveigh in set terms against such naked self-indulgence. The rudimentary lessons of philosophy had now been widely diffused. But as Christ called the poor into his kingdom, and addressed his invitation to those whom no reformer had hoped before to win, he was at the trouble to reason with this grossest egoism. On one occasion he told a homely tale of a man who, absorbed in the pursuit and enjoyment of wealth, was struck at the very moment of complete self-satisfaction by sudden death, and compelled to relinquish the treasures he had sacrificed every lasting good to amass. At another time he went further, and described tortures and agonies which might await on the further side of death some whose lot had been most enviable on this. And in the discourse before us he expostulates, though in a gentler tone, with the same class of sensualists.

There are two principal ways of rebuking lawless sensuality: it is most important to consider whether Christ's method coincides with either of them. The first is to admit the sensualist to be right in his end, but charge him with clumsiness in his choice of means. To get the greatest amount of pleasure, it may be said, is the only rational object which a man can propose to himself; but to suppose that this object can be attained either by recklessly gratifying every desire as it arises, or by collecting huge heaps of the ordinary material of pleasure, such as money or food or fine clothes, is childish. Pleasure is a delicate plant, and cannot be cultivated without much study and practice. Any excess of it is followed by a reaction of disgust and by a diminution in the power of entertaining it. If you would live in the constant enjoyment of it, you must carefully ascertain how large a dose it will be safe to take at a time, and then you must drill yourself by a constant discipline never to exceed that dose. Again, what is pleasant to one man is not equally so to another; you must study your own disposition; you must learn to know your own mind, and not slavishly enjoy through another man's senses. Once more, pleasant things, such as food or fine clothes, are indeed among the conditions of pleasure, but they do not by themselves constitute it. He who devotes himself to the acquisition of these, and neglects to prepare his own mind for the full enjoyment of them, will defeat his own object and sacrifice the end to the means. We must therefore tell the

Christ's Legislation

sensualist not that he loves pleasure too much, but that he ought to love it more, that he ought to seek it more exclusively, and not to suffer himself to be cheated by the mere external semblance and counterfeit of it.

Of course it is quite unjust to represent this theory as repudiating moral virtue. Among the indispensable conditions of pleasure virtue may very well be reckoned: it is perfectly open to an Epicurean philosopher to declare all other instruments of pleasure to be inoperative and useless compared with or independent of virtue. And those who think that we should not make pleasure our chief object, yet commonly maintain that he who lives best will actually attain the greatest amount and the best kind of pleasure; so that the most successful votary of pleasure would coincide with the ideal man of the very schools which most vehemently denounce pleasure-worship. The practical objection to Epicureanism is not so much that it makes pleasure the *summum bonum*, as that it recommends us to keep this *summum bonum* always in view. For it is far from being universally true that to get a thing you must aim at it. There are some things which can only be gained by renouncing them. To use a familiar illustration: it is easy to breathe evenly so long as you do not think about it; but as soon as you try, it becomes impossible. Many of the moral virtues are of this kind. Simplicity of character cannot be produced by thinking of it; rather, the more you think of it the further you travel into the opposite extreme of self-consciousness. The grace of humility is not to be won by constantly comparing yourself with others and cataloguing your deficiencies; this method is more likely to issue in hypocritical self-conceit. Now, a practical survey of life seems to show that pleasure in its largest sense—a true and deep enjoyment of life—is also not to be gained artificially. Much of what Epicureans say is doubtless true and valuable; our pleasures may be considerably heightened by a little common sense; we often break the cup or upset it in our excessive eagerness to drain it to the bottom. Still, we destroy pleasure by making it our chief object; its essential nature is corrupted when it is made into a business: the highest perfection of it is not among the prizes of exertion, the rewards of industry or ingenuity, but a bounty of nature, a grace of God. By contrivance and skill only an inferior sort can be attained, to which the keenness, the glee, the racy bitter of the sweet, is wanting. And this is the utmost that can be attained; this is what can be made of pleasure by the most skilful artificers of it. What, then, would the poor and simple-minded gain from such a principle? Epicureanism popularised inevitably turns to vice; no skill in the preachers of it will avail for a moment to prevent the obscene transformation. It would probably be safe to go farther, and say that Epicureanism means vice in all cases except where a rare refinement and tenderness of nature creates a natural propensity to virtue so strong as to disarm the most corrupting influence.

We need not, then, be surprised to find that Christ, whose purpose was entirely practical, and who was legislating not for a small minority but for mankind, did not place his reproof of sensuality on this ground. When he said, " Fret not yourself about your life what ye shall eat, nor about your body what ye shall put on," he did not go on to say, " Remember for what end food and clothing are intended; remember that they are only the appliances of pleasure, and make it your object to gain pleasure not through these means only, but by every means within your reach, including moral virtue." But he proposes another object altogether—" the kingdom of God and his righteousness."

There is another way in which it has been common to argue with the sensualist. It has been said that the sensualist makes bodily pleasure his object, and that in so doing he forgets that man possesses a soul as well as a body. This soul, it is said, is the nobler part of the man; the body is but a base appendage more or less useful, but so far inferior that it should be treated as a slave, and so intractable that it requires to be coerced, punished, kept to hard labour, and stinted of sustenance and pleasure. The interests of the body are not worth considering; the man should occupy himself with those of the soul—that is, the acquisition of knowledge, self-sufficiency, and virtue.

Christ's Legislation

But this reasoning, in the first place, convinces very few, and, in the second, has an injurious effect upon those whom it convinces. The soul and body are inextricably united. It is of no practical use to consider them apart; and if we do so, it is clear that the human body is not a base or mean thing, but, on the contrary, one of the most noble and glorious things known. Again, if it is to be made subservient to the soul, experience abundantly shows that the soul does not advance its own interests by maltreating its slave. Discipline and coercion may sometimes be necessary, but the soul loses its tone and health if the interests of the body are not consulted, and if its desires are not in a moderate degree satisfied. And those who learn from these reasoners to depreciate the body, first become inhumanly cold to natural beauty and out of sympathy with the material universe, and secondly, while they slight their own bodily comforts, disregard the physical well-being of their neighbours, and become unfeeling and cruel.

Christ, then, as a practical legislator, did not depreciate the body. On the contrary, he showed, both in this Sermon and in his whole career, a tenderness of the bodily well-being of men, such as no philosophical school except the Epicureans had shown, and such as the Epicureans themselves had not surpassed. He spent the greater part of his short life in healing sick people, and of the comforts which he restored to others he did not disdain himself to partake. He was to be met at weddings; many of the discourses which his biographies preserve were suggested by the incidents of feasts and banquets at which he was present; and so marked was the absence of asceticism both in his own life and in that which he prescribed for his disciples, that his enemies called him a glutton and a wine-bibber, and he had to apologise for the indulgent character of his discipline by pointing with sad foresight to the sufferings which his followers would all too soon have to endure. But the words of this Sermon are even more striking. He divides himself at once from the ascetic and the Stoic. They had said, " Make yourselves independent of bodily comforts " ; *he* says, " Ye have need of these things. But if the Epicurean or the sensualist take advantage of these words and say, " If you have need of these things, make it your study to obtain them," he parts company not less decidedly with these, and says, " True pleasure is not thus to be had. It is the healthy bloom of the spirit which must come naturally or not at all. Those who think about it lose it, or, if not, produce with all their labour but a poor imitation of it. Self-consciousness and sensualism is the enemy of true delight. Solomon on his throne was gaudy; the lilies of the field are better drest. Epicurus in his garden was languid; the birds of the air have more enjoyment of their food."

We are therefore to dismiss pleasure from our thoughts as a thing which we are indeed made to possess, yet are unable by our own efforts to obtain. We are to expect that it will come of itself, and in the meanwhile we are to adopt a mode of life which has no reference to it. But if this rule should prescribe a course of conduct which so far from producing pleasure should involve us in the most painful difficulties and hardships, shall we then turn back as though the promise were unfulfilled? And if it should issue in death itself, and thus absolutely prevent to all appearance the promise from being fulfilled, what shall we think? Christ anticipates our perplexity. Such cases he tells us will frequently arise. His rule of life *will* often, nay generally, involve us in hardships, and at certain periods in death itself. But the Creator of the world, our Father in Heaven, from whom alone, in all cases, genuine pleasure and satisfaction comes, is more to be trusted than these adverse appearances. Pleasure shall assuredly be ours, but in no extremity are we to make it our object. You shall suffer and yet you shall enjoy. Both are certain, and it is not worth while to attempt to reconcile the apparent contradiction. " Some of you shall they put to death . . . and there shall not a hair of your head perish."

This paradoxical position—that pleasure is necessary for us, and yet that it is not to be sought; that this world is to be renounced, and yet that it is noble and glorious—

Christ's Legislation

might, if it had been taken up by a philosopher, have been regarded as a subtlety which it would be impossible to act upon. But as the law laid down by a King and Master of mankind, every word of whom was treasured up and acted out with devotion, it has had a surprising influence upon human affairs. In the times of the Roman Emperors there appeared a sect which distinguished itself by the assiduous attention which it bestowed upon the bodily wants of mankind. This sect set the first example of a homely practical philanthropy, occupying itself with the relief of ordinary human sufferings, dispensing food and clothing to the destitute and starving. At the same period there appeared a sect which was remarkable for the contempt in which it held human suffering. Roman magistrates were perplexed to find, when it became necessary to coerce this sect by penal inflictions, that bodily pains, tortures, and death itself were not regarded as evils by its members. These two sects appeared to run into contrary extremes. The one seemed to carry their regard for the body to the borders of effeminacy; the other pushed Stoical apathy almost to madness. Yet these two sects were one and the same—the Christian Church. And though within that body every conceivable corruption has at some time or other sprung up, this tradition has never been long lost, and in every age the Christian temper has shivered at the touch of Stoic apathy and shuddered at that of Epicurean indolence.

But we have not yet, except by negatives, answered the question how Christ argued with the sensualist. We have discovered as yet only that he did *not* employ two common arguments. For a lawless pursuit of bodily enjoyment he did not exhort him to substitute either a methodical pursuit of the same object or a pursuit of intellectual and moral well-being. What, then, did he substitute? What was that " kingdom of God and his righteousness " which he bade men make the first object of their search?

CHAPTER XI

THE CHRISTIAN REPUBLIC

" SEEK ye first the kingdom of God and his righteousness." This exhortation is precisely what we had reason to expect, for we have already remarked that the cry which John raised in the desert, " The kingdom of heaven is at hand," was taken up by Christ, and that his life was devoted to proclaiming this new political constitution, to collecting adherents to it, and promulgating its laws. That kingdom of God into which he called men he elevates in this passage into the *summum bonum* of human life, and represents it as the secret of happiness and of all enduring good to belong to the divine society, and to understand and keep the rules prescribed for its members.

Before we enquire into the nature of this society and of its rules, it is important to consider what is implied in the fact that Christ placed the happiness of man in a political constitution. The philosophical schemes which we have described Christ as rejecting consider man as an independent being, and provide for him an isolated happiness or welfare. The ideal Epicurean is described as indifferent to public affairs and falling kingdoms, and exempt from the pain alike of pity for the poor and jealousy of the rich. To be self-sufficient was a principal ambition of the rival school. But a member of a state is one who has ceased to have a personal object, and who has made his welfare dependent on that of others. He sacrifices himself to the body of which he has become a member. In giving up present pleasure he does not differ from the isolated man of the philosophers, but he differs from him in giving it up not prudentially that he may get more of it in the end or something better than it, but disinterestedly and for the sake of other people. It is no doubt true that a man's

The Christian Republic

personal happiness is much increased by becoming a member of a community and having an object apart from himself; for, according to the paradox already stated, no man is so happy as he who does not aim at happiness. But that such personal happiness is not the ultimate object of the social union is plain from this, that men are expected to sacrifice not a part of their happiness, but all of it, for the state, and to die in battle for a cause in which they may have no personal interest, and which they may even hold to be unjust. It was not with any personal object whatever, it was with no hope of reward in a future state, it was not for glory, if their poet may be believed, but in obedience to the laws of Sparta, that the three hundred laid down their lives in the pass of Thermopylæ. Such a disinterested surrender is implied in the very notion of a political community. It is accordingly inculcated throughout this discourse as the great duty of those who enter the kingdom of God. They are to surrender all personal claims—not only, as Christ said often on other occasions, goods and property, life and family ties, but other claims, which it seems not painful merely but degrading to waive—the claims of wounded honour, of just resentment of injuries. All these things we are to be prepared to surrender, as he said elsewhere, " hoping for nothing again."

And yet it may be said the sacrifice which Christ exacts is no more genuine than that recommended by the Epicurean, for he never fails to promise a full recompense in the world to come. Scarcely once in this Sermon does he inculcate self-sacrifice without a reference to the other side of the account—to the treasures God has in store for those who despise the gold and silver of the earth. And however much we may admire the Christian martyrs, yet how can we compare their self-devotion with that of the Spartan three hundred or the Roman Decius? Those heroes surrendered *all*, and looked forward to nothing but the joyless asphodel meadow or " drear Cocytus with its languid stream." But the Christian martyr might well die with exultation, for what he lost was poor compared with that which he hoped instantly to gain. The happiness he expected may not have been sensual; it was not " the sparkle of female eyes, the handkerchief of green silk, the cap of precious stones," [1] that comforted him for the loss of this life, but he expected a personal and real, if not a sensual happiness.

It is most true that Christ's society, like all other political societies, does promise happiness to its members; it is further true that it promises this happiness, not as other societies in general, but to every individual member. The *most* complete self-sacrifice therefore, the love that gives up *all*, is impossible in the Christian Church, as it is *rarely* possible in any society, as one must suppose it impossible in the ideal society. Still the paradox must be repeated: though self-surrender lead in general, though it lead infallibly, to happiness, yet happiness is not its object. And if this seem a pedantic refinement outrageous to common sense, it will not appear so when we consider the nature of the self-surrender which Christ enjoins. For such self-surrender with such an object is simply impossible. A man can no doubt do any specific acts, however painful, with a view to his ultimate interest. With a view to his ultimate interest a man may fast, may impose painful penances on himself; nay, with a view to his ultimate interest a man may go two miles with one who has compelled him to go one, may turn the left cheek to one who has smitten him on the right, nay, may even *pray* for those that use him spitefully, although in doing so he will be guilty of the most hideous hypocrisy. But can a man, with a view to his ultimate interest, in order that he may go to heaven, *love* his enemies?

It appears throughout the Sermon on the Mount that there was a class of persons whom Christ regarded with peculiar aversion—the persons who call themselves one thing and are another. He describes them by a word which originally meant an " actor." Probably it may in Christ's time have already become current in the sense which we give to the word " hypocrite." But no doubt whenever it was used the original sense of the word was distinctly remembered. And in this Sermon, whenever

[1] The vision of the dying Islamite. See Gibbon, cap. li.

The Christian Republic

Christ denounces any vice, it is with the words, " Be not you like the actors." In common with all great reformers, Christ felt that honesty in word and deed was the fundamental virtue; dishonesty, including affectation, self-consciousness, love of stage-effect, the one incurable vice. Our thoughts, words, and deeds are to be of a piece. For example, if we would pray to God, let us go into some inner room where none but God shall see us; to pray at the corner of the streets, where the passing crowd may admire our devotion, is to *act* a prayer. If we would keep down the rebellious flesh by fasting, this concerns ourselves only; it is acting to parade before the world our self-mortification. And if we would put down sin, let us put it down in ourselves first; it is only the actor who begins by frowning at it in others. But there are subtler forms of hypocrisy, which Christ does not denounce, probably because they have sprung since out of the corruption of a subtler creed. The hypocrite of that age wanted simply money or credit with the people. His ends were those of the vulgar, though his means were different. Christ endeavoured to cure both alike of their vulgarity by telling them of other riches and another happiness laid up in heaven. Some of course would neither understand nor regard his words, others would understand and receive them. But a third class would receive them without understanding them, and, instead of being cured of their avarice and sensuality, would simply transfer them to new objects of desire. Shrewd enough to discern Christ's greatness, instinctively believing what he said to be true, they would set out with a triumphant eagerness in pursuit of the heavenly riches, and laugh at the short-sighted and weak-minded speculator who contented himself with the easy but insignificant profits of a worldly life. They would practise assiduously the rules by which Christ said heaven was to be won. They would patiently turn the left cheek, indefatigably walk the two miles, they would bless with effusion those who cursed them, and pray fluently for those who used them spitefully. To love their enemies, to love anyone, they would certainly find impossible, but the outward signs of love might easily be learnt. And thus there would arise a new class of actors, not like those whom Christ denounced, exhibiting before an earthly audience and receiving their pay from human managers, but hoping to be paid for their performance out of the incorruptible treasures, and to impose by their dramatic talent upon their Father in heaven.

Christ's meaning, however, is not doubtful. The principle is distinctly laid down. Our thoughts and deeds are to be of a piece. A pious and devout life will undoubtedly win for a man the reverence of the multitude, and yet Christ tells us when we pray we are to think of God and not of the credit we may gain. And so though by loving our neighbour and our enemy we shall win heaven, we are not to think of the heaven we shall win, we are to think of our neighbour and our enemy.

Noble-minded men [1] have often been scandalised by the appearance which Christ's law is made to wear, as if it were a system in which all virtue is corrupted by being made mercenary. The same moralists, however, would have been among the first to assert that the only true and lasting happiness is that which is gained by the practice of virtue. Christ adds nothing to this except a promise that those exceptional cases in which virtue appears to lose its reward shall prove in the end not to be exceptions. By defining virtue to consist in *love*, he brings into prominence its unselfish character; and by denouncing at the same time with vehemence all insincerity and hypocrisy, he sufficiently shows with what horror he would have regarded any interested beneficence or calculating philanthropy which may usurp the name of love.

It may, therefore, be affirmed that Christ's Kingdom is a true brotherhood founded in devotion and self-sacrifice. Nothing less, indeed, would have satisfied those disciples who had begun to feel the spell of his character. A philosophic school or sect may found itself on the prudential instincts of man, may attract empty hearts, and attach them by a loose bond to each other. But a king-

[1] Schiller, for example.

The Christian Republic 101

dom stands on self-devotion, and the hearts of Christ's disciples were not empty. They had not gathered themselves round him to be told how they might avoid the evils of life, but to know what they might do for him, how they might serve him, how they might prove their loyalty to him. It was the art of self-devotion that they wished to learn, and he taught it as a master teaches, not sparing words but resting most on deeds; by the Sermon on the Mount, but also by the Agony and the Crucifixion.

CHAPTER XII

UNIVERSALITY OF THE CHRISTIAN REPUBLIC

We discover, then, that Christ's society resembles other political societies in requiring from its members a disinterested devotion and patriotism. But to understand its essential nature it is necessary to know, not in what respects it resembles other things of the same kind, but in what respects it differs from them. We must therefore continue our investigation until we discover this difference.

It is one of the most obvious features of the Sermon on the Mount that it treats men as standing in the relation of brothers to one another under a common Father in heaven. Let us consider what is involved in this.

The earliest condition of mankind of which we have any knowledge was one of perpetual war. Homer describes a state of society in which a man was safe in the possession of his lands and flocks only so long as there was strength enough in his right arm to defend them. As soon as the primitive man began to grow old and to lose his vigour, there was danger that his neighbours would drive his cattle and encroach upon his estate. Ulysses in the early part of his wanderings, before he has lost his fleet and army, lands on the Thracian coast, and finds a city. He instantly sacks it and kills all the inhabitants. This is not because there has been a quarrel, but because there has been no treaty; the normal condition of men at that time being mutual enmity. To this mutual enmity, however, there is an exception established by an imperative law of nature. Persons of the same family live in perpetual alliance. This seems to have been originally the only tie between man and man, the only consideration that could prevent them from

The Christian Republic 103

murdering each other. Peleus in his old age will be in the greatest danger if he is deprived of Achilles, and the very children will persecute the child Astyanax after his father's death. Woe to the orphan, and woe to the old man who has not surrounded himself with children! They are the only arrows with which his quiver can be filled, the only defenders whom he can trust to speak with his enemies in the gate.

Thus in the earliest condition of things there was only one kind of community. The primitive man had no obligations, no duties, to any except his parents, his brothers, and his parents' brothers and their families. When he met with a man unrelated to him he would without hesitation take his life and his property. But the life and property of a relation were sacred, and the Greeks held that there were certain supernatural powers called Erinyes, who vindicated the rights of relatives. This sense of relationship being natural and universal and extending even to the brute creation, we cannot imagine a time when the family with its rights and obligations did not exist. But the family is a community which constantly expands until it loses itself in a more comprehensive one. It becomes a clan, the members of which may in many cases be strangers to each other, while they are, notwithstanding, bound together by the sacred tie of relationship. Again, in primitive times, when men had little power of verifying facts or weighing evidence, relationship was often supposed to exist between persons who were really of different stocks. Any resemblance was supposed to furnish a proof of relationship, and so those who spoke the same language were presumed to be descended from a common ancestor. In this way the family passed ultimately into the nation, and political constitutions and codes of law came to bind men together, grounded all alike on the supposition, true or false, that they were relations by blood. When states had once been founded and began to flourish, men began to associate with each other more freely; other grounds of obligation besides blood-relationship were gradually admitted, and finally Rome, binding together in the unity of common subjection a number of tribes strange to each other, gave a basis of fact and law to universal morality. But in states which had been isolated, and had mixed little with foreigners either by conquest or by trade, the original tradition did not die out, and men continued to say and to think that they owed obligations only to those of the same blood. This was especially true of the Jews, the most isolated of all ancient nations. Their common descent from Abraham was always present to their minds, and was the tie which bound them together. A sense of obligation they expressed by the formula, " He also is a child of Abraham "; their very religion was a worship paid to the God of Abraham, Isaac, and Jacob. And Christ himself sometimes adopted the same style, as when he reproved the vice of selfishness by representing Dives as repudiated by Abraham, and Lazarus welcomed to his bosom in the invisible world.

It was, therefore, no novelty when, in the Sermon on the Mount, Christ described those who entered the Kingdom of God as standing in the relation of brothers to one another. In doing so he only used the ordinary language of what may be called ethnic morality. The novelty lies here that he does not ground the mutual obligations of men upon a common descent from Abraham, but upon a common descent from God.

It is not difficult to see what follows from this change of style. By substituting the Father in Heaven for father Abraham, Christ made morality universal. This phrase, which places not a certain number of men, but all men, in the relation of brotherhood to each other, destroys at once the partition-wall between Jew and Gentile, Greek and barbarian, German and Welsh, white man and Negro, or under whatever names the families of the earth have justified and legalised the savage instinct of antipathy. It is not to be imagined that the thought was new or original; Christ was no theorist or philosopher, but a legislator. The thought had existed in the mind of Socrates, when he called himself a citizen of the world; it had become a commonplace of the Stoic philosophy; it was taken up by Roman jurists, and worked into the imperial legislation.

The Christian Republic 105

But to work it into the hearts and consciences of men required a much higher and rarer power, the power of a ruler, not of a philosopher. It may have been the thought of a Julianus or a Papinianus that all the Roman world had a right to Roman citizenship; but it was the Cæsar, Antoninus Caracalla, who gave the right; and, in like manner, what a Socrates and a Zeno and many Hebrew prophets had claimed for men, was given to them by this Edict from the Mount.

The first law, then, of the Kingdom of God, is that all men, however divided from each other by blood or language, have certain mutual duties arising out of their common relation to God. It may, however, be urged that this law was superfluous. Without denying the fact that at an earlier time nations had regarded each other as natural enemies, without maintaining that the philosophic doctrine of a unity in the human race had had much practical influence, it may still be urged that the Roman Empire had already realised that unity which philosophers had imagined and to which Christ now gives a late sanction. By the Roman conquests a number of different nations had been brought together and united under a common government. In the period immediately succeeding their subjugation they had, no doubt, been treated by their conquerors with insolent oppression. It was plain that proconsuls and proprætors had little sense of duty in regard to their subjects. The principal object of their government was to preserve to the state its acquisition, and the secondary object to reap some personal advantage from it. But time had produced a great improvement. The sense of duty, which at first was wanting, had been awakened. A morality not founded on blood-relation had certainly come into existence. The Roman citizenship had been thrown open to nations which were not of Roman blood. A hundred years before the Sermon on the Mount was delivered Cicero had roused public indignation against an unjust and rapacious proprætor. Since that time foreigners had been admitted by the Roman state to the highest civic honours. And in the centuries that followed, the process by which nations were being fused into one universal society went steadily forward without any help from Christian maxims. So signally, so much more than in later and Christian ages, were national distinctions obliterated under the Empire, that men of all nations and languages competed freely under the same political system for the highest honours of the state and of literature. The good Aurelius and the great Trajan were Spaniards. So were Seneca and Martial. Severus was an African. The leading jurists were of Oriental extraction.

All this is true. A number of nations which had before waged incessant war with one another had been forced into a sort of unity. What court-poets call a golden age had set in. Round the whole shore of the Mediterranean Sea, and northward to the Danube and beyond the British Channel, national antipathies had been suppressed, and war had ceased, while the lives of men were regulated by an admirable code of laws. Yet, except to court-poets, this age did not seem golden to those who lived in it. On the contrary, they said it was something worse than an iron age; there was no metal from which they could name it. Never did men live under such a crushing sense of degradation, never did they look back with more bitter regret, never were the vices that spring out of despair so rife, never was sensuality cultivated more methodically, never did poetry curdle so readily into satire, never was genius so much soured by cynicism, and never was calumny so abundant or so gross or so easily believed. If morality depended on laws, or happiness could be measured by comfort, this would have been the most glorious era in the past history of mankind. It was in fact one of the meanest and foulest, because a tone or spirit is necessary to morality, and self-respect is needful to happiness.

Ancient morality, as it has been already remarked, was essentially national and exclusive. Its creed was that a man is born not for himself, but for his parents, his family, and the state. The state was surrounded by others with which, unless some treaty had been concluded,

The Christian Republic 107

it was at war. To do as much good as possible to one's own state, and as much harm as possible to all other states, was therefore the whole duty of a man. Those who performed this duty manfully might look for the protection of the gods who lived in temples built for them within the walls of the city, and who were feasted and enriched with the spoils of other nations. Now this whole scheme of morality had been overturned by the Roman conquests. For they had destroyed the very principle of nationality both among conquerors and conquered. Among the conquered nations, for their gods had left them, and their freedom, which, as they said themselves, was half their virtue, and their isolation, which was the other half, were taken away. Among the Romans themselves, for they had been compelled to raise the conquered to their own level, and they knew not what to make of their new condition when their own country no longer required to be defended or enriched, and there were scarcely any more foreign countries to be invaded. Yet, their poets thought, they might at least have occupied themselves with conquering these. " Shame on you! " says Lucan, " You turned your arms against each other, *when you might have been sacking Babylon.*"

The nations were thus forced into a unity for which they were not prepared. Ethnic morality, the light under which their fathers had lived, which had given them self-respect, strength in hardships, and a sense of satisfaction in the hour of death, was now useless, and universal morality was a thing unknown, or at least untried. On this new path they were cheered by no great memories, guided by no acknowledged rules. When they treated a foreigner as a fellow-citizen, the spirits of their fathers seemed to reproach them, and they derived but cold comfort from the approval of Stoic philosophers. Men did what was right with the feeling that they were doing wrong. The most mortal evil that can befall mankind had befallen them—conscience took the wrong side.

It was not a repetition of the Stoic maxim in more emphatic terms that purified the human conscience. It was the personality of Christ exciting a veneration and worship which effaced in the minds of his followers their hereditary and habitual worships. No theory, says a Greek poet, will throw down ancestral traditions. This is true; but they can be overthrown by a passionate personal devotion. Father Abraham, seceding from his Chaldean community in obedience to a divine Call, and thus dividing Jew from Gentile as strongly as he united Jew with Jew, would have resisted many generations of Rabbinical teachers. Father Æneas bearing from the flames of Troy the venerated symbols of Roman unity and isolation would have been too strong for the Stoic philosophy. Both alike faded like phantoms, both alike were superannuated, the moment the heart is touched. And in order that those who worshipped his person might not forget his fundamental law, Christ assumed a title expressing the universality of his dominion, as kings have often borne titles taken from the nations they have added to the empire, and called himself the Son of Man.

How opportune this Edict of Comprehension was we may learn by considering for a moment the writings of Juvenal. This poet reflects the deep dissatisfaction, the bitter sense of degeneracy and degradation, which characterised his age. Now what is the ground of his despondency? what provokes the savage indignation, which made him a satirist? If we examine, we shall find that it is one and the same grievance which inspires almost every fierce tirade, namely, the mixture of races. Life seems to him not worth having when the Roman cannot walk the *Via Sacra* unelbowed by Greeks and Syrians. All distinctions, he complains, are lost; the Roman worships the Egyptian monster-deities whom his own national gods vanquished at Actium; Orontes empties itself into Tiber; it is time for a Roman to turn his back on his own city when it has become a thing of no account that his infancy breathed the air of Aventine and was fed upon the Sabine berry. Now this very writer is a Stoic, familiar of necessity with the speculations which made the wise and good of all nations citizens alike in the city of

The Christian Republic 109

God. So little power had any such philosophic theory to supply the place of a morality founded on usage, on filial reverence, on great and dear examples. Yet that theory, if it had presented itself to him, not as an ambitious speculation of philosophers, but as a sober account of an actual fact, would have dried up the source of his satire. He would not have regretted the downfall of national distinctions, if they had been abolished by an authority equal in his mind to that which had created them. To minds perplexed like his it was, therefore, the beginning of a new life and hope when a new Romulus gathered into a new republic the chaos of nations. The city of God, of which the Stoics doubtfully and feebly spoke, was now set up before the eyes of men. It was no insubstantial city, such as we fancy in the clouds, no invisible pattern such as Plato thought might be laid up in heaven, but a visible corporation whose members met together to eat bread and drink wine, and into which they were initiated by bodily immersion in water. Here the Gentile met the Jew whom he had been accustomed to regard as an enemy of the human race; the Roman met the lying Greek sophist, the Syrian slave the gladiator born beside the Danube. In brotherhood they met, the natural birth and kindred of each forgotten, the baptism alone remembered in which they had been born again to God and to each other.

The mention of slaves and gladiators reminds us that ethnic morality had, besides putting discord between states, created certain positive institutions. As under that system obligations subsisted only between blood-relations, and each tribe might without provocation or pretext attack and slaughter any foreign community, so had it the right of reducing foreigners to slavery. Whether death or slavery should be inflicted on the conquered enemy was, in fact, not a question of morality or mercy, but simply of calculation. In either case the captive was deprived of life so far as life is a valuable or desirable possession; if he was allowed to exist, it was not for his own sake, but as a property more or less valuable to his master. Not that the lot of the slave was always or inevitably miserable; natural kindness, which was not killed but only partially paralysed by ethnic morality, and which was always essentially Christian, might indefinitely and in an indefinite number of instances mitigate the bitterness of his lot; but theoretically he had no more claim to consideration or care at the hand of his master, no more right to happiness, than if he had been slain at the moment of his capture. Everywhere then throughout the Roman world there was a class of outcasts whom it was supposed lawful to treat with heartless cruelty, such as would have been held unlawful if the objects of it had been fellow-citizens. The ground on which this right had originally been founded was that the class in question consisted either of prisoners taken in war, or of the descendants of such prisoners; and that as they were protected by no treaties, their lives and fortunes were at the disposal of their captors, or of others to whom the rights of the captor had passed by purchase.

Now although Christ never, so far as we know, had occasion to pronounce judgment on the question of slavery, yet we do not require the testimony of his earliest followers (declaring that in Christ Jesus there is neither bond nor free) to assure us that, considered in this sense, slavery could not be reconciled with his law. The Edict of Comprehension conferred citizenship upon the whole outcast class. Under it, whatever law of mutual help and consideration had obtained between citizen and citizen, began to obtain between the citizen and his slaves. The words " foreign "and" barbarous " lost their meaning; all nations and tribes were gathered within the pomœrium of the city of God; and on the baptised earth the Rhine and the Thames became as Jordan, and every sullen desert-girdled settlement of German savages as sacred as Jerusalem.

Therefore it is that St. Paul, writing to Philemon, exhorts him to receive back Onesimus " no longer as a servant, but as a brother beloved." It may, however, surprise us that he does not exhort Philemon to emancipate him. But this does not seem to occur to the apostle; and it has been made matter of complaint against the Christian

The Christian Republic

Church, that, though it announced principle fundamentally irreconcilable with slavery, it never pronounced the institution itself unlawful. Nor can it be denied that, instead of telling the slave that he was wronged, and exhorting him in the name of human nature, degraded in his person, to take the first opportunity of shaking off the yoke, the first Christian teachers exhorted him to obedience, and declared it particularly meritorious to be submissive to a cruel and unreasonable master, while, on the other hand, they exhorted the masters not to set their slaves free, but simply to treat them well.

The explanation of this is, that under the name of slavery two essentially different institutions were confounded, only one of which was irreconcilable with Christian principle. Slavery may mean the degradation of a person into a thing, the condition of a man who has no claims upon his fellow-men. This is essentially monstrous, and has always been condemned by Christianity. But it may mean merely a condition of dependence, differing from that of a free servant only in its being compulsory, and in the rights of the master being transferable by purchase. The latter kind of slavery does not depend upon the theory of ethnic morality; it does not deny that the slave has rights or claims upon his master; it depends upon the assumption of a natural inferiority in the slave incapacitating him for judging of his own rights or for living in happiness except under guardianship or restraint. Now, as Christianity, in asserting the unity of the human race, and their equality in the sight of God and Christ, did not declare war upon the social system which arranges men according to " degree, priority, and place," and binds them together by ties of loyalty and obedience, as it did not deny, but strongly confirmed, the authority of the father over the child and the husband over the wife, an authority grounded on a similar assumption of a natural inferiority and incapacity for liberty in the woman and child, it acted consistently in withholding liberty from the slave while it gave him citizenship. As it often happens that a usage introduced for one reason is afterwards retained for another, so had slavery, originally the most savage abuse of ethnic morality, come to be differently understood and differently defended. The servile condition has a natural tendency to degrade human nature; of the slaves of antiquity a large proportion belonged originally to the lowest and rudest nations; and from these two causes it was a patent and undeniable fact that the slave population was in an incalculable degree inferior to the free. It might reasonably be considered rebellion against an ordinance of nature to give freedom to those who appeared so little fit for it; and if it seems to us a false and cruel argument to turn the consequence of slavery into a justification of it, and to pronounce the slave naturally incapable of liberty because he had been artificially incapacitated for it, yet we must remember that the social speculations of antiquity were seldom dictated by philanthropy, and we must not expect the refined tenderness of adult Christianity from its earliest developments.

False and cruel to a certain extent the argument was; but if the earliest Christian teachers had rejected it absolutely, and inferred from their Master's Law of Comprehension that all men are not only to be respected alike, but to be treated in the same manner, put in possession of the same privileges, directed to seek happiness in the same pursuits, they would have run into the opposite extreme. Christ declares all men alike to be the sons of God, and the least of mankind he adopts as a brother. By doing so he makes all mankind equal to this extent, that the interests and the happiness of all members of the race are declared to be of equal importance. But he does not declare them to be equally gifted. Each individual is equally entitled to whatever dignity he is capable of supporting; but the early Church, at least, was in possession of no proof that all men are equally capable of sustaining the dignity of a free condition. If this discovery has been made since, there was at that time nothing that could suggest it. Dependence and subjection were then regarded as the natural condition of women; the son under the Roman Law was literally his father's slave, incapable of owning a penny of personal

The Christian Republic

property, even though he might have held the highest honours of the state. And if such appeared to the Roman jurists to be a natural ordinance, even when there was no visible inferiority between the father and the son who was thus enslaved to him, who could question that the slave population, visibly characterised by all the faults, vices, and deficiencies that make men unfit for freedom, were intended by nature to live under the control of those whom she had made wise and intelligent?

In the Universal Republic therefore, while in one sense there were no slaves, in another sense slavery was admitted. The position given to the outcast class was what we may call citizenship without emancipation. Their welfare was regarded as not less important than that of the most exalted. They were Christ's brothers, and he had pronounced the solemn sentence, " Whoso offendeth one of these little ones that believe in me, it were better for him that a mill-stone should be hanged round his neck, and that he should be cast into the depths of the sea." This sentence contained the abolition of all the horrible usages of ancient slavery, the tortures of the ergastulum, the gladiatorial show. But, notwithstanding, the slave was left under a control which might be harsh and rigorous, if harshness and rigour appear necessary, because it was believed that men were called to different offices in life, and that while it was the glory and dignity of some to feel nothing between themselves and God, to others it was given only to see God reflected in wiser and nobler spirits than themselves.

CHAPTER XIII

THE CHRISTIAN A LAW TO HIMSELF

Our investigation has led us to three conclusions respecting Christ's legislation:—1, that he does not direct us to adopt a private or isolated rule of life, but to occupy ourselves with the affairs of the society; 2, that he expects us to merge our private interests absolutely in those of this society; 3, that this society is not exclusive, but catholic or universal—that is, that all mankind have a right to admission to it. Or we should rather say re-admission, for Christ does not regard the society as new, but rather as one which had subsisted from the beginning in the Maker's plan, but had been broken up through the jealousies and narrowness of men. For this reason, though baptism is the essential condition of membership, yet those who refuse baptism are not to be treated as the foreigner would be treated under the system of ethnic morality, but to be pitied as fellow-citizens who madly refuse to take up their birthright, to be abandoned only after their perverseness has shown itself incorrigible, and even then not to be punished, but left to the judgment of God.

A universal society, then, being founded, and a life strictly social and civic being enjoined upon its members, by what rule is this social life to be guided? How are Christians to behave towards each other? This question must be carefully separated from others which naturally connect themselves with it. We are not now concerned with the constitution of the society, its system of magistrates and public assemblies—questions which in fact Christ left entirely to the decision of the society itself. Nor do we here consider the injunctions which he laid upon them, so to speak, as a politician—for example, concerning the way in which they were to comport

The Christian a Law to Himself 115

themselves towards the governments of the earth, or what they were to do in times of persecution. Nor are we concerned at present with the theology of the society, nor with its relation to God and Christ. When, however, we have gone through the recorded discourses and sayings of Christ, and eliminated everything in them referring to theology, or the occasional duties of the society, or arising out of the polemic in which Christ occasionally engaged with the Jewish doctors, we may be surprised to find how small is the residue which contains his system of morality. The truth is that he did not leave a code of morals in the ordinary sense of the word—that is, an enumeration of actions prescribed and prohibited. Two or three prohibitions, two or three commands, he is indeed recorded to have delivered, but on the greater number of questions on which men require moral guidance he has left no direction whatever.

Are we then, after being brought together into a universal society, left without a rule by which to guide our intercourse in this society? Not so; we are to consider what is the origin of laws in human communities. They arise from a certain instinct in human nature, which it is not necessary here to analyse, but which supports itself by a constant struggle against other anarchic and lawless instincts, and which is so far the same in all men that all the systems of law which have ever appeared among men are, in certain grand features, alike. This we may call the law-making power in men. Now anyone set to organise a new community, if he had it in his power either to deliver an elaborate and minute code of rules to the community, or to increase indefinitely the law-making power in each member of it, would certainly without hesitation choose the latter course. For, not to speak of the trouble that would be saved both in compiling the code at first and in remodelling it as new circumstances demanded new provisions, the morality of the citizens would be of a much higher and more vital kind if they could be made, as it were, a law to themselves, and could always hear, in the language of Hebrew poetry, a voice behind them saying, " This is the way, walk ye in it."

Now this was what Christ undertook to do. Instead of giving laws to his Society, he would give to every member of it a power of making laws for himself. He frequently repeated that to make the fruit of a tree good you must put the tree into a healthy state, and, slightly altering the illustration, that fruit can only be expected from a fruit-tree, not from a thistle or thorn. The meaning of this plainly is that a man's actions result from the state of his mind; that if that is healthy they will be right, and if not, they will be wrong. Such language was new in the mouth of a legislator, but not at all new in itself. It was an adoption of the style of philosophy. Philosophers had always made it their study to bring their minds into a healthy condition, *"frui emendato animo."* When, however, we enquire what Christ considered a healthy condition of the mind to be, we do not find him in agreement with philosophers. The law-making power of which mention has been made, which, raised to predominance, issues in an unerring tact or instinct of right action, was differently conceived by him and by them. They placed it in reason, and regarded passion as the antagonistic power which must be controlled and coerced by it. Christ also considers it necessary to control the passions, but he places them under the dominion not of reason but of a new and more powerful passion. The healthy mind of the philosophers is in a composed, tranquil, and impartial state; the healthy mind of Christ is in an elevated and enthusiastic state. Both are exempt from perturbation and unsteadiness, but the one by being immovably fixed, the other by being always powerfully attracted in one direction.

This is collected from the following facts. Christ was once asked to pronounce which commandment in the law was the greatest. He answered by quoting a sentence from the Book of Deuteronomy, in which devoted love to God and man is solemnly enjoined upon the Israelite, and by declaring that upon this commandment the whole Mosaic and prophetic legislation depended. In other words, he declared an ardent, passionate, or devoted state of mind to be the root of virtue. Again, he directed one who declared that he had kept all the commandments

The Christian a Law to Himself

and asked what remained for him to do, if he would be perfect, to sell all his goods and give them to the poor, and devote himself to the kingdom of God. What does this imply but that the morality which is sound must be no mere self-restraint, no mechanical movement within prescribed rules, no mere punctiliousness, but ardent and active, exceeding duty and outstripping requirement? He taught the same doctrine in a striking form when he bade his followers exhibit their virtue conspicuously, so that all might see it and none might mistake it. They were to be, he said, a city set on a hill, a candle set on a candlestick and lighting the whole room, salt with a strong taste in it. These exhortations are peculiarly striking, because no teacher has ever insisted more strongly than Christ on the unobtrusive character of true virtue. We are not, he says, to sound a trumpet before us; if we would pray we are to go into a closet and shut the door behind us; we are to do good by stealth; our left hand is not to know what our right hand does. These two sets of injunctions appear, as is often the case in the many-sided wisdom of Christ, to be in direct contradiction to each other. But they are not really so; if taken together there results from them the following perfectly clear and consistent doctrine: True goodness does not study to attract attention; nevertheless, wherever it appears, such is the warmth, fire, and energy inherent in it, that it does and must attract attention. And so strongly does Christ feel this, that he solemnly declares the virtue which does not make itself felt and recognised to be worth nothing. If the very salt have lost its taste, what remains? it is good for nothing but to be thrown away and trodden under foot.

All other faults or deficiencies he could tolerate, but he could have neither part nor lot with men destitute of enthusiasm. He thought it a bad, almost a fatal sign, in one who proposed to become a disciple that he asked leave first to bid farewell to his relations. Another asked permission to bury his father, and was advised to let the dead (that is, those whose hearts were not animated by any strong passion or impulse) bury their dead. And once when it seemed that the magic of his presence and words would draw his entire audience into the number of his followers, alarmed lest he should find himself surrounded by half-hearted or superficial and merely excitable adherents, he turned suddenly upon the crowd, and with one of those startling expressions which he seldom, and yet like all great reformers sometimes, employed, declared that he could receive no man who did not *hate* his father and mother and his own life.

These passages will help us to understand the allegory of the strong man armed keeping secure possession of his palace until he is expelled by a stronger than himself. The strong man armed is the anarchic passions of human nature, against which the law-making power contends. Nothing can control them, says Christ, but a stronger passion still. And he goes on to explain that an empty condition of mind, a quiescence or temporary absence of the anarchic passion, is a hollow and dangerous state. The demon may leave his abode for a time, but he finds no sustenance abroad, and so at last back he comes hungry and brings congenial guests with him.

It was fully understood in the early Church that this enthusiastic or elevated condition of mind was the distinctive and essential mark of a Christian. St. Paul, having asked some converts whether they had received this divine inspiration since their conversion, and receiving for answer that they had not heard there was any such divine inspiration abroad, demanded in amazement what then they had been baptised into.

Before we investigate the nature of the enthusiasm or divine inspiration which Christ proposed to kindle in the minds of his disciples, let us consider what is involved in the fact that he made morality dependent upon such an enthusiasm, and not upon any activity of the reasoning power. It is the essence of morality to place a restraint upon our natural desires in such a manner that in certain cases we refrain from doing that which we have a natural desire to do, or force ourselves to do that to which we feel a repugnance. Now, he who refrains from gratifying a wish on some ground of reason, at the same time feels the

The Christian a Law to Himself 119

wish as strongly as if he gratified it. The object seems to him desirable, he cannot think of it without wishing for it; he can, indeed, force his mind not to dwell upon the object of desire, but so long as the mind dwells upon it so long it desires it. On the other hand, when a stronger passion controls a weaker, the weaker altogether ceases to be felt. For example, let us suppose two men, one of whom has learnt and believes that he owes fidelity to his country, but has no ardour of patriotism, and the other an enthusiastic patriot. Suppose a bribe offered to these two men to betray their country. Neither will take the bribe. But the former, if we suppose the bribe large enough, will feel his fingers itch as he handles the gold; his mind will run upon the advantages it would bring him, the things he might buy, the life he might lead, if he had the money; he will find it prudent to divert his mind from the subject, to plunge desperately into occupations which may absorb him until the time of temptation has passed. The other will have no such feelings; the gold will not make his fingers itch with desire, but perhaps rather seem to scorch them; he will not picture to himself happiness or pleasure as a consequence of taking it, but, on the contrary, insupportable degradation and despair; his mind will need no distraction, it will be perfectly at ease however long the period of temptation may continue.

The difference between the men is briefly this, that the one has his anarchic or lower desires under control, the other feels no such desires; the one, so far as he is virtuous, is incapable of crime, the other, so far as he is virtuous, is incapable of temptation.

Now, as Christ demands virtue of the latter or enthusiastic kind, we shall be prepared to find that he prohibits evil desires as well as wrong acts. Accordingly, it is one of the most remarkable features of his moral teaching that he does not command us to regulate or control our unlawful desires, but pronounces it unlawful to have such desires at all. A considerable part of the Sermon on the Mount is devoted to the exposition of this doctrine. Christ quotes several prohibitions from the

Mosaic law, and proceeds to declare the desire from which each prohibited act springs equally culpable with the act itself. This is at first sight perplexing, because the desire out of which an unlawful act springs is often or generally a mere natural appetite which in itself is perfectly innocent. The truth is, that Christ requires that such natural appetite, when the gratification of it would be unlawful, be not merely left ungratified, but altogether destroyed, and a feeling of aversion substituted for it by the enthusiasm of virtue within the soul.

This higher form of goodness, though of course it had existed among the heathen nations, yet had never among them been sufficiently distinguished from the lower to receive a separate name. The earliest Christians, like the Christians of later times, felt a natural repugnance to describe the ardent enthusiastic goodness at which they aimed by the name of *virtue*. This name suited exactly the kind of goodness which Christ expressly commanded them to rise above. They therefore adopted another. Regarding the ardour they felt as an express inspiration or spiritual presence of God within them, they borrowed from the language of religious worship a word for which our equivalent is " holy "; and the inspiring power they consistently called the Spirit of Holiness or the Holy Spirit. Accordingly, while a virtuous man is one who controls and coerces the anarchic passions within him so as to conform his actions to law, a holy man is one in whom a passionate enthusiasm absorbs and annuls the anarchic passions altogether, so that no internal struggle takes place, and the lawful action is that which presents itself first and seems the one most natural and most easy to be done.

But now, of what nature is the enthusiasm Christ requires? We have seen that a particular passion may raise a man above a particular sin. The enthusiastic patriot is incapable of treason. He who passionately loves one woman may be made by that love incapable of a licentious thought; and an elevated self-love may make it impossible for a man to lie. But these passions are partial in their operation. The patriot, incapable of

The Christian a Law to Himself 121

public treason, may be capable of private treachery. The chaste man may be a traitor. The honest man may be cruel. What is the passion, if such a passion there be, which can lift a man clean out of all sin whatever?

As it has been shown that Christ founded a society the peculiarity of which is that it was intended to include the whole human race, it may occur to us that the *esprit de corps* which would naturally spring up in such a society may be the passion we seek. It would be a passion of the same nature as patriotism, but without its exclusiveness. For the patriot, though incapable of injuring his own country, is not less but perhaps more capable of being unjust or treacherous towards foreign nations, while the Christian patriot, whose country is the world, will, it may be supposed, be equally incapable of wrong-doing towards all alike.

But it must be remembered that an enthusiastic attachment to a state or a community is very different from an attachment to the members of that community. The patriot, it has just been said, is not by any means above the temptation to private injustice or treachery, nor will he become more so when his country is the world. An example was given in the first French Revolution of the operation of this passion of universal patriotism. It was in the cause not so much of France as of universal man that the revolutionary party agitated and fought, and they displayed a disregard of private rights and individual happiness quite as catholic as their philanthropy. Universal patriotism, taken by itself, is not Christianity but Jacobinism.

The all-purifying passion must, it is plain, be a passion for individuals. Let us imagine, then, a love for every human being. This answers the conditions of the problem to this extent, that he who loves everybody will of course willingly injure nobody, that is, will not commit sin. And if, leaving conjecture, we turn again to Christ's discourses, we find him, as it appears, mentioning this very passion as the essence of all legislation, or as what we called above the law-making power in man. The great commandment of the law, he says, is to love God with all your heart and your neighbour *as yourself*, and the maxim for practice corresponding to this law of feeling is, " Do unto others as you would that they should do to you."

Here then, it appears, is our panacea for all diseases of the soul; here is that passion which once conceived in the breast is to make laws superfluous, to redeem our nature, to make " our days bright and serene, love being an unerring light and joy its own security." We are to love every human being alike. The discovery, it cannot be concealed, seems rather an empty one. We will not at present enquire where are the agencies which are to excite in us so strange a passion: men *do* conceive strange attachments; they learn, for example, to love their country, though it seems surprising that such an abstraction should excite so much interest. But is not the feeling now enjoined upon us one plainly impossible because self-contradictory? There exist men of opposite qualities. Love is a name we give to a feeling aroused in us by certain qualities, and hatred is the feeling aroused by qualities of the opposite kind. How then is it possible to love at the same time persons of opposite qualities?

Obvious and forcible as this objection seems, there is something in us which rebels against it as soon as it is stated. Manifest as it may seem that we can only love what is lovely, and that what is hateful must, in the nature of things, be hated, we are yet aware that practically our feelings towards our fellow-creatures are more complex. It is not merely that almost all men have qualities we can love even when the hateful qualities preponderate, nor merely that we are conscious how our self-interest makes many things hateful to us which are not hateful in themselves and would not be so to us if our self-love were diminished or at rest, but even in the extreme case, when our hatred seems most just and necessary, when monsters appear in the form of man whose crimes strike us with horror, even for such we sometimes detect in ourselves a feeling opposite to hatred. When they fall into calamity and death, a feeling of awe, aye, of pity, mixes with our rejoicing. Even in primitive times, when men's feelings

The Christian a Law to Himself 123

towards each other were for the most part simple and clear, when hatred was unmixed and had not begun to lose its " raven gloss " we find these pangs of tenderness. When the housekeeper Euryclea was admitted by Ulysses into the hall where the oppressors of the house lay slaughtered, her first impulse, woman though she was—such was the fierceness of the time—was to utter a shout of triumph. But the hero stopped her and said, " Rejoice in silence, woman, and restrain thyself, and utter no shout: it is not right to triumph over slaughtered men."

If we consider these singular relentings, the thoughts with which they are accompanied, and the words in which they most naturally express themselves, we shall find that it is the ideal of man in each man which calls them forth. When we think of the fallen criminal or tyrant we say, " He too was once an innocent child," or " Who knows what he might have been had circumstances been more favourable or temptation less! " In thoughts like these we betray that there is a third kind of love which we may bear to our fellow-creatures, and which is neither that love of the whole race which has been called above Jacobinism, nor that independent love of each individual which appears impossible when we consider that different individuals exhibit opposite qualities. This third feeling is the love not of the race nor of the individual, but of the race *in* the individual; it is the love not of all men nor yet of every man, but of *the man* in every man.

This ought not to be regarded as a mere Platonic dream. Though it finds expression most easily and naturally in Platonic language, it is in reality one of the most hackneyed and familiar of truths. There is a fellow-feeling, a yearning of kindness towards a human being as such, which is not dependent upon the character of the particular human being who excites it, but rises before that character displays itself, and does not at once or altogether subside when it exhibits itself as unamiable. We save a man from drowning whether he is amiable or the contrary, and we should consider it right to do so even though we knew him to be a very great criminal, simply because he is a man. By examples like this we may discover that a love for humanity as such exists, and that it is a natural passion which would be universal if special causes did not extinguish it in special cases, but like all other human passions, it may be indefinitely increased and purified by training and by extraordinary agencies that may be brought to bear upon it. Now this was the passion upon which Christ seized, and treating it as the law-making power or root of morality in human nature, trained and developed it into that Christian spirit which received the new name of ἀγάπη.

The objection is then removed which represents Christ's rule of universal love as impracticable because different men may exhibit opposite qualities, for it is shown that there is a kind of love which may be felt for unamiable persons. And though it must be admitted that there is an extreme degree of unamiability which quenches this love in us, yet it is conceivable that when the passion has been cultivated and strengthened by the means which Christ may employ, it may become a passion in the strictest sense all-embracing. What these means were, and what character the passion assumes in its full development, it is now necessary to consider.

CHAPTER XIV

THE ENTHUSIASM OF HUMANITY

THE first method of training this passion which Christ employed was the direct one of making it a point of duty to feel it. To love one's neighbour as oneself was, he said, the first and greatest *law*. And in the Sermon on the Mount he requires the passion to be felt in such strength as to include those whom we have most reason to hate— our enemies and those who maliciously injure us—and delivers an imperative precept, " Love your enemies."

It has been shown that to do this is not, as might at first appear, in the nature of things impossible, but the further question suggests itself, Can it be done to order? Has the verb to love really an imperative mood? Certainly, to say that we can love at pleasure, and by a mere effort of will summon up a passion which does not arise of itself, is to take up a paradoxical and novel position. Yet if this position be really untenable, how is it possible to obey Christ's commands?

The difficulty seems to admit of only one solution. We are not commanded to create by an effort of will a feeling of love in ourselves which otherwise would have had no existence; the feeling must arise naturally or it cannot arise at all. But a number of causes which are removable may interfere to prevent the feeling from arising or to stifle it as it arises, and we are commanded to remove these hindrances. It is natural to man to love his kind, and Christ commands us only to give nature play. He does not expect us to procure for ourselves hearts of some new supernatural texture, but merely the heart of flesh for the heart of stone.

What, then, are the causes of this paralysis of the heart? The experience of human life furnishes us readily with the answer. It constantly happens that one whose affections were originally not less lively than those of most men is thrown into the society of persons destitute of sympathy or tenderness. In this society each person is either totally indifferent to his neighbour or secretly endeavouring to injure or overreach him. The new-comer is at first open-hearted and cordial; he presumes every one he meets to be a friend, and is disposed to serve and expects to be served by all alike. But his advances are met by some with cautious reserve, by others with icy coldness, by others with hypocritical warmth followed by treacherous injury, by others with open hostility. The heart which naturally grew warm at the mere sight of a human being, under the operation of this new experience slowly becomes paralysed. There seats itself gradually in the man's mind a presumption concerning every new face that it is the face of an enemy, and a habit of gathering himself into an attitude of self-defence whenever he deals with a fellow-creature. If when this new disposition has grown confirmed and habitual, he be introduced into a society of an opposite kind and meet with people as friendly and kind as he himself was originally, he will not at first be able to believe in their sincerity, and the old kindly affections from long disuse will be slow to rouse themselves within him. Now to such a person the imperative mood of the verb to love may fairly be used. He may properly be told to make an effort, to shake off the distrust that oppresses him, not to suffer unproved suspicions, causeless jealousies, to stifle by the mere force of prejudice and mistaken opinion the warmth of feeling natural to him.

But we shall have a closer illustration if we suppose the cold-hearted society itself to be addressed by a preacher who wishes to bring them to a better mind. He too may fairly use the imperative mood of the verb to love. For he may say, " Your mutual coldness does not spring from an original want of the power of sympathy. If it did, admonitions would indeed be useless. But it springs from a habit of thought which you have formed, a maxim which has been received among you, that all men are

The Enthusiasm of Humanity 127

devoted to self-interest, that kindness is but feebleness and invites injury. If you will at once and by a common act throw off this false opinion of human nature, and adopt a new plan of life for yourselves and new expectations of each other, you will find the old affections natural to all of you, weakened indeed and chilled, but existing and capable of being revived by an effort."

Such a preacher might go further and say, " If but a small minority are convinced by my words, yet let that minority for itself abandon the selfish theory, let it renounce the safety which that theory affords in dealing with selfish men, let it treat the enemy as if he were indeed the friend he ought to be, let it dare to forego retaliation and even self-defence. By this means it will shame many into kindness; by despising self-interest for itself it will sometimes make it seem despicable to others, by sincerity and persistency it will gradually convert the majority to a higher law of intercourse.

The world has been always more or less like this coldhearted society; the natural kindness and fellow-feeling of men have always been more or less repressed by lowminded maxims and cynicism. But in the time of Christ, and in the last decrepitude of ethnic morality, the selfishness of human intercourse was much greater than the present age can easily understand. That system of morality, even in the times when it was powerful and in many respects beneficial, had made it almost as much a duty to hate foreigners as to love fellow-citizens. Plato congratulates the Athenians on having shown in their relations to Persia, beyond all the other Greeks, " a pure and heartfelt hatred of the foreign nature." [1] Instead of opposing, it had sanctioned and consecrated the savage instinct which leads us to hate whatever is strange or unintelligible, to distrust those who live on the further side of a river, to suppose that those whom we hear talking

[1] οὕτω δή τοι τό γε τῆς πόλεως γενναῖον καὶ ἐλεύθερον βέβαιόν τε καὶ ὑγιές ἐστι καὶ φύσει μισοβάρβαρον διὰ τὸ εἰλικρινῶς εἶναι Ἕλληνες καὶ ἀμιγεῖς βαρβάρων. . . . ἀλλ' αὐτοὶ Ἕλληνες, οὐ μιξοβάρβαροι οἰκοῦμεν ὅθεν καθαρὸν τὸ μῖσος ἐντέτηκε τῇ πόλει τῆς ἀλλοτρίας φύσεως.—Plato, Menexenus, p. 245.

together in a foreign tongue must be plotting some mischief against ourselves. The lapse of time and the fusion of races doubtless diminished this antipathy considerably, but at the utmost it could but be transformed into an icy indifference, for no cause was in operation to convert it into kindness. On the other hand, the closeness of the bond which united fellow-citizens was considerably relaxed. Common interests and common dangers had drawn it close; these in the wide security of the Roman Empire had no longer a place. It had depended upon an imagined blood-relationship; fellow-citizens could now no longer feel themselves to be united by the tie of blood. Every town was full of resident aliens and emancipated slaves, persons between whom and the citizens nature had established no connection, and whose presence in the city had originally been barely tolerated from motives of expediency. The selfishness of modern times exists in defiance of morality, in ancient times it was approved, sheltered, and even in part enjoined by morality.

We are therefore to consider the ancient world as a society of men in whom natural humanity existed but had been, as it were, crusted or frosted over. Inveterate feuds and narrow-minded local jealousies, arising out of an isolated position or differences of language and institutions, had created endless divisions between man and man. And as the special virtues of antiquity, patriotism and all that it implies, had been in a manner caused and fostered by these very divisions, they were not regarded as evils but rather cherished as essential to morality. Selfishness, therefore, was not a mere abuse or corruption arising out of the infirmity of human nature, but a theory and almost a part of moral philosophy. Humanity was cramped by a mistaken prejudice, by a perverse presumption of the intellect. In a case like this it was necessary and proper to prescribe humanity by direct authoritative precept. Such a precept would have been powerless to create the feeling, nor would it have done much to protect it from being overpowered by the opposite passion; but the opposite passion of selfishness was at this period justified by

The Enthusiasm of Humanity 129

authority and claimed to be on the side of reason and law. Precept is fairly matched against precept, and what the law of love and the golden rule did for mankind was to place for the first time the love of man as man distinctly in the list of virtues, to dissipate the exclusive prejudices of ethnic morality, and to give selfishness the character of sin.

When a theory of selfishness is rife in a whole community, it is a bold and hazardous step for a part of the community to abandon it. For in the society of selfish people selfishness is simply self-defence; to renounce it is to evacuate one's entrenched position, to surrender at discretion to the enemy. If society is to disarm, it should do so by common consent. Christ, however, though he confidently expected ultimately to gather all mankind into his society, did not expect to do so soon. Accordingly he commands his followers not to wait for this consummation, but, in spite of the hazardous nature of the step, to disarm at once. They are sent forth " as sheep in the midst of wolves." Injuries they are to expect, but they are neither to shun nor to retaliate them. Harmless they are to be as *doves*. The discipline of suffering will wean them more and more from self, and make the channels of humanity freer within them; and sometimes their patience may shame the spoiler; he may grow weary of rapacity which meets with no resistance, and be induced to envy those who can forego without reluctance that which he devotes every thought to acquire.

But we shall soon be convinced that Christ could not design by a mere edict, however authoritative, to give this passion of humanity strength enough to make it a living and infallible principle of morality in every man, when we consider, first, what an ardent enthusiasm he demanded from his followers, and secondly, how frail and tender a germ this passion naturally is in human nature. Widely diffused indeed it is, and seldom entirely eradicated, but for the most part, at least in the ancient world, it was crushed under a weight of predominant passions and interests; it had seldom power enough to dictate any action, but made itself felt in faint misgivings and relentings, which sometimes restrained men from extremes of cruelty. Like Enceladus under Ætna, it lay fettered at the bottom of human nature, now and then making the mass above it quake by an uneasy change of posture. To make this outraged and enslaved passion predominant, to give it, instead of a veto rarely used, the whole power of government, to train it from a dim misgiving into a clear and strong passion, required much more than a precept. The precept had its use; it could make men feel it right to be humane and desire to be so, but it could never inspire them with an enthusiasm of humanity. From what source was this inspiration to be derived?

Humanity, we have already observed, is neither a love for the whole human race, nor a love for each individual of it, but a love for the race, or for the ideal of man, in each individual. In other and less pedantic words, he who is truly humane considers every human being as such interesting and important, and without waiting to criticise each individual specimen, pays in advance to all alike the tribute of good wishes and sympathy. Now this favourable presumption with regard to human beings is not a causeless prepossession, it is no idle superstition of the mind, nor is it a natural instinct. It is a feeling founded on the actual observation and discovery of interesting and noble qualities in particular human beings, and it is strong or weak in proportion as the person who has the feeling has known many or few noble and amiable human beings. There are men who have been so unfortunate as to live in the perpetual society of the mean and the base; they have never, except in a few faint glimpses, seen anything glorious or good in human nature. With these the feeling of humanity has a perpetual struggle for existence, their minds tend by a fatal gravitation to the belief that the happiness or misery of such a paltry race is wholly unimportant; they may arrive finally at a fixed condition, in which it may be said of them without qualification, that " man delights not them, nor woman neither." In this final stage they are men who, beyond the routine of life, should not be trusted, being " fit for treasons, stratagems, and spoils." On the other hand, there are

The Enthusiasm of Humanity 131

those whose lot it has been from earliest childhood to see the fair side of humanity, who have been surrounded with clear and candid countenances, in the changes of which might be traced the working of passions strong and simple, the impress of a firm and tender nature, wearing when it looked abroad the glow of sympathy, and when it looked within the bloom of modesty. They have seen, and not once or twice, a man forget himself; they have witnessed devotion, unselfish sorrow, unaffected delicacy, spontaneous charity, ingenuous self-reproach; and it may be that on seeing a human being surrender for another's good not something but his uttermost all, they have dimly suspected in human nature a glory connecting it with the divine. In these the passion of humanity is warm and ready to become on occasion a burning flame; their whole minds are elevated, because they are possessed with the dignity of that nature they share, and of the society in the midst of which they move.

But it is not absolutely necessary to humanity that a man shall have seen *many* men whom he can respect. The most lost cynic will get a new heart by learning thoroughly to believe in the virtue of *one* man. Our estimate of human nature is in proportion to the best specimen of it we have witnessed. This then it is which is wanted to raise the feeling of humanity into an enthusiasm; when the precept of love has been given, an image must be set before the eyes of those who are called upon to obey it, an ideal or type of man which may be noble and amiable enough to raise the whole race and make the meanest member of it sacred with reflected glory.

Did not Christ do this? Did the command to love go forth to those who had never seen a human being they could revere? Could his followers turn upon him and say, How can we love a creature so degraded, full of vile wants and contemptible passions, whose little life is most harmlessly spent when it is an empty round of eating and sleeping; a creature destined for the grave and for oblivion when his allotted term of fretfulness and folly has expired? Of this race Christ himself was a member, and to this day is it not the best answer to all blasphemers of the species, the best consolation when our sense of its degradation is keenest, that a human brain was behind his forehead and a human heart beating in his breast, and that within the whole creation of God nothing more elevated or more attractive has yet been found than he? And if it be answered that there was in his nature something exceptional and peculiar, that humanity must not be measured by the stature of Christ, let us remember that it was precisely thus that he wished it to be measured, delighting to call himself the Son of Man, delighting to call the meanest of mankind his brothers. If some human beings are abject and contemptible, if it be incredible to us that they can have any high dignity or destiny, do we regard them from so great a height as Christ? Are we likely to be more pained by their faults and deficiencies than he was? Is our standard higher than his? And yet he associated by preference with these meanest of the race; no contempt for them did he ever express, no suspicion that they might be less dear than the best and wisest to the common Father, no doubt that they were naturally capable of rising to a moral elevation like his own. There is nothing of which a man may be prouder than of this; it is the most hopeful and redeeming fact in history; it is precisely what was wanting to raise the love of man as man to enthusiasm. An eternal glory has been shed upon the human race by the love Christ bore to it. And it was because the Edict of Universal Love went forth to men whose hearts were in no cynical mood but possessed with a spirit of devotion to a man, that words which at any other time, however grandly they might sound, would have been but words, penetrated so deeply, and along with the law of love the power of love was given. Therefore also the first Christians were enabled to dispense with philosophical phrases, and instead of saying that they loved the ideal of man in man could simply say and feel that they loved Christ in every man.

We have here the very kernel of the Christian moral scheme. We have distinctly before us the end Christ proposed to himself, and the means he considered ade-

The Enthusiasm of Humanity 133

quate to the attainment of it. His object was, instead of drawing up, after the example of previous legislators, a list of actions prescribed, allowed, and prohibited, to give his disciples a universal test by which they might discover what it was right and what it was wrong to do. Now as the difficulty of discovering what is right arises commonly from the prevalence of self-interest in our minds, and as we commonly behave rightly to anyone for whom we feel affection or sympathy, Christ considered that he who could feel sympathy for all would behave rightly to all. But how to give to the meagre and narrow hearts of men such enlargement? How to make them capable of a universal sympathy? Christ believed it possible to bind men to their kind, but on one condition— that they were first bound fast to himself. He stood forth as the representative of men, he identified himself with the cause and with the interests of all human beings, he was destined, as he began before long obscurely to intimate, to lay down his life for them. Few of us sympathise originally and directly with this devotion; few of us can perceive in human nature itself any merit sufficient to evoke it. But it is not so hard to love and venerate him who felt it. So vast a passion of love, a devotion so comprehensive, elevated, deliberate and profound, has not elsewhere been in any degree approached save by some of his imitators. And as love provokes love, many have found it possible to conceive for Christ an attachment the closeness of which no words can describe, a veneration so possessing and absorbing the man within them, that they have said, " I live no more, but Christ lives in me." Now such a feeling carries with it of necessity the feeling of love for all human beings. It matters no longer what quality men may exhibit; amiable or unamiable, as the brothers of Christ, as belonging to his sacred and consecrated kind, as the objects of his love in life and death, they must be dear to all to whom he is dear. And those who would for a moment know his heart and understand his life must begin by thinking of the whole race of man, and of each member of the race, with awful reverence and hope.

Love, wheresoever it appears, is in its measure a law-making power. " Love is *dutiful* in thought and deed." And as the lover of his country is free from the temptation to treason, so is he who loves Christ secure from the temptation to injure any human being, whether it be himself or another. He is indeed much more than this. He is bound and he is eager to benefit and bless to the utmost of his power all that bear his Master's nature, and that not merely with the good gifts of the earth, but with whatever cherishes and trains best the Christ within them. But for the present we are concerned merely with the power of this passion to lift the man out of sin. The injuries he committed lightly when he regarded his fellow-creatures simply as animals who added to the fierceness of the brute an ingenuity and forethought that made them doubly noxious, become horrible sacrilege when he sees in them no longer the animal but the Christ. And that other class of crimes which belongs more especially to ages of civilisation, and arises out of a cynical contempt for the species, is rendered equally impossible to the man who hears with reverence the announcement, " The good deeds you did to the least of these my brethren you did to me."

There are two objections which may suggest themselves at this point, the one to intellectual, the other to practical men. The intellectual man may say, " To discover what it is right to do in any given case is not the province of any feeling or passion however sublime, but requires the application of the same intellectual power which solves mathematical problems. The common acts of life may no doubt be performed correctly by unintellectual people, but this is because these constantly recurring problems have been solved long ago by clever people, and the vulgar are now in possession of the results. Whenever a new combination occurs it is a matter for casuists; the best intentions will avail little; there is doubtless a great difference between a good man and a bad one; the one will do what is right when he knows it, and the other will not; but in respect for the power of ascertaining what it is right to do, supposing their knowledge of casuistry to

The Enthusiasm of Humanity 135

be equal, they are on a par. Goodness or the passion of humanity, or Christian love, may be a motive inducing men to keep the law, but it has no right to be called the law-making power. And what has Christianity added to our theoretic knowledge of morality? It may have made men practically more moral, but has it added anything to Aristotle's Ethics? "

Certainly Christianity has no ambition to invade the provinces of the moralist or the casuist. But the difficulties which beset the discovery of the right moral course are of two kinds. There are the difficulties which arise from the blinding and confusing effect of selfish passions, and which obscure from the view the end which should be aimed at in action; when these have been overcome there arises a new set of difficulties concerning the means by which the end should be attained. In dealing with your neighbour the first thing to be understood is that his interest is to be considered as well as your own; but when this has been settled, it remains to be considered what his interest is. The latter class of difficulties requires to be dealt witn by the intellectual or calculating faculty. The former class can only be dealt with by the moral force of sympathy. Now it is true that the right action will not be performed without the operation of both these agencies. But the moral agency is the dominant one throughout; it is that without which the very conception of law is impossible; it overcomes those difficulties which in the vast majority of practical cases are the most serious. The calculating casuistical faculty is, as it were, in its employ, and it is no more improper to call it the law-making power, although it does not ultimately decide what action is to be performed, than to say that a house was built by one who did not with his own hands lay the bricks and spread the mortar.

The objection which practical men take is a very important one, as the criticisms of such men always are, being founded commonly upon large observation and not perverted by theory. They say that the love of Christ does not in practice produce the nobleness and largeness of character which has been represented as its proper and natural result; that instead of inspiring those who feel it with reverence and hope for their kind, it makes them exceedingly narrow in their sympathies, disposed to deny and explain away even the most manifest virtues displayed by men, and to despair of the future destiny of the great majority of their fellow-creatures; that instead of binding them to their kind, it divides them from it by a gulf which they themselves proclaim to be impassable and eternal, and unites them only in a gloomy conspiracy of misanthropy with each other; that it is indeed a law-making power, but that the laws it makes are little-minded and vexatious prohibitions of things innocent, demoralising restraints upon the freedom of joy and the healthy instincts of nature; that it favours hypocrisy, moroseness, and sometimes lunacy; that the only vice it has power to check is thoughtlessness, and its only beneficial effect is that of forcing into activity, though not always into healthy activity, the faculty of serious reflection.

This may be a just picture of a large class of religious men, but it is impossible in the nature of things that such effects should be produced by a pure personal devotion to Christ. We are to remember that nothing has been subjected to such multiform and grotesque perversion as Christianity. Certainly the direct love of Christ, as it was felt by his first followers, is a rare thing among modern Christians. His character has been so much obscured by scholasticism, as to have lost in a great measure its attractive power. The prevalent feeling towards him now among religious men is an awful fear of his supernatural greatness, and a disposition to obey his commands arising partly from dread of future punishment and hope of reward, and partly from a nobler feeling of loyalty, which, however, is inspired rather by his office than his person. Beyond this we may discern in them an uneasy conviction that he requires a more personal devotion, which leads to spasmodic efforts to kindle the feeling by means of violent raptures of panegyric and by repeating over and getting by rote the ardent expressions of those who really had it. That is wanting for the most part which Christ held to be all in all, spontaneous warmth, free and generous devotion.

The Enthusiasm of Humanity 137

That the fruits of a Christianity so hollow should be poor and sickly is not surprising.

But that Christ's method, when rightly applied, is really of mighty force may be shown by an argument which the severest censor of Christians will hardly refuse to admit. Compare the ancient with the modern world; " Look on this picture and on that." One broad distinction in the characters of men forces itself into prominence. Among all the men of the ancient heathen world there were scarcely one or two to whom we might venture to apply the epithet " holy." In other words, there were not more than one or two, if any, who besides being virtuous in their actions were possessed with an unaffected enthusiasm of goodness, and besides abstaining from vice regarded even a vicious thought with horror. Probably no one will deny that in Christian countries this higher-toned goodness, which we call holiness, has existed. Few will maintain that it has been exceedingly rare. Perhaps the truth is, that there has scarcely been a town in any Christian country since the time of Christ where a century has passed without exhibiting a character of such elevation that his mere presence has shamed the bad and made the good better, and has been felt at times like the presence of God Himself. And if this be so, has Christ failed? or can Christianity die?

CHAPTER XV

THE LORD'S SUPPER

THAT Christ had but a slight esteem for rites and ceremonies may be argued negatively from his establishing so few, and positively from the contempt he poured on the traditional formalities prized so highly by the Scribes and Pharisees. But he well understood their use, and we have already observed with what rigorous firmness he insisted on his followers submitting to the initiatory rite of baptism. The kingdom he was founding was to be everywhere *imperium in imperio ;* its members were to be at the same time members of secular states and national bodies. It was therefore a matter of extreme importance to preserve the distinctness of the Christian society and to prevent its members from being drawn apart from each other by the distractions of worldly claims and engagements. For this purpose certain *sacramenta* or solemn observances renewing and reminding them of their union were most desirable, and Christ ordained two, the one expressing the distinctness of the Church from the world, and the other the unity of the Church within itself. Of the former, Baptism, mention was made when we considered Christ's Call, concerning the latter, the Common Supper or συσσίτιον of Christians, it is convenient to say something now.

A common meal is the most natural and universal way of expressing, maintaining, and as it were ratifying relations of friendship. The spirit of antiquity regarded the meals of human beings as having the nature of sacred rites (sacra mensæ). If therefore it sounds degrading to compare the Christian Communion to a club-dinner, this is not owing to any essential difference between the two things, but to the fact that the moderns connect less dignified associations with meals than the ancients did, and

The Lord's Supper

that most clubs have a far less serious object than the Christian Society. The Christian Communion *is* a club-dinner: but the club is the New Jerusalem; God and Christ are members of it; death makes no vacancy in its lists, but at its banquet-table the perfected spirits of just men, with an innumerable company of angels, sit down beside those who have not yet surrendered their bodies to the grave.

Goethe thought that Protestant Christians have too few sacraments, and this opinion is not refuted by the fact that Christ himself only instituted two. We are to suppose, however, that these two are the most essential, and indeed without them we can scarcely imagine the Church maintaining its distinct existence. Without a solemn form of entrance, and without occasional solemn meetings, Christians would forget that they were Christians. But in these meetings it was obviously desirable, if it were possible, that not only the fact of the union of Christians, but also the nature and manner of their union, should be symbolically expressed. We have now considered at some length the nature and conditions of the Christian Society, without referring to or producing in evidence the Lord's Supper. If therefore the form of the Lord's Supper expresses symbolically such a union as we have described, we shall derive from this fact a confirmation of the results at which we had independently arrived.

Of those results some do not require confirmation, being in themselves obvious and disputed by none. It has never been questioned that the doctrine of the brotherhood of mankind and of the duty of universal benevolence and charity is a main feature of Christianity. This doctrine, then, is very plainly symbolised in the Lord's Supper. As a meeting or communion it is clearly designed to express a certain fellowship between those who share it; by admitting all Christians without distinction on equal terms, it expresses the universal character of the society. The extreme simplicity of the ceremony makes its symbolical character more impressive, and averts, as far as that is possible, the danger which all venerated symbols incur of being valued for their own sake and confounded with the thing symbolised. The meal consisted of bread and wine, the simplest and in those countries most universal elements of food; and when men of different nations or degrees sat or knelt together and received, as from the hand of God, this simple repast, they were reminded in the most forcible manner of their common human wants, and their common character of pensioners on the bounty of the Universal Father.

But Christ added something to the ceremony. He bade his followers consider the bread they ate as his body, and the wine they drank as his blood. And in a discourse recorded by St. John, which we may quote without distrust, as it is so manifestly confirmed by the accounts given by the other Evangelists of the institution of the Supper, he says, " Except ye eat the flesh and drink the blood of the Son of Man, ye have no life in you." What Christ meant by *life* is not now difficult to discover. It is that healthy condition of the mind which issues of necessity in right action. This health of the soul we know Christ regarded as consisting in a certain enthusiasm of love for human beings as such. This enthusiasm then, we are now informed, will not spring up in us spontaneously nor by any efforts we may make to kindle it in ourselves, nor is the message of Christianity fully delivered when love to the human race is declared to be a duty; human beings will not unite merely because they are told to do so, nor will the anarchic passions submit to a mere reproof. Men cannot learn to love each other, says Christ, but " by eating his flesh and drinking his blood."

The Lord's Supper, then, confirms by its symbolism the view of Christian morality which was taken in the last chapter. It was there asserted that Christ did not regard it as possible to unite men to each other but by first uniting them to himself. And in the Lord's Supper, in which the union of Christians is symbolised, it is represented as depending not merely on the natural passion of humanity implanted in their breasts, nor merely on the command of Christ calling that passion into activity, but upon a certain intimate personal contact between Christ and his followers. The union of mankind, but a union begun and subsisting

The Lord's Supper

only in Christ, is what the Lord's Supper sacramentally expresses.

As to the metaphor itself, if it seems at first violent and unnatural, we are to observe that on the subject of the personal devotion required by Christ from his followers his language was often of this vehement kind, and that his first followers in describing their relation to him in like manner overleap the bounds of ordinary figurative language. Christ, in a passage to which allusion has already been made, demanded of his followers that they should *hate* their father and mother for his sake, and St. Paul in many passages declares that Christ is his life and his very self. It is precisely this intense personal devotion, this habitual feeding on the character of Christ, so that the essential nature of the Master seems to pass into and become the essential nature of the servant — loyalty carried to the point of self-annihilation—that is expressed by the words " eating the flesh and drinking the blood of Christ."

Much remains to be said about the details of Christian morality, but the reader should already be in a condition to understand and judge of its scope. And let us pause once more to consider that which remains throughout a subject of ever-recurring astonishment, the unbounded personal pretensions which Christ advances. It is common in human history to meet with those who claim some superiority over their fellows. Men assert a preeminence over their fellow-citizens or fellow-countrymen and become rulers of those who at first were their equals, but they dream of nothing greater than some partial control over the actions of others for the short space of a lifetime. Few indeed are those to whom it is given to influence future ages. Yet some men have appeared who have been " as levers to uplift the earth and roll it in another course." Homer by creating literature, Socrates by creating science, Cæsar by carrying civilisation inland from the shores of the Mediterranean, Newton by starting science upon a career of steady progress, may be said to have attained this eminence. But these men gave a single impact like that which is conceived to have first set the planets in motion, Christ claims to be a perpetual attractive power like the sun which determines their orbit. They contributed to men some discovery and passed away; Christ's discovery is himself. To humanity struggling with its passions and its destiny he says, Cling to me, cling ever closer to me. If we believe St. John, he represented himself as the Light of the World, as the Shepherd of the Souls of men, as the Way to immortality, as the Vine or Life-Tree of Humanity. And if we refuse to believe that he used those words, we cannot deny, without rejecting all the evidence before us, that he used words which have substantially the same meaning. We cannot deny that he commanded men to leave everything and attach themselves to him; that he declared himself king, master, and judge of men; that he promised to give rest to all the weary and heavy-laden; that he instructed his followers to hope for life from feeding on his body and blood.

But it is doubly surprising to observe that these enormous pretensions were advanced by one whose special peculiarity, not only among his contemporaries but among the remarkable men that have appeared before and since, was an almost feminine tenderness and humanity. This characteristic was remarked, as we have seen, by the Baptist, and Christ himself was fully conscious of it. Yet so clear to him was his own dignity and infinite importance to the human race as an objective fact with which his own opinion of himself had nothing to do, that in the same breath in which he asserts it in the most unmeasured language he alludes, apparently with entire unconsciousness, to his *humility*. " Take my yoke upon you and learn of me, *for I am meek and lowly of heart*." And again, when speaking to his followers of the arrogance of the Pharisees, he says, " they love to be called Rabbi; but be not you called Rabbi, *for one is your master, even Christ*."

Who is the humble man? It is he who resists with special watchfulness and success the temptations which the conditions of his life may offer to exaggerate his own importance. He, for example, is humble who, born into a high station, remembers that those who are placed lower in society are also men and may have more intrinsic merit

The Lord's Supper 143

and dignity than himself. Christ could not show his humility in this way, for he was poor and obscure. But there are peculiar temptations which assail the thinker. He is in danger of being intoxicated by the influence which he gains over others, he feels himself elevated by the greatness of the thoughts with which his mind habitually deals and which from time to time it originates. If besides intellectual gifts the thinker possess acute sensibility, strong moral intuitions, heroic powers of indignation and pity, his temptation is to suppose that he is made of finer clay than other men, and that he has a natural title to pre-eminence and sovereignty over them. Such is the temptation of moral reformers such as Christ, and if Christ was humble he resisted this temptation with exceptional success. If he judged himself correctly, and if the Baptist described him well when he compared him to a lamb, and, we may add, if his biographers have delineated his character faithfully, Christ was one naturally contented with obscurity, wanting the restless desire for distinction and eminence which is common in great men, hating to put forward personal claims, disliking competition and " disputes who should be greatest," finding something bombastic in the titles of royalty, fond of what is simple and homely, of children, of poor people, occupying himself so much with the concerns of others, with the relief of sickness and want, that the temptation to exaggerate the importance of his own thoughts and plans was not likely to master him; lastly, entertaining for the human race a feeling so singularly fraternal that he was likely to reject as a sort of treason the impulse to set himself in any manner above them. Christ, it appears, was this humble man. When we have fully pondered the fact, we may be in a condition to estimate the force of the evidence, which, submitted to his mind, could induce him, in direct opposition to all his tastes and instincts, to lay claim, persistently, with the calmness of entire conviction, in opposition to the whole religious world, in spite of the offence which his own followers conceived, to a dominion more transcendent, more universal, more complete, than the most delirious votary of glory ever aspired to in his dreams.

CHAPTER XVI

POSITIVE MORALITY

Our investigation into the character of the law under which the members of the Christian Commonwealth are called to live has led us to the discovery that in the strict sense of the word no such law exists, it being characteristic of this commonwealth that every member of it is a lawgiver to himself. Every Christian, we learn, has a divine inspiration which dictates to him in all circumstances the right course of action, which inspiration is the passion of humanity raised to a high energy by contemplation of Christ's character, and by the society of those in whom the same enthusiasm exists. We cease, therefore, henceforth to speak of a Christian law, and endeavour instead to describe in its large outlines the Christian character; that is to say, the new views, feelings, and habits produced in the Christian by his guiding enthusiasm.

The tendency and operation of this enthusiasm will be most clearly apprehended if we consider the way in which it led those who felt it to regard the current morality of their time and country, in other words, the Jewish law. In this law they had been bred; it was their rule of life up to the time when they awoke to a new life. How, then, did they regard this system after their regeneration?

In the first place they regarded it critically, as something of which they were independent and with which they could dispense. They had in their own breasts an inexhaustible spring of morality; of written and formulated morality they had henceforth no need. Feeling a sure foundation under their feet, they gathered courage for the first time to examine and criticise what before they had felt it their wisdom to receive without criticism. As Jews their piety had consisted in a certain timid caution,

Positive Morality

a wary walking in the old paths, and when they became Christians, it is remarkable that they gave to those who continued to be what they had originally been the title of " the cautious men."

In periods which are wanting in inspiration piety always assumes this character of caution. It degenerates from a free and joyful devotion to a melancholy and anxious slavery. The first work of the Divine Spirit was a work of encouragement, and the humblest man was found the most courageous of all. He scrutinised fearlessly the mass of traditions which then went by the name of the Law, and unhesitatingly pronounced a great part of them wanting in authority. Some of these time - honoured usages he stigmatised as immoral and mischievous, others, which were in themselves indifferent, he treated with contemptuous neglect. We may imagine that by this conduct he gave grievous offence to some honest, " cautious," conservative spirits. Doubtless—thus they may have expostulated—the washing of cups and pots is in itself unimportant, but wise men, our ancestors, have prescribed the usage; by such symbolism we may learn the lesson and form the habit of purity. These men Christ perhaps regarded as Milton regarded the versifier who did not know whether his lines were of the right length till he had counted the syllables. As the poet consulted on such questions only the soul of rhythm within him, so were all mysteries of purity made clear to Christ by the Spirit of purity which he had received from above. It was not, indeed, in his nature to despise anything which might be useful to the ignorant and the weak, however unnecessary for himself. As he stooped to receive baptism from John, so he would, no doubt, have sanctified these usages by his own observance if he had seen any good in them at all. But he seems to have considered that the time for these methods was gone by; and as all such contrivances begin to be mischievous the moment they cease to be beneficial, he condemned them as fettering the freedom of that inspiration which was for the future to take the place of law.

Of the Scriptures of the Old Testament he always spoke with the utmost reverence, and he seems never to have called in question the Jewish view of them as infallible oracles of God. Some parts of them, particularly the book of Deuteronomy, seem to have been often present to his thoughts. Yet even the Old Testament he regarded in a sense critically, and he introduced canons of interpretation which must have astonished by their boldness the religious men of the day. For he regarded the laws of Moses, though divine, as capable of becoming obsolete and also as incomplete. On the question of divorce he declared the Mosaic arrangement to have been well suited for the " hard-heartedness " of a semi-barbarous age, but to be no longer justifiable in the advanced condition of morals. So too in the matter of oaths, the permission of private revenge, and other points in which the Mosaic legislation had necessarily something of a barbaric character, he unhesitatingly repealed the acts of the lawgiver and introduced new provisions.

It is easy to imagine the alarm which such freedom of interpretation must have excited in the " cautious." They would declare it destructive of the authority of the Scriptures. Were not the Scriptures given, they would say, to save man from his own reason? Does not their priceless value consist in this, that for all conceivable circumstances they furnish a rule which simple men may follow with simple obedience? But if these divine rules can in any case become obsolete, if human affairs can change so far that the Scriptures can cease to be a guide to our feet, if the words of the Eternal can be subject to the accidents of time and mutability, what further use can there be in the Scriptures, and how henceforth shall our steps be guided?

It was the inspiration, the law-making power, that gave Christ and his disciples courage to shake themselves free from the fetters even of a divine law. Their position was a new and delicate one, and nothing but such an inspiration could have enabled them to maintain it. To pronounce the old law entirely true or entirely false would have been easy, but to consider it as true and divine yet no longer true for them, no longer their authoritative guide, must have seemed, and must seem even to us, at first sight unnatural and paradoxical. It may be illustrated, how-

Positive Morality

ever, by what everyone has observed to happen in the process of learning any art. For the beginner rigid rules are prescribed, which it will be well for him for a time to follow punctiliously and blindly. He may believe that under these rules a principle is concealed, that a reason could be given why they should be followed, but it is well for a time that the principle should remain concealed and that the rules should be followed simply because they are prescribed. At any rate, so long as he actually has not discovered the principle, he must abide strictly by the rules, and it would be foolish to abandon them in order to go in search of it. But there comes a time when the discovery is made, a golden moment of silent expansion and enlargement. Then the reason of all the discipline to which he has submitted becomes clear to him, the principle reveals itself and makes the confused and ill-apprehended multitude of details in a moment harmonious and luminous. But the principle at the same moment that it explains the rules supersedes them. They may be not less true than before, they may be seen to be true far more clearly than before. But they are obsolete; their use is gone; they can for the future tell only that which is already well known, which can never again be forgotten or misunderstood. If the student refers to them at a later time it is with a feeling of wonder that they should ever have delayed his attention for a moment, and probably in the rude and peremptory particularity of their form he may discover that which, though well enough adapted for the beginner under certain circumstances, is yet in itself not true and is calculated under other circumstances to mislead.

It was in this manner that Christ found the Mosaic law at once divine and in part obsolete. But not only did he find it in part obsolete, he found it throughout utterly meagre and imperfect. And this was inevitable. Between the rude clans that had listened to Moses in the Arabian desert and the Jews who in the reign of Tiberius visited the temple courts there was a great gulf. The " hard-heartedness " of the primitive nation had given way under the gradual influence of law and peace and trade and literature. Laws which in the earlier time the best men had probably found it hard to keep could now serve only as a curb upon the worst. The disciples of Moses were subject to lawless passions which they could not control, and the fiercest ebullitions of which seemed to them venial, misfortunes rather than crimes. Self-restraint of any kind was to them a new and hard lesson. They listened with awe to the inspired teacher who taught them not to covet their neighbour's wife or property; and when they were commanded not to commit murder, they wondered doubtless by what art, by what contrivance, it might be possible to put a bridle on the thing called *anger*—" anger which far sweeter than trickling drops of honey rises in the bosom of a man like smoke." But how much was all this changed! If one like Paul had gone to a Christian teacher after the new enthusiasm of humanity had been excited in him, and asked for instruction in morality, would it have satisfied him to be told that he must abstain from committing murder and robbery? These laws, to be sure, were not obsolete, but the better class of men had been raised to an elevation of goodness at which they were absolutely unassailable by temptations to commit them. Their moral sense required a different training, far more advanced instruction. It is true that in the later books of the Old Testament there might be found a morality considerably more advanced, but through the life and example of Christ the humblest of his followers was advanced a long stage beyond even this. No one who had felt, however feebly, the Christian enthusiasm could fail to find even in Deuteronomy and Isaiah something narrow, antiquated, and insufficient for his needs.

Now in what consisted precisely the addition made by Christ to morality?

It has been already shown that Christ raised the feeling of humanity from being a feeble restraining power to be an inspiring passion. The Christian moral reformation may indeed be summed up in this—humanity changed from a restraint to a motive. We shall be prepared therefore to find that while earlier moralities had dealt chiefly in prohibitions, Christianity deals in positive commands. And precisely this is the case, precisely this difference

Positive Morality 149

made the Old Testament seem antiquated to the first Christians. They had passed from a region of passive into a region of active morality. The old legal formula began " *thou shalt not,*" the new begins with " *thou shalt.*" The young man who had kept the whole law—that is, who had refrained from a number of actions—is commanded to do something, to sell his goods and feed the poor. Condemnation passed under the Mosaic law upon him who had sinned, who had done something forbidden— the soul that sinneth shall die;—Christ's condemnation is pronounced upon those who had not done good. " I was an hungered and ye gave me no meat." The sinner whom Christ habitually denounces is he who has done nothing. This character comes repeatedly forward in his parables. It is the priest and Levite who passed by on the other side. It is Dives, of whom no ill is recorded except that a beggar lay at his gate full of sores and yet no man gave unto him. It is the servant who hid in a napkin the talent committed to him. It is the unprofitable servant, who has only done what it was his duty to do.

Putting together these parables delivered at different times and to different audiences, yet all teaching the same doctrine, and adding to them the positive exhortations to almsgiving, to free and lavish charity, we see that Christ's conception of practical goodness answers to his ideal of a right state of mind. We observed that he considered the healthy condition of character to be an enthusiastic or inspired condition; we now find that he prescribes just such conduct as would be prompted by such enthusiastic feelings. And this consistency or unity of his teaching will appear still more plainly when we consider what the tenor of his own life was. It may sometimes strike us that the time which he devoted to acts of beneficence and the relief of ordinary physical evils might have been given to works more permanently beneficial to the race. Of his two great gifts, the power over nature and the high moral wisdom and ascendency over men, the former might be the more astonishing, but it is the latter which gives him his everlasting dominion. He might have left to all subsequent ages more instruction if he had bestowed less time upon diminishing slightly the mass of evil around him, and lengthening by a span the short lives of the generation in the midst of which he lived. The whole amount of good done by such works of charity could not be great, compared with Christ's powers of doing good; and if they were intended, as is often supposed, merely as attestations of his divine mission, a few acts of the kind would have served this purpose as well as many. Yet we may see that they were in fact the great work of his life; his biography may be summed up in the words, " he went about doing good "; his wise words were secondary to his beneficial deeds; the latter were not introductory to the former, but the former grew occasionally, and, as it were, accidentally out of the latter. The explanation of this is that Christ merely reduced to practice his own principle. His morality required that the welfare and happiness of others should not merely be remembered as a restraint upon action, but should be made the principal motive of action, and what he preached in words he preached still more impressively and zealously in deeds. He set the first and greatest example of a life wholly governed and guided by the passion of humanity. The very scheme and plan of his life differed from that of other men. He had no personal prospects, no fortune to push, no ambitions. A good man before had been understood to be one who in the pursuit of his own personal happiness is careful to consider also the happiness of those around him, declines all prosperity gained at their expense, employs his leisure in relieving some of their wants, and who, lastly, in some extreme need or danger of those connected with him, his relations or his country, consents to sacrifice his own life or welfare to theirs. In this scheme of life humanity in its rudimentary forms of family feeling or patriotism enters as a restraining or regulating principle; only in the extreme case does it become the mainspring of action. What with other good men was the extreme case, with Christ was the rule. In many countries and at many different times the lives of heroes had been offered up on the altar of filial or parental or patriotic love. A great impulse had overmastered them; personal interests, the love of life and of the pleasures of life, had yielded to a higher motive; the names of

Positive Morality

those who had made the great oblation had been held in honour by succeeding ages, the place where it was made pointed out, the circumstances of it proudly recounted. Such a sacrifice, the crowning act of human goodness when it rises above itself, was made by Christ, not in some moment of elevation, not in some extreme emergency, but *habitually ;* this is meant when it is said, he went about doing good; nor was the sacrifice made for relative or friend or country, but for all everywhere who bear the name of man.

Those who stood by watching his career felt that his teaching, but probably still more his deeds, were creating a revolution in morality and were setting to all previous legislations, Mosaic or Gentile, that seal which is at once ratification and abolition. While they watched, they felt the rules and maxims by which they had hitherto lived die into a higher and larger life. They felt the freedom which is gained by destroying selfishness instead of restraining it, by crucifying the flesh instead of circumcising it. In this new rule they perceived all old rules to be included, but so included as to seem insignificant, axioms of moral science, beggarly elements. It no longer seemed to them necessary to prohibit in detail and with laborious enumeration the different acts by which a man may injure his neighbour. Now that they had at heart as the first of interests the happiness of all with whom they might be brought in contact, they no longer required a law, for they had acquired a quick and sensitive instinct, which restrained them from doing harm. But while the new morality incorporated into itself the old, how much ampler was its compass! A new continent in the moral globe was discovered. Positive morality took its place by the side of Negative. To the duty of not doing harm, which may be called justice, was added the duty of doing good, which may properly receive the distinctively Christian name of Charity.

And this is the meaning of that prediction which certain shepherds reported to have come to them in a mystic song heard under the open sky of night (" carmine perfidiæ quod post nulla arguet ætas ") proclaiming the commencement of an era of " *good will to men.*"

CHAPTER XVII

THE LAW OF PHILANTHROPY

Thus there rises before us the image of a commonwealth in which a universal enthusiasm not only takes the place of law, but by converting into a motive what was before but a passive restraint, enlarges the compass of morality and calls into existence a number of positive obligations which under the dominion of law had not been acknowledged. It is a commonwealth sustained and governed by the desire existing in the mind of each of its members to do as much good as possible to every other member.

Doubtless, a commonwealth fully answering this description has never existed on the earth, nor can exist. It is an ideal. True that Christ always spoke of the kingdom of God as an actual and present commonwealth into which men were actually introduced by baptism. Nevertheless he fully acknowledged its ideal character, and therefore spoke of it as at the same time future and still waiting to be realised. Those who were already members of God's kingdom were notwithstanding instructed to pray that that kingdom might come. And if we look at the facts around us we shall discover that the kingdom of God has always been in this manner at once present and future, at once realised and waiting to be realised. In other words, it has always fallen far short of its ideal, and yet it has never ceased in some degree to resemble that ideal. It has never ceased to abide by the positive or active scheme of morality, and to occupy itself more or less zealously with works of beneficence and charity. We may go further, and say that the Christian view of morality has become universal, so that now no man is called or considered good, whether he bear the Christian name or not,

The Law of Philanthropy 153

who does not in some form or other exhibit an active love for his kind and go out of his way to do good.

The enthusiasm of humanity in Christians is not only their supreme but their only law. It has been remarked that Christ's plan was to kindle in the hearts of his followers a feeling which should dictate to them the right course of action in all circumstances. It follows that when we have considered the nature of this feeling we have exhausted the subject of Christian morality. If Christ delivered any other more special commands besides the command to love, they must be either deducible from it, if it be the law-making power which he pronounced it to be, or if they do not agree with its dictates—if those who have the genuine enthusiasm in them find that the literal obedience to Christ's special commands is in any instance irreconcilable with obedience to his universal command— they must bear in mind the boldness with which he himself treated the Mosaic law while acknowledging it to be divine. They must remember that principles last for ever, but special rules pass away with the things and conditions to which they refer. As Christ relaxed the sabbatical obligation by referring to the object of the ordinance—the Sabbath was made for man—so should his disciples boldly and reverently interpret his precepts by the light of the principle which governed them, the principle of humanity, and obey as freemen not as slaves.

But to us considering what are likely to be the characteristics, the modes of life and action, of a person in whom the Enthusiasm of Humanity has been kindled, these special commands of Christ are likely to afford the very information we seek. A principle is best seen in its practical applications, a rule in its examples. It may be said, then, that besides the great and one law of love Christ delivered three special injunctions.

First he enjoined his followers to apply themselves to relieving the physical needs and distresses of their fellow-creatures. Next he commanded them to add new members to the Christian Church, and especially to seek the amendment of the neglected, outcast, and depraved part of society. Thirdly he enjoined them to forgive all personal injuries. These three injunctions we will proceed to consider in order.

The command to relieve physical distress is many times repeated. Christians are to give alms; in some cases they were commanded to give all their wealth to the poor; in all cases they were assured that their final acceptance before the Judge would depend upon the zeal they had shown in feeding the hungry, welcoming the stranger, and visiting the sick. The first definite duty which Christ imposed upon his followers when they began to form an organised society was that of travelling over the whole country in order to cure diseases. Lastly, as has been already remarked, he was himself constantly and principally occupied in the same way.

No rule of life is more plainly deducible from the general law of love than this. Higher benefits may be conferred upon men than the alleviation of their physical sufferings, but there can be no more natural expression and no better test of humanity. Nothing is more certain than that he who can witness suffering without an attempt to relieve it, when such attempt is not hopeless, is not humane. The proposition is one of the most obvious that can be expressed in words; all nations not utterly savage have in a sense admitted it. Christ's command had nothing in it which to a heathen could have seemed novel, and yet, on the other hand, it was not at all superfluous. For though there was humanity among the ancients, there was no philanthropy. In other words, humanity was known to them as an occasional impulse, but not as a standing rule of life. A case of distress made painfully manifest and prominent would often excite compassion; the feeling might lead to a single act of beneficence; but it had not strength enough to give birth to reflection or to develop itself into a speculative compassion for other persons equally distressed whose distresses were not equally manifest. Exceptional sufferings had therefore a chance of relief, but the ordinary sufferings which affected whole classes of men excited no pity, and were treated as part of the natural order of things, providential dispensations which it might even be impious to endeavour to counter-

The Law of Philanthropy

act. Let us consider the example of slavery. There were in antiquity kind masters who refrained from treating their slaves with cruelty; when a slave was to be punished, it was not hard to find good-humoured " precatores " who would intercede for him; there was humanity enough to cause sometimes a general feeling of displeasure when a slave was treated with outrageous cruelty. But no general protest was ever made against the cruelty of slave-owners. No man, still less any body of men, thought it worth while to give time and trouble either to alleviating the miseries of the slave or to mitigating the harshness of the institution itself. If it became clear to any, as to a few philosophers it did, that the institution was unjust, and if unjust then of necessity a monstrous injustice, they quietly noted the fact, but never stirred hand or foot to remedy it, and the majority of mankind were not sufficiently interested in each other's happiness to discover the existence of any such social injustice at all.

When this lethargy passed away and humanity became a passion in the first Christians, it issued by the lips of Christ an imperative ordinance making the sorrows of each a burden upon all. Henceforth it became the duty of every man gravely to consider the condition of the world around him. It became his duty to extend his regards beyond the circle of his personal interests, and sometimes to open the gate of his privacy and relieve the beggar who might be lying outside full of sores. Nor was he to wait till the misery of some fellow-creature forced itself rudely upon his notice and affected his sensibility. On the contrary he was to bear habitually in his heart the load of the world's distress. Pity was to be henceforth no stranger greeted occasionally, but a familiar companion and bosom-friend. Nor was he to make philanthropy the amusement of his leisure, but one of the occupations of his life. He was to give alms; that is, he was to relieve his fellow-creature at the cost of some personal loss to himself, and Christ held that a despicable Christianity which flung to the poor some unregarded superfluity; he valued more the mite which the widow spared out of her poverty.

156 Ecce Homo

The obligation of philanthropy is for all ages, but if we consider the particular modes of philanthropy which Christ prescribed to his followers we shall find that they were suggested by the special conditions of that age. The same spirit of love which dictated them, working in this age upon the same problems, would find them utterly insufficient. No man who loves his kind can in these days rest content with waiting as a servant upon human misery, when it is in so many cases possible to anticipate and avert it. Prevention is better than cure, and it is now clear to all that a large part of human suffering is preventible by improved social arrangements. Charity will now, if it be genuine, fix upon this enterprise as greater, more widely and permanently beneficial, and therefore more Christian than the other. It will not, indeed, neglect the lower task of relieving and consoling those who, whether through the errors and unskilful arrangements of society or through causes not yet preventible, have actually fallen into calamity. Its compassion will be all the deeper, its relief more prompt and zealous, because it does not generally, as former generations did, recognise such calamities to be part of man's inevitable destiny. It will hurry with the more painful eagerness to remedy evils which it feels ought never to have befallen. But when it has done all which the New Testament enjoins, it will feel that its task is not half fulfilled. When the sick man has been visited and everything done which skill and assiduity can do to cure him, modern charity will go on to consider the causes of his malady, what noxious influence besetting his life, what contempt of the laws of health in his diet or habits, may have caused it, and then to enquire whether others incur the same dangers and may be warned in time. When the starving man has been relieved, modern charity enquires whether any fault in the social system deprived him of his share of nature's bounty, any unjust advantage taken by the strong over the weak, any rudeness or want of culture in himself wrecking his virtue and his habits of thrift. The truth is, that though the morality of Christ is theoretically perfect and not subject, as the Mosaic morality was, to a further development,

The Law of Philanthropy

the practical morality of the first Christians has been in a great degree rendered obsolete by the later experience of mankind, which has taught us to hope more and undertake more for the happiness of our fellow-creatures. The command to care for the sick and suffering remains as divine as ever and as necessary as ever to be obeyed, but it has become, like the Decalogue, an elementary part of morality, early learnt, and not sufficient to satisfy the Christian enthusiasm. As the early Christians learnt that it was not enough to do no harm and that they were bound to give meat to the hungry and clothing to the naked, we have learnt that a still further obligation lies upon us to prevent, if possible, the pains of hunger and nakedness from being ever felt.

This last duty was as far beyond the conception of the earliest Christians as the second was beyond the conception of those for whom Moses legislated. Many things concealed it from the eye of the conscience. First the obscure social position of the first Christians. They belonged for the most part to the subject races of the Roman Empire. The government of affairs, the ordering of the social system, was in other hands. Their masters were jealous and reserved. Little concerted action of any kind was allowed to them. Any protest they might have made against social inequalities and injustices would have died away utterly unheeded. There was no channel through which those who discerned an evil could communicate with those who had the power of removing it. At such a time reforms were out of the question. It would have been simply useless and perilous to lay a hand upon the ponderous wheels of the social system which crushed the lives and limbs of men at every revolution. All that could be done was to be at hand to tend the victims, to rescue as many wounded as possible, and shed a tear over the dead.

But the principal reason why the philanthropy prescribed by the Gospel is so rudimentary was probably a different one. The first Christians were probably not so much hopeless of accomplishing great social reforms as unripe for the conception of them. The instinct of compassion, which joined to a sanguine spirit of hope produces the modern systematic Reformer, was newborn and infantine in them. It had as yet everything to learn, both as to the evils which were to be cured and as to the possibility and means of curing them. On both points the ancients laboured under a blindness which we can only understand by an effort of reflection. They did not easily recognise evil to be evil, and they did not believe, or rather they had never dreamed, that it could be cured. Habit dulls the senses and puts the critical faculty to sleep. The fierceness and hardness of ancient manners is apparent to us, but the ancients themselves were not shocked by sights which were familiar to them. To us it is sickening to think of the gladiatorial show, of the massacres common in Roman warfare, of the infanticide practised by grave and respectable citizens, who did not merely condemn their children to death, but often in practice, as they well knew, to what was still worse—a life of prostitution and beggary. The Roman regarded a gladiatorial show as we regard a hunt; the news of the slaughter of two hundred thousand Helvetians by Cæsar or half-a-million Jews by Titus excited in his mind a thrill of triumph; infanticide committed by a friend appeared to him a prudent measure of household economy. To shake off this paralysis of the moral sense produced by habit, to see misery to be misery and cruelty to be cruelty, requires not merely a strong but a trained and matured compassion. It was probably as much as the first Christians could learn at once to relieve the sick, the starving, and the desolate. Only after centuries of this simple philanthropy could they learn to criticise the fundamental usages of society itself, and acquire courage to pronounce that, however deeply-rooted and time-honoured, they were in many cases shocking to humanity.

Closely connected with this insensibility to the real character of common usages is a positive unwillingness to reform them. The argument of prejudice is twofold. It is not only that what has lasted a long time must be right, but also that what has lasted a long time, right or wrong, must be intended to continue. That reverence

The Law of Philanthropy

for existing usages, which is always strong in human nature, was far stronger in antiquity than it is now. The belief in the wisdom of ancestors, which seems to be caused by the curious delusion that ancestors must needs be old and therefore deeply-experienced men, was stronger among the ancients than among the moderns, because their impression of their ancestors was derived not from history but from poetry. They traced their institutions to semi-divine or inspired legislators, and held it almost impious to change what came to them marked with such authority, while we, however proud we may be of our ancestors, do not disguise from ourselves that they were barbarians, and can hardly fancy their handiwork incapable of improvement.

Thus the Enthusiasm of Humanity, if it move us in this age to consider the physical needs of our fellow-creatures, will not be contented with the rules and methods which satisfied those who first felt its power. Breathed from the lips of Christ or descending from heaven at the Pentecostal feast, it entered into men who had grown to manhood in a cruel and hard-hearted world and who were accustomed to selfishness. When Love was waked in his dungeon and his fetters struck off, he must at first have found his joints too stiff for easy motion. It entered into the subjects of a world-wide tyranny, who never raised their thoughts to large or public interests, over which they could not hope to have influence. It entered into men of narrow cultivation, who had no conception of progress or of the purpose that runs through the ages, no high ideal of the happiness that the race may attain through the labours of the good of every generation in its cause, no suspicion that the whole framework of society compared to what it might be was as the hut of a savage to a Grecian temple. It entered into men who in their simplicity revered the barbaric past and placed behind them that golden age for which they should have looked forwards. And therefore it could but rouse them to a philanthropy which, though glorious in the spirit that animated it, was faint and feeble in its enterprises, the half-despairing attempt of a generation which had more love than hope.

We are advanced by eighteen hundred years beyond the apostolic generation. All the narrowing influences which have been enumerated have ceased to operate. Our minds are set free, so that we may boldly criticise the usages around us, knowing them to be but imperfect essays towards order and happiness, and no divinely or supernaturally ordained constitution which it would be impious to change. We have witnessed improvements in physical well-being which incline us to expect further progress and make us keen-sighted to detect the evils and miseries that remain. The channels of communication between nations and their governments are free, so that the thought of the private philanthropist may mould a whole community. And, finally, we have at our disposal a vast treasure of science, from which we may discover what physical well-being is and on what conditions it depends. In these circumstances the Gospel precepts of philanthropy become utterly insufficient. It is not now enough to visit the sick and give alms to the poor. We may still use the words as a kind of motto, but we must understand under them a multitude of things which they do not express. If we would make them express the whole duty of philanthropy in this age, we must treat them as preachers sometimes treat the Decalogue, when they represent it as containing by implication a whole system of morality. Christ commanded his first followers to heal the sick and give alms, but he commands the Christians of this age, if we may use the expression, to investigate the causes of all physical evil, to master the science of health, to consider the question of education with a view to health, the question of labour with a view to health, the question of trade with a view to health; and while all these investigations are made, with free expense of energy and time and means, to work out the rearrangement of human life in accordance with the results they give.

Thus ought the Enthusiasm of Humanity to work in these days, and thus, plainly enough, it does work. These investigations are constantly being made, these reforms commenced. But perhaps it is rather among those who

The Law of Philanthropy

are influenced by general philanthropy and generosity, that is, by indirect or secondary Christianity, than among those who profess to draw the Enthusiasm directly from its fount, that this spirit reigns. Perhaps those who appear the most devoted Christians are somewhat jealous of what they may consider this worldly machinery. They think they must needs be most Christian when they stick most closely to the New Testament, and that what is utterly absent from the New Testament cannot possibly be an important part of Christianity. A great mistake, arising from a wide-spread paralysis of true Christian feeling in the modern Church! The New Testament is not the Christian law; the precepts of Apostles, the special commands of Christ, are not the Christian law. To make them such is to throw the Church back into that legal system from which Christ would have set it free. The Christian law is the spirit of Christ, that Enthusiasm of Humanity which he declared to be the source from which all right action flows. What it dictates, and that alone, is law for the Christian. And if the progress of science and civilisation has put into our hands the means of benefiting our kind more and more comprehensively than the first Christians could hope to do—if instead of undoing a little harm and comforting a few unfortunates we have the means of averting countless misfortunes and raising, by the right employment of our knowledge and power of contrivance, the general standard of happiness—we are not to enquire whether the New Testament commands us to use these means, but whether the spirit of humanity commands it.

But, say the cautious, is it safe to follow a mere enthusiasm? If Christ is to be believed, it is not safe to follow anything else. According to him this Spirit was expressly given to guide men into all truth. But, they will rejoin—and here the truth comes out—we like to feel the stay of a written precept; we are not conscious of any such ardent impulse directing us infallibly what to do. In reply to which what can we do but repeat the question of St. Paul, " Into what then were ye baptised? "

CHAPTER XVIII

THE LAW OF EDIFICATION

PHILANTHROPY is the first and easiest lesson in positive morality. It is a duty in which all Christian sects agree and which with more or less zeal they perform. The means used may differ; the means used in this age differ widely from those used in the first ages; but the obligation which the first Christians acknowledged is substantially the same as that acknowledged now. When they visited the sick and made provision for widows and orphans and gave alms to the poor, they were doing to the best of their light and knowledge what philanthropists of the present day do when they study the science of physical well-being, search into the causes of disease and suffering, and endeavour systematically to raise the standard of happiness to the highest possible point.

Did the Enthusiasm of Humanity rest content with this? It might have done so. Perhaps there are some who believe that this is in fact the substance of Christianity, and that all the rest has been overlaid upon the original system. This is not true, and it will hardly seem plausible to a reader who has given even a general assent thus far to the results of the present investigation. But we shall find it easier to understand what the substance of Christianity really is, if we consider attentively what Christianity would have been and how it would have worked if this theory of it were true. How the persons who hold this theory regard Christianity we may make clear to ourselves by a comparison. The present century has witnessed a remarkable softening of manners. A number of cruel practices and severities, that excited no disgust a hundred years ago, have now been either swept away as intolerable or are reluctantly tolerated from a feeling of

The Law of Edification 163

necessity. Among these are the torture of the wheel, the pillory, the punishment of death. And in private life during the same period men have greatly advanced in tenderness, sympathy, and unwillingness to inflict pain. This improvement was doubtless caused by the decay of feudal, chivalrous, and semi-barbaric institutions which had cherished hard and warlike habits of life. Society in the last century entered upon a new period. For this new period there arose new legislators, and it may probably be said that the fashion of gentleness in feelings and manners was introduced mainly through the influence of Jean Jacques Rousseau.

Now the first century, like the eighteenth, was a period of transition. It was a period when for the first time the civilised nations of the world lived together in almost unbroken peace. War had ceased to be the main business of life, the support of virtue and almost the only means by which eminent virtue could show itself. In these circumstances the world was prepared for, was calling for, a theory of virtue which should be adapted to its new condition. It wanted a new pursuit in place of war, a pursuit in which, as before in war, the moral feelings might find satisfaction and in which heroism might be displayed. Christ, it may be maintained, was the social legislator who appeared in answer to this call. He induced a large number of people by his eloquence and enthusiasm to devote themselves to philanthropy. He opened their eyes to the suffering and horrors of which the world was full, and pointed out to them a noble and satisfying occupation for their energies and a path to the truest glory in the enterprise of alleviating this misery.

There is no doubt that a philanthropic movement such as is here supposed was possible and would have been highly beneficial in the first century. As five centuries before, a ferment in the Greek mind, arising out of a general advance in civilisation and the influence of several remarkable men, led to the appearance in the world of an entirely new character which has never since disappeared—the *sophist* or *philosopher*, so it was natural enough that in the first century of the Christian era *philanthropists* should be heard of for the first time, and that they should take their rise out of a moral ferment excited by a great preacher. A sect of philanthropists might have spread everywhere, and gradually influenced rulers, and by this means manners might have been considerably softened. The Christians were no doubt such a sect, but were they merely this? Suppose the philanthropical scheme to be far more successful than it was likely to be, suppose it to succeed perfectly in producing physical comfort everywhere, and banishing from human life all forms of pain and suffering, such a result would certainly not have been satisfactory to Christ. He described in one of his parables a man such as philanthropy might produce if it were perfectly successful, a man enjoying every physical comfort and determining to give himself up to enjoyment, but he describes him rather with horror than with satisfaction. And though so much of his life was passed in relieving distress, we never find him representing physical happiness as a desirable condition; on the contrary, most of his beatitudes are pronounced upon those who suffer. The ideal of the economist, the ideal of the Old Testament writers, does not appear to be Christ's. He feeds the poor, but it is not his great object to bring about a state of things in which the poorest shall be sure of a meal; he recalls dead men to life, but his wisdom does not, like Solomon's, carry length of days in her right hand, and in her left hand riches and honour. Rather does it carry with it suffering, persecution, and the martyr's death. He corrects him who said, Blessed are they who shall *eat bread* in the kingdom of God. The kingdom of God does not exist for the sake of eating and drinking. He preaches peace, and yet he says, I am not come to send peace but a *sword*.

The paradox is not very difficult to explain. A good parent will be careful of the physical condition of his child, will tend him assiduously in sickness, relieve his wants, and endeavour in every way to make him happy. But a good parent will not rest content with seeing his child comfortable and secure from pain. He will consider that other and greater things than physical comfort

The Law of Edification 165

are to be procured for him, and for the sake of these greater things he will even sacrifice some of his comforts and see with satisfaction that the child suffers a certain amount of pain and wants some pleasures. The affection which pets and pampers its object is not excessive, as it is sometimes described, but a feeble affection, or at least the affection of a feeble nature. Now the love of Christ for human nature was no such feeble affection. It was not an exceedingly keen sensibility which made him feel more painfully than other men the sufferings of which the world is full. It was a powerful, calm, and contemplative love. It was a love of men for what they may be, a love of the ideal man in each man, or, as Christ himself might have said, a love of the image of God in each man. Accordingly the Enthusiasm of Humanity in him did not propose to itself principally to procure gratifications and enjoyments for the senses of men, but to make the divine image more glorious in them and to purge it as far as possible of impurities.

That ideal which Christ contemplated directly in God his followers found in him. And thus arises the second great obligation of Positive Morality, the obligation, namely, to use every means to raise men to the moral elevation of Christ. This obligation was brought home to the Christian by the natural working of the Enthusiasm of Humanity in him. Excited as it was by the contemplation of Christ, it could not be contented with diffusing physical well-being. He who had himself become humane desired indeed that others should be happy, but still more that they too should become humane. This dictate of the Christian spirit Christ threw into the form of a special command when he bade his disciples go everywhere, not merely healing diseases, but also proclaiming the kingdom of God and baptising. It was natural that the command should take this particular form, because, as we have seen, Christ regarded it as essential to the diffusion of true humanity that men should form themselves into a society of which humanity should be the law, and that they should signalise their entrance into it by undergoing a special rite of purification.

But here again we remark that the command is limited by the peculiar condition of the nascent Church, and that if it were performed to the utmost the Enthusiasm of Humanity would still remain entirely unsatisfied. There comes a time when the work of baptism has been already accomplished. We, for example, live in the midst of a baptised community; the command has become for us unnecessary or rather impossible to be fulfilled. But to meet the new circumstances, though Christ is silent, the spirit of Christ issues a new command. The Enthusiasm of Humanity tells us that though all are baptised all are not yet truly humane. It may be true that almost all are conscious of impulses and compunctions which are due directly or indirectly to Christianity, but the glowing humanity which alone Christ valued is surely not even common, much less universal, among the baptised. To rekindle this in those who have lost it, or in those who though nominally Christians have never really conceived it, or in those who have adopted one of the countless perversions of Christianity, and have never understood that this enthusiasm is the true Christian law, here is work for the Christian concerning which Christ left no command because it could not arise in the infant Church. As early, however, as the Apostolic age itself, it had begun to be the principal occupation of Christians. St. Paul's Epistles throughout regard the Christian Enthusiasm as liable to remission, depression, and languor. Continually therefore he exhorts the Christians to whom he writes to remember their ideal. His admonitions to activity in philanthropical works are brief and few though always earnest; but when he endeavours to keep alive their humanity, when he admonishes them to excite and cherish it in each other, then he is copious and vehement. This is the subject nearest his heart. His anxiety is not so much to hear that the widows and orphans are duly supplied, and that within the circle of the Christian community want is disappearing and the ills of life are sensibly diminished, as to be informed that his converts are conforming gradually more and more to their ideal. This conformity he expresses by various figures of speech.

The Law of Edification

It is to "put on Christ," "to put on the new man, the new Adam"; it is "to have Christ dwelling in the heart," "Christ formed within"; it is "to fill up the measure of the stature of the fulness of Christ."

So important a duty necessarily received a name. As the moral science of that time furnished no term which could describe it, the Christians denoted it by a metaphorical expression which has passed into modern languages. It has been remarked that the Christian *summum bonum* was a social one; it was the welfare of the Christian society. The whole duty of the Christian was to fill satisfactorily his place in that society. Now it is a universal usage of language that the building in which any society meets may be put for the society itself, and *vice versâ* that the building may be called after the society. The word *house* means sometimes the building in which a family lives, sometimes the family that lives in such a building; a college is sometimes a building in which learning is cultivated, sometimes the society that cultivate learning in such a building. The same remark applies to all similar words, such as club, bank, hospital, city. Among others it applies to the word church, which in like manner may be used either to describe a building or a society. This inveterate habit of language indicates the intimate association which forms itself in every mind between the two notions of a *corporation* and an *edifice*. No one can speak long in impassioned or rhetorical style about any society whatever without introducing metaphors drawn from architecture. The Christian writers fell immediately into the practice, and in doing so followed the example of Christ who said, "Upon this rock will I *build* my church." In this style of language, then, as the Church is a building, so each member of it is a stone, and the prosperity of the Church is expressed by the orderly arrangement and secure cementing of the stones. It follows that the labour of making men Christians and inspiring them with the Enthusiasm of Humanity is nothing else but the arrangement and cementing of the stones. In other words, it is *building*. This then was the name which the Christians adopted. " Let everything be done," says St. Paul, " with a view to *building.*" The phrase has been adopted into modern languages, yet in such a way as to destroy all its force. Instead of being translated, it has been directly transferred from the ecclesiastical Latin of the first centuries in the form of *edification.* The Christian law, then, which we are now discussing, may be called the Law of Edification.

This second Christian obligation—the obligation, as the same Apostle expresses it, to " provoke others to love "— is as much greater than the obligation of philanthropy as it is a better thing for a man to be good than to be prosperous. And in all cases of conflict between the two obligations the greater of course suspends the less. Christianity therefore is not identical with philanthropy, nor does it always dictate the course of action which may directly issue in happiness and prosperity for others. It regards temporal prosperity as no indispensable or unmixed blessing; its *summum bonum* is that healthy condition of the soul in which, influenced by the instinct of humanity, it becomes incapable of sin. This healthy condition is called in the dialect of Christianity " life " or " salvation," and Christ was in the habit of declaring it to be a blessing in comparison of which temporal happiness is utterly insignificant. There is nothing, he says, which a man can give in exchange for his *soul;* if he gain the whole world and lose *that,* what is he the better? All manner of physical suffering, therefore, is to be cheerfully endured rather than that the life of the soul should be sacrificed or enfeebled. If danger assail the soul through the right hand or the right eye, and it can be averted in no other way, we are to cut off the hand or pluck out the eye. He gives us at the same time to understand that not only have we sometimes to choose between temporal happiness and spiritual health, but that suffering and sorrow have often a direct tendency to produce spiritual health. They may serve the purpose of a wholesome discipline. Accordingly he pronounces a blessing on those that mourn, and speaks ominously and forebodingly of the temptations attending riches and a state of temporal prosperity.

If we are not to regard prosperity as the first of bless-

The Law of Edification 169

ings for ourselves, if we are not to seek it in preference to everything else for ourselves, if we are to acquiesce sometimes for ourselves in a state of suffering, it follows that we ought to do so for our neighbours. A humane man will certainly be pleased to see his fellow-creatures enjoying comfort, but if he be deeply humane he will never be satisfied with this; if their prosperity last long and be unalloyed he will even become dissatisfied, he will jealously watch for the appearance of those vices which prosperity breeds — insolence, selfishness, superficiality in thought, infirmity in purpose, and a luxurious baseness which is the death of the soul. If he discern these vices, if they show themselves visibly, the humane man may at last come to call out for sorrow; or, if this be too boldly said, yet at least if to men thus demoralised calamities happen at last, and wholesome labours be imposed, and they be made to support some stern agony of endurance, he will witness the visitation with a solemn satisfaction, and far more than he rejoiced before to see their pleasure will he exult to see the gates of that delusive Paradise closed again, and the fiery cherubim return to guard from man the fruit he cannot see without temptation nor taste without ruin.

Christ, therefore, is not merely the originator of philanthropy; and indeed the Church has sustained another part on earth besides that of the Sister of Charity. She has not merely sat by sick-beds, and played the Lady Bountiful to poor people, and rushed between meeting armies on the field of battle to reconcile the combatants by reminding them of their brotherhood. Christianity is not quite the mild and gentle system it is sometimes represented to be. Christ was meek and lowly, but he was something beside. What was he when he faced the leading men among his countrymen and denounced them as a brood of vipers on their way to the infernal fires? That speech which has been quoted above, " I am not come to send peace but a sword," will appear, when considered, to be the most tremendous speech ever uttered. Burke's wish that the war with France which he foresaw might prove a *long* war has been stigmatised as horrible. It was certainly an awful wish; it may well cause those who look only to physical and immediate happiness to shudder; but from Burke's premises it was justifiable. Christ's solemn resolution to persevere in what he felt to be his mission, in spite of the clearest foreknowledge of the suffering and endless bloodshed which his perseverance would cause to that race of which he was the martyr, was grounded on a similar confidence that the evil was preparatory to a greater good, and that if some happiness was to be sacrificed, it would be the price of a great moral advance. But the resolution was notwithstanding a most awful one, and should impressively teach us not to confound Christianity with mere philanthropy, not to suppose that what is shocking is of necessity unchristian, not to confound warmheartedness, bonhommie, or feminine sensibilities with the Enthusiasm of Humanity.

It has been remarked above that the machinery of philanthropy among the early Christians had all the rudeness which it might be expected to have at a time of little freedom, either of action or organisation. Instead of studying comprehensively the science of human well-being and devising systematic methods of producing and increasing it, they contented themselves with tending the sick, pensioning widows and orphans, and distributing alms. The means they adopted for performing the second great obligation, that of converting mankind to Christian humanity or holiness, were equally simple and below the requirements and powers of the present age. They used the one instrument of direct moral suasion. To the heathen they *preached*, to those already baptised they *prophesied*. They related to their converts the principal facts of Christ's life, they told the story of his death and resurrection, they instructed them in the morality and theology he had given to his Church. More effectively than this, but without organisation or contrivance, there worked within the Church and outwards round its whole circumference the living, diffusive, assimilative power of the Christian Humanity. As there are still many Christians who cling to the old modes of philanthropy because they are the only modes prescribed by the New Testament,

The Law of Edification

so may the modern Church be fairly charged with confining itself too exclusively to preaching and catechising in the work of conversion and edification. Preaching and catechising may still be useful and important, but many other instruments are now at our command, and these instruments it is none the less the duty of Christians to use because the New Testament says nothing about them.

The enthusiasm can indeed hardly be kindled except by a personal influence acting through example or impassioned exhortation. When Christ would kindle it in his disciples he *breathed* on them and said, " Receive the Holy Spirit "; intimating by this great symbolical act that life passes into the soul of a man, as it were by contagion from another living soul. It may indeed come to a man through the mere bounty of God, but of means that men can use to kindle it there is none beside their personal influence passing either directly from man to man or diffused by means of books. Contrivance, however, and organisation may do much in marshalling this personal influence, in bringing it to bear upon the greatest number and in the most effective way; it may also do much in preventing men's natural susceptibility to the enthusiasm from being dulled by adverse circumstances, and in giving fuel to the enthusiasm when it already burns. As it is the duty of Christians to study human well-being systematically with a view to philanthropy, so is it their duty with a view to edification to consider at large the conditions most favourable to goodness, and by what social arrangements temptations to vice may be reduced to the lowest point and goodness have the most and the most powerful motives. Here is a whole field of investigation upon which Christians are bound to enter; much doubtless has been already done in it, but not perhaps with much system, nor has it been sufficiently felt that it is a principal part of the work belonging properly to the Church.

The conditions most favourable to goodness! It will be well to consider in some detail what these are, remembering always that by goodness is meant the Christian Enthusiasm of Humanity. How may men be made most susceptible of this Enthusiasm?

It has been shown that the attractive power which throughout has acted upon men, which has preserved them from that isolation which is the opposite of Christianity, and which has united them in those communities of clan or city or state which were the germs and embryos of the Universal Christian Republic, is the tie of kindred. The state, we have seen, was founded on a fiction of blood-relationship, and Christianity uses the dialect of blood-relationship when it pronounces all mankind to be brothers. What is true of mankind in general will be found to be true in this case of the individual man. He in whom the *family affections* have been awakened will have a heart most open to the passion of humanity. It is useless to tell a man to love all mankind if he has never loved any individual of mankind and only knows by report what love is. It should be recognised that family affection in some form is the almost indispensable root of Christianity. This family affection is rightly called natural, that is to say, it will come of itself if it be not artificially hindered. It becomes therefore a principal duty of Christians to remove all hindrances out of the way of family affection.

Now what are these hindrances? They are innumerable, arising out of the endless incompatibilities of temperament and taste, incompatibilities of natural difference and those finer incompatibilities, which are more exquisitely painful and more malignant, arising out of small differences in general resemblance. For the removal of such hindrances no general rules can be laid down. In resisting and removing them the higher degrees of Christian tact win their triumphs. Meanwhile there are other hindrances of a simpler kind which are, to an indefinite degree, removable and of which some may here be mentioned. We may here mention marriages of interest or convenience, the children of which, often originally of dull and poor organisation, grow up in an atmosphere of cynical coldness which speedily kills whatever blossoms of kindliness their nature may put forth. In another class of society there rages another terrible destroyer of natural affection, hunger. Christ spoke of suffering as a wholesome discipline, but there is an extreme degree of suffering

The Law of Edification 173

which seems more ruinous to the soul than the most enervating prosperity. When existence itself cannot be supported without an unceasing and absorbing struggle, then there is no room in the heart for any desire but the wretched animal instinct of self-preservation, which merges in an intense, pitiable, but scarcely blamable selfishness. What tenderness, what gratitude, what human virtue can be expected of the man who is holding a wolf by the ears?

To persons who, from either of these causes or from others that might be mentioned, have become destitute of natural affection, preaching and catechising are almost useless. Your declamations will rouse in them no Enthusiasm of Humanity, but, it may be, an ecstasy of fright or fanaticism. Instruction in morality or theology will not make them moral or religious, but only a little more knowing and self-satisfied. A great example of humanity put visibly before them may indeed rouse in them the sense they want, but it will never have the healthy keenness and calmness it might have had, if it had been roused in the manner appointed by nature. Therefore all Christians who take an adequate view of Christian obligations will consider that the removal of all such social abuses as destroy natural affection, and by doing so kill Christian humanity in its germ, is among the first of those obligations.

But again, where natural affection exists, a peculiar perversion of it requires to be guarded against, which often makes it hostile to that very Humanity of which it is properly the rudimentary form. It is apt to take a clannish, exclusive shape, and to inspire not merely no love but positive hatred towards those who are without the circle of blood-relationship. It has been shown above how the very same attraction which created states, isolated them, created national distinctions, and, arising out of national distinctions, a permanent condition of international hostility. This state of things is still far indeed from being obsolete, and the same abuse exists within the bosom of states in another form. Divisions arise, embittered by superciliousness on the one side and envy on the other, between the high-born and the low-born, and other advantages such as wealth and acquired station are eagerly seized by family affection as an excuse for turning itself into an exclusive partiality. The distinctions themselves of birth and wealth are substantial realities which cannot be treated as if they did not exist. There are superior and inferior breeds of men as of other animals, and the rich man will be led by his wealth into a mode of life which must remove him to a certain distance from the poor man. The danger is lest the distinction and the distance should turn to a moral division, to a separation of interests and sympathies in which Christian union perishes. Therefore against all unjust privilege, against all social arrangements which make the prosperity of one man incompatible with the prosperity of another, the Christian is bound by his humanity to watch and protest.

But if this danger also is escaped, and natural affection be present without exclusiveness, to develop it into the full Christian Enthusiasm, there remain many other means besides preaching and purely religious instruction. Of these the most important is *education*, which is certainly a far more powerful agent than preaching, inasmuch as in the first place it acts upon the human being at an age when he is more susceptible of all influences, and particularly of moral ones, than he afterwards becomes, and in the second place it acts upon him incessantly, intensely, and by countless different methods for a series of years, whereas preaching acts upon him intermittently, for the most part faintly, and by one uniform method. Preaching is moral suasion delivered formally at stated intervals. In good education there is an equal amount of moral suasion, delivered far more impressively because delivered to individuals and at the moment when the need arises, while besides moral suasion other instruments are employed. Of these the principal is Authority, a most potent and indispensable agent. We have traced above the process by which mankind were ripened for the reception of Christianity. For many ages peremptory laws were imposed upon different nations and enforced by a machinery of punishment. During these ages, out of the

The Law of Edification

whole number of persons who obeyed these laws very few either knew or enquired why they had been imposed. But all the time these nations were forming habits of action which gradually became so familiar to them that the nations who wanted similar habits became to them objects of contempt and disgust as savages. At last the time came when the hidden principle of all law was revealed and Christian humanity became the self-legislating life of mankind. Thus did the Law bring men to Christ. Now what the Law did for the race the schoolmaster does for the individual. He imposes rules, assigning a penalty for disobedience. Under this rule the pupil grows up, until order, punctuality, industry, justice and mercy to his school-fellows become the habits of his life. Then when the time comes, the strict rule relaxes, the pupil is taken into the master's confidence, his obedience becomes reasonable, a living morality. If the teacher be one whose own morality attains the standard of the Christian Enthusiasm, the pupil is more likely to be initiated into the same supreme mystery than if he stood in any other relation to him. There is no moral influence in the world, excepting that occasionally exerted by great men, comparable to that of a good teacher; there is no position in which a man's merits, considered as moral levers, have so much purchase. Therefore the whole question of education—what the method of it should be, what men should be employed in it—is pre-eminently a question in which Christians are bound by their Humanity to interest themselves.

Let us advance a step further, and in considering the conditions favourable to goodness it will be convenient to isolate a particular case. We have before us, then, the child of parents to whose mutual love he owes a healthy organisation and a fresh flow of natural feeling, to the moderate prosperity of whose condition he owes an exemption from brutalising anxieties, and who have instilled into him no prejudices of caste. He has had a teacher who trained him as Providence trained mankind, assuming at the proper season the part of Moses, then that of Isaiah, then that of the Baptist, ushering him into the very presence of Christ. Into that presence he has entered, and we see a young man in whose mind there has ripened by natural development out of the sense of duty to kindred and country a commanding sense of duty to that Universal Commonwealth of men whose majesty he worships gathered up in the person of its Eternal Sovereign, Christ Jesus. Does manhood bring new dangers to such a person? What are they? And what safeguards can be provided against them?

The most formidable temptation of manhood is that which Christ described in a phrase hardly translatable as μέριμναι βιωτικαί. To boys and youths work is assigned by their parents or tutors. The judicious parent takes care not to assign so much work as to make his son a slave. We cherish as much as possible the freedom, the discursiveness of thought and feeling natural to youth. We cherish it as that which life is likely sooner or later to diminish, and if we curb it, we do so that it may not exhaust itself by its own vivacity. But in manhood work is not assigned to us by others who are interested in our welfare, but by a ruthless and tyrannous necessity which takes small account of our powers or our happiness. And the source of the happiness of manhood, a family, doubles its anxieties. Hence middle life tends continually to routine, to the mechanic tracing of a contracted circle. A man finds or fancies that the care of his own family is as much as he can undertake, and excuses himself from most of his duties to humanity. In many cases, owing to the natural difficulty of obtaining a livelihood in a particular country or to remediable social abuses, such a man's conduct is justified by necessity, but in many more it arises from the blindness of natural affection, making it difficult for him to think that he has done enough for his family while it is possible for him to do more. Christ bids us look to it that we be not weighed down by these worldly cares, which indeed if not resisted must evidently undo all that Christianity has done and throw men back into the clannish condition out of which it redeemed them. How many a man who at twenty was full of zeal, high-minded designs and plans of a life devoted to humanity,

The Law of Edification

after the cares of middle life have come upon him and one or two schemes contrived with the inexperience of youth have failed, retains nothing of the Enthusiasm with which he set out but a willingness to relieve distress whenever it crosses his path, and perhaps a habit of devoting an annual sum of money to charitable purposes!

To protect the lives of men from sinking into a routine of narrow-minded drudgery, the Christian Church has introduced the invaluable institution of *the Sunday*. Following the example of the old Jewish Church, it proclaims a truce once in seven days to all personal anxieties and degrading thoughts about the means of subsistence and success in life, and bids us meet together to indulge in larger thoughts, to give ourselves time to taste Heaven's bounty, and to drink together out of " the chalice of the grapes of God." In countries where life is a hard struggle, what more precious, more priceless public benefit can be imagined than this breathing-time, this recurring armistice between man and the hostile powers that beset his life, this solemn sabbatic festival? Connected with the Sunday is the institution of *preaching* or, as it is called in the New Testament, *prophesying*. The power of impassioned rhetoric over those whose occupations do not leave them much time for reading is very great, and when the preacher speaks out of the overflowing of a genuine Christian enthusiasm, his words will echo in the memories of many until the Sunday comes round again. In periods when the pulpits of a country are occupied by the foremost men of their time for genius and wisdom this institution may sway and form the whole mind of a nation.

Besides the Sunday and the institution of preaching there exist certain *societies* formed to war against social, political, or moral evils and in various ways to benefit mankind, by interesting himself in which the grown man may support the Christian humanity within him.

The μεριμναὶ βιωτικαί are an overwhelming host. It seems desirable to supply as many and as potent instruments as possible to him who would combat them. Valuable as the three instruments just mentioned are, it may be urged in deduction from the advantage of the Sunday and of preaching that they leave him passive; that if they free him for a time from his persecutors and revive in him the aspiration after a higher life, they do not supply him with the activities and the interests of that higher life. Societies do this, but for the most part at present in a very insufficient way. They do require from their members an effort of will, a deed, and one involving self-denial; they require a subscription of money. The money goes to furnish that comparatively small proportion of the members of the society who are personally grappling with the evil to remove which the society was formed. But from the majority nothing further is required; all personal service in the cause of humanity is commuted for a money-payment. So customary has this become that the word charity has acquired a new meaning; a man's charity, that is, his love for his fellow-creatures, is commonly estimated in pounds, shillings, and pence. But it is a question whether this commutation, however customary, is altogether legal in the Christian Republic. It would appear that St. Paul recognised a broad distinction between charity and money-donations. He seems to have thought that a man might give away all his property and yet have no charity. Perhaps we are rather to compare the Christian Republic with those famous states of antiquity which in their best days required the personal service of every citizen in the field, and only accepted a money-equivalent from those who were incapacitated from such service. It is characteristic of the Christian State that it depends for its very existence on the public spirit of its citizens. The states of the world are distinguished from each other visibly by geographical boundaries and language. But the Christian Republic scarcely exists apart from the Enthusiasm which animates it; if that dies it vanishes like a fairy city, and leaves no trace of its existence but empty churches and luxurious sinecurists. And assuredly he who remembers his citizenship in it only by the taxes he pays is but one step removed from forgetting it altogether.

If then the Christian Humanity is to be maintained at the point of enthusiasm in a man upon whom the cares of

The Law of Edification

middle life have come, he must not content himself with paying others to do Christian work. He must contribute of his gifts, not merely of his money. He must be a soldier in the campaign against evil, and not merely pay the war-tax. But then it is too much to expect that he should find work for himself. Spenser allegorises ill when he represents his Red Cross Knight as pricking forth alone in quest of adventures. At least this sort of soldiering is long out of date. In civilised war men are marshalled in companies and put under the orders of a superior officer. To drop the figure, a flourishing Church requires a vast and complicated organisation, which should afford a place for everyone who is ready to work in the service of humanity. The enthusiasm should not be suffered to die out in anyone for want of the occupation best calculated to keep it alive. Those who meet within the church walls on Sunday should not meet as strangers who find themselves together in the same lecture-hall, but as co-operators in a public work the object of which all understand and to his own department of which each man habitually applies his mind and contriving power. Thus meeting, with the *esprit de corps* strong among them, and with a clear perception of the purpose of their union and their meeting, they would not desire that the exhortation of the preacher should be, what in the nature of things it seldom can be, eloquent. It might cease then to be either a despairing and overwrought appeal to feelings which grow more callous the oftener they are thus excited to no definite purpose, or a childish discussion of some deep point in morality or divinity better left to philosophers. It might then become weighty with business, and impressive as an officer's address to his troops before a battle. For it would be addressed by a soldier to soldiers in the presence of an enemy whose character they understood and in the war with whom they had given and received telling blows. It would be addressed to an ardent and hopeful association who had united for the purpose of contending within a given district against disease and distress, of diminishing by every contrivance of kindly sympathy the rudeness, coarseness, ignorance, and imprudence of the poor and the heartlessness and hardness of the rich, for the purpose of securing to all that moderate happiness which gives leisure for virtue, and that moderate occupation which removes the temptations of vice, for the purpose of providing a large and wise education for the young; lastly, for the purpose of handing on the tradition of Christ's life, death, and resurrection, maintaining the Enthusiasm of Humanity in all the baptised, and preserving, in opposition to all temptations to superstition or fanaticism, the filial freedom of their worship of God.

Thus far have we carried our analysis of the conditions most favourable to the Christian spirit or Spirit of Humanity. It must remain incomplete. To finish it would lead us too far and answer no purpose. Our purpose in it is already answered if it has shown how much is involved in the great Law of Edification, how many duties that Law includes, and how large-minded and comprehensive in his studies and observations, how free from the fetters of tradition or Scripture, must be the man who would thoroughly fulfil it.

CHAPTER XIX

THE LAW OF MERCY

But there is another aspect of the Law of Edification. Hitherto we have considered it as imposing upon Christians the obligation of developing the domestic and patriotic virtue which is natural to men into that Christian Humanity which is its proper completion, and of cherishing, as much as possible, that natural virtue with a view to the development of the Christian Humanity, and of cherishing the Christian Humanity itself when developed. But it continually happens that all methods fail of accomplishing these results. There is a class of men in every community in whom both natural and Christian humanity is at the lowest ebb. These will not only do nothing for their kind, but they are capable of committing crimes against society and against those nearest to them. Under temptation from self-interest they actually commit such crimes, and the precedent being once established, they for the most part fall gradually into the condition of avowed enemies of their kind, and constitute a criminal or outcast class, which is not merely destitute of virtue but is, as it were, an Evil Church sustaining its evil by its union and propagating its anarchic law on every side. In exceptional cases men equally devoid of virtue are restrained by prudence or timidity or fortunate circumstances from committing grave crimes, and remain in the midst of the good undetected or tolerated but not morally better than the outcast on whom all turn their backs. How does Christianity command us to treat bad men? Let us first consider whether Christ taught anything on this special point by precept or example, and, secondly, let us consider what the Spirit of Humanity itself teaches.

He made a great difference between the avowed and

recognised criminal and the criminal whose vices were concealed under a veil of sanctimonious profession. The latter case, however, is a complicated one, which it will be convenient to consider apart. How then did he treat the recognised criminal? In Palestine the distinction between the virtuous and the vicious class seems to have been much more marked than in other countries of the ancient world, and as much as in Christian countries at the present day. We read of " the publicans," the tools of the rapacious farmers-general, and of " the sinners," among whom are included the prostitutes: these two classes of people were under the ban of public opinion, and those who laid claim to a reputation for sanctity avoided their contact as a pollution. This social excommunication may of course in certain special cases have been unjust, but that it was on the whole deserved by those who suffered it Christ did not call in question. Now before we enquire how he treated these outcasts, let us consider how, from the knowledge of his doctrine and character which we have now acquired, we should expect him to treat them.

In the course of our investigation we have seen Christ tightening in an incredible degree all obligations of morality. He rejects as utterly insufficient what had been considered by the Jews as the highest moral attainment. It is in vain, he says, to refrain from injuring your neighbour, if, notwithstanding, you have the wish and impulse to injure him; a movement of hatred is, according to him, morally equivalent to a murder. And even if you have no such immoral impulses, yet if your disposition towards your fellow-creatures be purely negative, if you are not actuated by an ardent, by an enthusiastic love and benevolence towards all mankind, you are morally good for nothing, tasteless salt not good even for the dunghill. He thus raises the standard of morality to the highest possible point. But further, he insists far more vehemently than previous moralists had done upon the absolute necessity of attaining the standard. He does not say, This is morality, but, as it is difficult to be moral, God will forgive your shortcomings. On the contrary he says, To be moral in this high sense is life and peace, not to be so is

The Law of Mercy

death and eternal damnation. In his eyes a man's moral character was everything. He went through life looking upon men with the eyes of a King or Judge, confounding false estimates of human merit, separating the sheep from the goats, disregarding all other distinctions that can exist between men as unimportant in comparison with the radical distinction between the good and the bad. How then would such a moralist act when he found among his countrymen this distinction already drawn and firmly marked in practice? If it was incorrectly drawn, he might rectify it; he might also point out that it must needs be inadequate as not distinguishing immoral persons simply from moral, but only those whose immorality had ripened into criminal actions, and whose crimes had been detected, from those who could not be proved immoral. These important reservations he would undoubtedly make, but having done so, would he not be likely to stamp the distinction with his approval and make it ten times more stringent?

Another train of reflection leads to the same conclusion. One who loves his kind is likely to regard injuries done to human beings with greater indignation than one who does not. If the Jews, under the dominion of formularies and a somewhat outworn legislation, had arrived at so much energy of moral resentment as to reject from their society and personal contact those who had perpetrated such injuries, was it not to be expected that Christ and his followers, in whom humanity was an enthusiasm, would regard with tenfold indignation the plunderers of the poor, and the tempters who waylaid the chastity of men?

The fact, however, is, that Christ, instead of sanctioning the excommunication of the publican and sinner, openly associated with them. He chose a publican to be among the number of his Apostles, and earned for himself from his ill wishers the invidious epithet of the " Friend of publicans and sinners." Not, indeed, that his intercourse with them could possibly be mistaken for a connivance at their immoral courses. We may be very sure that he carried his own commanding personality into these degraded societies, and that the conversations he held in them were upon the topics he chose, not the topics most usual or most welcome there. He himself asserts this in justifying his novel course—" I am not come to call the righteous, but sinners to *repentance* "; " They that are whole need not a *physician*, but they that are sick ";— words implying that he appeared among the outcasts as a missionary or physician of the soul. If it had been otherwise his conduct would indeed have been inexplicable, but even so it needs explanation. The paradox lies in his allowing himself to feel compassion for criminals, and in his supposing it possible that their crimes could be forgiven. Criminality certainly appeared to Christ more odious and detestable than it appeared to his contemporaries. How strange then to find him treating it more leniently! Those, it appears, whose moral sense was moderately strong, who hated vice moderately, yet punished it so severely that they utterly excluded those who were deeply infected with it from their society and their sympathy; he who hated it infinitely was, at the same time, the first to regard it as venial, to relent towards it, to parley and make terms with it. He who thought most seriously of the disease held it to be curable, while those who thought less seriously of it pronounced it incurable. Those who loved their race a little made war to the knife against its enemies and oppressors; he who loved it so much as to die for it, made overtures of peace to them. The half-just judge punished the convicted criminal; the thoroughly-just judge offered him forgiveness. Perfect justice here appears to take the very course which would be taken by injustice.

It is true that the two extremes do in a manner meet. Christ, representing the highest humanity, treats crime in a manner which superficially resembles the treatment of it by those in whom humanity is at the lowest stage. He tolerates it in a certain sense, as it was tolerated before the institution of law. But the other toleration was barbarous, Christ's toleration is the newly revealed virtue of Mercy.

In explaining this we must once more recur to the

The Law of Mercy

fundamental principle that Christianity is natural fellow-feeling, or humanity raised to the point of enthusiasm. Now, it will be found that where this fellow-feeling is dormant, vice is regarded with simple indifference, where it is partially developed, with the anger of justice, but where it is developed completely, not with fiercer anger, but with Mercy, i.e. pity and disapprobation mixed.

Let us imagine a person devoid of sympathy, a person to whom the welfare of his fellow-creatures is a matter of complete indifference. On him a wrong action will make no more impression than a right one, so long as he is himself affected by neither. He will feel neither the indignation of justice, nor the mixed indignation and compassion of mercy. Next let us imagine a person of limited sympathy. The limitations of sympathy may be of two kinds. The person we imagine may sympathise only with certain people, as for example his relations, or he may sympathise with only moderate ardour. Such a person will feel dissatisfaction when wrong is committed (this is the instinct of justice) in the latter case always, in the former case when the person wronged is of those to whom his sympathy extends. But he will not feel pity for the criminal mixed with his indignation (which is mercy) in the latter case, because his moderate sympathy will be neutralised by his indignation, in the former case, because he will not perceive the criminality. But suppose a person whose sympathy is unlimited, that is, one who sympathises intensely and with all persons alike: he will feel at the same time indignation at a crime, and pity for the degradation and immoral condition of the criminal; in other words, he will have mercy as well as justice.

It is to be noted that the word *justice* is here used in the sense of resentment against a criminal, mercy in the sense of mixed pity and resentment. Now it may in some cases be a man's duty to punish, and in other cases to pardon, but it is in all cases a man's duty to be merciful to a criminal, that is, to mix pity for him with the resentment inspired by his deed; and, the words being used in this sense, it may be asserted that mercy is not in any way inconsistent with justice, but only the riper form of it; in other words, the form which justice assumes when the instinct which is the source of justice is exceptionally powerful. Now, of the ancients, for the most part, it may be said that they had not enough justice to have any mercy. Their feelings with respect to wrong-doing were almost always either those of the perfectly unsympathetic man or of the partially sympathetic man. They regarded the criminal either with indifference or with unmixed indignation. In Christ's treatment of the publicans and sinners we have that ripest humanity, that fully developed justice, which we call by the name of mercy, and which combines the utmost sympathy with the injured party and the utmost sympathy for the offender.

It may be well to pause a moment on the three stages in the history of the treatment of crime: the stage of barbarous insensibility, the stage of law or justice, and that of mercy or humanity.

We have in the Iliad an interesting record of the stage of insensibility. In that poem the distinction between right and wrong is barely recognised, and the division of mankind into the good and the bad is not recognised at all. It has often been remarked that it contains no villain. The reason of this is not that the poet does not represent his characters as doing wicked deeds, for, in fact, there is not one among them who is not capable of deeds the most atrocious and shameful. But the poet does not regard these deeds with any strong disapprobation, and the feeling of moral indignation which has been so strong in later poets was in him so feeble that he is quite incapable of hating any of his characters for their crimes. He can no more conceive the notion of a villain than of an habitually virtuous man. The few deeds that he recognises as wrong, or at least as strange and dangerous,—killing a suppliant,[1] or killing

---

[1] Δμωὰς δ' ἐκκαλέσας λοῦσαι κέλετ', ἀμφί τ' ἀλεῖψαι,
νόσφιν ἀειράσας, ὡς μὴ Πρίαμος ἴδοι υἱὸν·
μὴ ὁ μὲν ἀχνυμένῃ κραδίῃ χόλον οὐκ ἐρύσαιτο,
παῖδα ἰδών, Ἀχιλῆϊ δ' ὀρινθείη φίλον ἦτορ,
καί ἑ κατακτείνειε, Διὸς δ' ἀλίτηται ἐφετμάς.—xxiv. 582.

The Law of Mercy 187

a father [1]— he, notwithstanding, conceives all persons alike as capable of perpetrating under the influence of passion or some heaven-sent bewilderment of the understanding.

But there comes a time, probably coincident with the first consolidation of ancestral custom or usage into written law, when a sense of *justice* begins to diffuse itself through the community. By the law comes the knowledge of sin. A standard of action is set up, which serves to each man both as a rule of life for himself and a rule of criticism upon his neighbours. Then comes the division of mankind into those who habitually conform to this rule and those who violate it, into the good and the bad, and feelings soon spring up to sanction the classification, feelings of respect for the one class and hatred for the other. This new hatred of criminals spreads slowly, and is only perhaps keenly felt when the crime is very heinous. But it is unmixed. In this second stage a criminal may be regarded with indifference as in the first, but if he is not so regarded then he is simply hated. It cannot be necessary to produce examples of this pitiless hatred from classical antiquity; in the Hebrew Psalms, which are morally so much in advance of even much later Gentile writings, it is sufficiently apparent. "The man that privily slandereth his neighbour," says David, "him will I *destroy*;" and he expresses a hope of "soon *destroying* all that are ungodly in the land." That he does not regard this work of vengeance as a painful necessity imposed on him by his royal office is plain from other expressions, e.g. "the righteous shall rejoice when he seeth the vengeance, he shall wash his footsteps in the blood of the ungodly."

We may be sure, however, that there was one tolerably numerous class of exceptions to this unmixed hatred. Natural affection, it has already been remarked, was always Christian. We may be sure that in the homes of

---
[1] τὸν μὲν ἐγὼ βούλευσα κατακτάμεν ὀξέϊ χαλκῷ
ἀλλά τις ἀθανάτων παῦσεν χόλον, ὅς ῥ' ἐνὶ θυμῷ
δήμου θῆκε φάτιν καὶ ὀνείδεα πόλλ' ἀνθρώπων
ὡς μὴ πατροφόνος μετ' Ἀχαιοῖσιν καλεοίμην.—ix. 458.

antiquity there were disobedient sons, to whom the father, urged by the strong instinct of nature, was sometimes merciful as well as just. Hebrew antiquity presents us with some pathetic instances of forgiveness between brothers, and the prophets are full of the tenderest expressions of the mercy of Jehovah towards his disobedient children. It is true that here, in accordance with the conceptions of archaic society, it is to the state rather than the individual members of it that pardon is offered. But doubtless the prophets, who presented so noble an image of the Invisible Father, had found in the hearts of earthly fathers the mercy they attributed to Him, and accordingly it was by family relations that Christ taught his disciples and they taught themselves to understand the law of mercy. " How often shall my *brother* offend against me and I forgive him, until seven times? " " I will arise and go to my *Father*, and will say unto him, *Father*, I have sinned."

While the Gentile nations in their feelings towards vice oscillated between the stage of insensibility and the stage of hatred, the Jews, who in all such matters were more mature, were for the most part in the stage of hatred. Among them the division between the virtuous and the vicious was most decidedly drawn, and the enmity between the two parties most irreconcilable. Let us now consider how such a division must work. In the first place it plainly affords a valuable encouragement to virtuous dispositions. It separates the wheat from the chaff, it throws the good into the society of the good and saves them from demoralising example and contagion, and, far more than all, through this division there arises that which is to virtue what air is to life, a tone or fashion of goodness. But the bad consequences it produces are scarcely of less magnitude than the good ones. These bad consequences are manifold, but the most serious is the effect of the system upon the criminal himself. The law which condemns sin binds in a most fatal manner the sin to the sinner. It exulcerates the sore and makes the disease chronic. In the stage of insensibility, men, easily tempted into crime, flung off the effects of it as easily. Agamemnon, after violating outrageously the rights of property, has but to say ἀασάμην, "My mind was bewildered," and the excuse is sufficient to appease his own conscience, and is accepted by the public and even by the injured party himself, who feels himself equally liable to such temporary mental perplexities. When such a view of sin prevailed no high virtue was possible, but at the same time that moral degradation was equally unknown which follows the loss of self-respect. After the introduction of law crime could never again be thus lightly expiated and forgotten. By solemn trial and public punishment the criminal was made conspicuously visible to his fellow-citizens, he was held up to their criticism, and it became part of their duty and of their education to hate him. For them this was beneficial; but how did it operate on the criminal himself? When the law was satisfied and the punishment inflicted, could he return to his former estimation and rank in the community? Not so; beyond the legal punishment another was inflicted of endless duration and fatal severity. He might be condemned to fine or imprisonment or exile, but in all cases he incurred another sentence, in all cases he was condemned to a place among the bad, to excommunication from the society and league of the virtuous. A fatal prejudice rested upon him for the future, a clinging suspicion oppressed him; crime was expected of him; his virtuous acts required explanation; his endeavour after virtue was distrusted by the good or passed unobserved by them; he lived among the bad, the bad were now the censors of his behaviour, to their standard it was most expedient for him to conform. And as a man's opinions are commonly those of the society in which he lives, the criminal accepted in most cases the ignominy as just, believed himself to be incapable of virtue, to be made for crime, and resolved at last to give the reins to his nature. By this process the momentary lapse, the human infirmity, from which the best have no exemption, under the dreadful hands of law was converted into an abiding curse. It was, as it were, bound to the sinner and became a millstone dragging him down to perdition. Justly have great authors described sin, deriving its strength from law, as a burden laid upon the back, or, still more graphically, as a dead body tied to a living one.

And when the criminal is the father of children the curse descends even upon those who are wholly innocent. Before they are old enough to distinguish right and wrong they are, as it were, received into the Evil Church by infant baptism, their parents or their parents' friends standing sponsors and promising for them that which when they come to age they take upon themselves but too willingly. Cut off from all contact with virtue, instructed in vice, which is itself an easy art, and strangers to goodness, which is difficult to learn, they enter into perdition by a natural title, and the same law, which favours so much, as it were, the formation of large properties in vice, provides also that they shall pass by inheritance.

The sole reign of Law, then, is a despotism, beneficent and necessary at a certain stage of social development, but yet terrible, and, if maintained too long, mischievous. It is a preparatory discipline destined to fit the pupil for another teacher, a proper condition for the childhood of society, but not well adapted for its maturity. It accompishes a great work in elevating men out of the savage levity of primitive manners, in delivering them from passions which by indulgence had grown to resemble insanity, from the fierceness of appetite and anger. It brings out the instinct of sympathy, it develops the power man possesses of identifying himself with his neighbour, and teaches a whole community to interest itself in redressing the wrong done to one of its members. As has been already remarked, it is in its nature tender and not cruel, for it protects the weak who before were helpless and arms itself to avenge the injured. Though Law inflicts punishment, yet it exists to reduce the whole amount of suffering, and though when we personify it we call it stern and relentless, yet, compared with lawlessness, it is soft-hearted. But there comes a time when mankind have learned all the lessons which Law has to teach and begin to leave their instructor behind them. For Law is

The Law of Mercy

an *esprit borné*, and does not perceive the legitimate consequences of his own principle. Sympathy, the instinct by which men identify themselves with their fellow-creatures, should not be partial or limited in its activity. Law teaches us to put ourselves in the place of those who are injured, but does not teach us, nay, he forbids us, to put ourselves in the place of those who commit injuries. And those who have learnt his lesson best, and in whom the power of sympathy is most highly trained, will be most discontented with his rule, and as to the lawless he was a preacher of pity, to these he will justly appear cruel. Such persons are ripe for that higher doctrine which Christ teaches.

Christ, representing all who are possessed by the Enthusiasm of Humanity, does not regard crime with less anger, is not less anxious for the punishment of it, than the legalists. But when it is punished, when the claims of the injured party are satisfied, he does not dismiss the matter from his thoughts. He considers that the criminal also has claims upon him, claims so strong that they are not forfeited by any atrocity of crime. Nay, they are rather strengthened by his criminality, as they would be by misery, for the humane man, who finds his own happiness in his humanity, does sincerely consider the criminal to be miserable. This doctrine that vice is essentially pitiable was advanced sometimes in antiquity, but plain men flouted it from them with irritation as one of those childish paradoxes with which philosophers amused and abused their leisure, and some of the philosophers themselves showed that they only half believed it by the self-complacency and affected preciseness with which they demonstrated it. Nevertheless he in whom humanity is an enthusiasm does honestly feel distressed when he thinks of those who are fallen and lost in character and whom society repudiates. Even when wickedness is prosperous and flourishes like a green bay tree, he understands pretty well and unaffectedly pities the uneasiness of remorse, the loneliness of pride, the moral paralysis that succeeds satiety, the essential poverty of vulgarity. Nor does he only feel such pity, but he has the courage to indulge it.

The legalist, if he is at any time surprised into a similar feeling for an unfortunate criminal, suppresses it as dangerous and weak. The anger which he feels, the punishment which he executes or approves, is his guarantee against falling back into insensibility. His disapprobation of wrong-doing, being not very strong, requires to be anxiously cherished lest it should die in him altogether. Any relentings of pity would be dangerous to it; he has not sympathy enough for both the injured party and the criminal; at least any that he might give to the latter must be taken from the former. Therefore in communities which are in the legal stage, mercy is always identified with laxity; the stage before them is mistaken for the stage behind them; and any tenderness towards criminals —*parum odisse malos cives*—is regarded as a portentous omen of the downfall of discipline and of public ruin. But the moment that sympathy ceases to be this invalid thing, needing constant artificial stimulants, the moment it kindles into the free Enthusiasm of Humanity, it gets the confidence to follow its own impulses. It perceives the truth of what has been explained above, that mercy is no relaxation of justice, but justice itself in a riper stage; it is not afraid that if it pities criminals it shall have no compassion left to bestow on the innocent sufferers from criminality. On the contrary, it is confident that if it can pity those with whom it is angry and at the very moment when it is most angry, and even at the very moment when it is inflicting the punishment suggested by a just anger, it will be able *à fortiori* to pity and sympathise with those who are suffering from no fault of their own.

Therefore it is that Christ went boldly among the publicans and sinners. Virtue, he considered, was not now so feebly supported that its soldiers must needs remain for ever within their entrenched camp. This had been necessary at an earlier stage of the war. A close and exclusive league of the virtuous had been necessary at an earlier time, that they might not forget their principles or be overwhelmed by numbers. But goodness had now become ten times more powerful in becoming an enthusiasm. It no longer contents itself with barely preserving

The Law of Mercy

its existence in the presence of prevailing vice. It turns against its enemy; it undertakes to take the hostile army prisoner. The children of Israel turn and pursue the Egyptians through the Red Sea. Under the command of Christ Jerusalem lays siege to Babylon. He announces a great mundane project of regeneration. He will not consent to lose those who have apostatised from virtue. He will not rest content with raising goodness to a higher standard in those who are good already, nor with making it easier for others to be good in future. He will go in search of those who have already fallen; no matter how deep their degradation, he will not willingly lose one. Besides the title of King, or Son of Man, he assumes that of Saviour or Redeemer, and in this work he seems to have his heart even more than in the other. The shepherd, he says, leaves without hesitation the ninety-nine sheep to seek the hundredth that is lost. A woman that has lost a single piece of money will sweep the whole house and search diligently till she find it. And what pleasure when such a search is successful! In heaven, among God's angels, there is more joy over one sinner that returns than over ninety and nine that never wandered.

CHAPTER XX

THE LAW OF MERCY—*continued*

CHRIST then undertakes the conversion of sinners. Of his success in this enterprise our biographies, particularly that of St. Luke, contain many examples. Christianity, by giving men a greater interest in each other than they had before, and by weakening the influence of artificial distinctions, and, at the same time, by its intense seriousness, gave those who were influenced by it a keen eye for character and an insight into human nature such as is very rarely found in antiquity. The stories of conversation recorded in the Gospels have a liveliness and truth which everyone can in some measure feel, but which are felt ten times as strongly by those who know and consider how perfectly new to literature such sketches were when they appeared. It was by them that the depth and complexity and mystery of the human heart were first brought to light, and their appearance involved a revolution in literature, the results of which are to be traced not so much in the writers of the long barbaric period which followed their diffusion as in Dante and Shakspeare. Of these stories we will find room here for two, the one containing the repentance of a man, the other of a woman.

Zacchæus held a high office under the farmers-general, and had become rich. His wealth, however, had not availed to relax the social excommunication under which, with all his fraternity, he lay. Either the Jews of that time were less dazzled by wealth than the Gentiles of the present, or they reflected with indignation that the riches he had amassed had been plundered from themselves. By some means he had heard of Christ, and conceived an intense curiosity to see him. That it was no vulgar curiosity, but that overpowering attraction towards great-

The Law of Mercy

ness and goodness—that *faith,* which is the germ of all that is good in human character—may be gathered from the sequel of the story. He may have heard it reported that Christ did not, like other religious men, disdain the company of publicans, and that he had condescended to be entertained at their houses. He was rich; he also was able, if only such an honour could be granted him, to entertain Christ. It is for this that riches are enviable, that while the poor must be content with glimpses of the hero or the saint as he passes in the street, the rich can bring him within their doors and contemplate him at their leisure. But Zacchæus had not the courage to use this privilege of his wealth. His conscience was ill at ease, the stigma of his infamous occupation had entered into his heart. He was afraid to show his wealth to Christ, lest the question should be asked him how it had been gained. He submitted therefore to look on among the poor, and to be satisfied with what he could see as the procession passed. But the crowd was dense, and, it may be, found a pleasure in elbowing aside the social tyrant who had thus put himself on a level with them. He was short, and saw himself in danger of losing even the passing glimpse of Christ's countenance with which he had resolved to be content. Determined to secure at least so much, he ran forward and climbed into a tree which overshadowed the road by which the train was to pass. By this means he saw Christ, and not only so but Christ saw him. Zacchæus was not one of the most pitiable of his excommunicated class. He might be hated, but he was successful; he was one of those who might say, " *Populus me sibilat, at mihi plaudo.*" In a word, he was a prosperous plunderer, living in abundance among the victims of his rapacity. But Christ was touched by the enthusiasm he displayed, and may have divined and understood the shame which, as we have conjectured, caused him to shrink from a personal interview. Such enthusiasm and shame seemed to Christ the first stirrings of humanity in the publican's heart, and by a single stroke he completed the change he perceived to be beginning, and ripened a half-hopeless yearning into a settled purpose of moral amendment. Without delay, or reserve, or conditions, or rebuke, he gave himself up to the publican. Adopting the royal style which was familiar to him, and which commends the loyalty of a vassal in the most delicate manner by freely exacting his services, he informed Zacchæus of his intention to visit him, and signified his pleasure that a banquet be instantly prepared. Such generous confidence put a new soul into Zacchæus; it snapped in a moment the spell of wickedness under which all his better instincts had remained in dull abeyance; and while the crowd murmured at the exceptional honour done to a public enemy, Zacchæus stood forth, and solemnly devoted half his property to the poor, and vowed fourfold restoration to all whom he had wronged.

This is the repentance of a man. Zacchæus shows no remarkable sensibility; he sheds no tears, he utters no striking reflections. The movement in his mind is strong, but not in the least peculiar or difficult to follow. It is a conflict between common honesty and the instincts of the thief, a conflict in which the former, fighting at great odds, gains a signal victory. Against all the might of inveterate habit, and bad society, and a crushing public prejudice, this man makes head, and by one great effort forces his way back into the class of good citizens and honest men. And this great but simple achievement he gained power to perform, not through reflection and reasoning, not through the eloquence of a preacher, not through supernatural terrors, but through the cordial, restoring influence of Mercy. It was Mercy, which is not Pity—a thing comparatively weak and vulgar—but Pity and Resentment blended at the highest power of each, the most powerful restorative agent known in the medicine of the soul; it was Mercy that revealed itself in Christ's words, the Pity slightly veiled under royal grace, the Resentment altogether unexpressed and yet not concealed because already too surely divined and anticipated by the roused conscience of the criminal. And Mercy, more powerful than Justice, redeemed the criminal while it judged him, increased his shame tenfold, but increased in the same proportion the wish and courage to amend.

The Law of Mercy

The second story describes the repentance of a woman. It is a fragment. A woman fallen from virtue, we know not who, entered a room in the house of a Pharisee who was entertaining Christ. We know not particularly what Christ had done for her, but we can conclude generally that he had roused her conscience as he did that of Zacchæus, that he had restored her to virtue by giving her hope and by inspiring her with an enthusiastic devotion to himself. She threw herself down before him and embraced his feet, weeping so abundantly over them that she was obliged to wipe them, which she did with her hair. This is the picture presented to us, and we know nothing further of the woman, although tradition has identified her with that Mary Magdalene of whose touching fidelity to Christ in the last scenes of his life so much is recorded. But fragmentary as the story is, it is all-important, as the turning-point in the history of women. Such wisdom is there in humanity that he who first looked upon his fellow-creatures with sympathetic eyes found himself, as it were, in another world and made mighty discoveries at every step. The female sex, in which antiquity saw nothing but inferiority, which Plato considered intended to do the same things as the male only not so well, was understood for the first time by Christ. His treatment brought out its characteristics, its superiorities, its peculiar power of gratitude and self-devotion. That woman who dried with her hair the feet she had bathed in grateful tears has raised her whole sex to a higher level. But we are concerned with her not merely as a woman, but as a fallen woman. And it is when we consider her as such that the prodigious force and originality of Christ's mercy makes itself felt. For it is probably in the case of this particular vice that justice ripens the slowest and the seldomest into mercy. Most persons in whom the moral sense is very strong are, as we have said, merciful; mercy is in general a measure of the higher degrees of keenness in the moral sense. But there is a limit beyond which it seems almost impossible for mercy, properly so called, to subsist. There are certain vices which seem to indicate a criminality so engrained, or at least so inveterate, that mercy is, as it were, choked in the deadly atmosphere that surrounds them, and dies for want of that hope upon which alone it can live. Vices that are incorrigible are no proper objects of mercy, and there are some vices which virtuous people are found particularly ready to pronounce incorrigible. Few brave men have any pity to spare for a confirmed coward. And as cowardice seems to him who has the instinct of manliness a fatal vice in man as implying an absence of the indispensable condition of masculine virtue, so does confirmed unchastity in woman seem a fatal vice to those who reverence womanhood. And therefore little mercy for it is felt by those who take a serious view of sexual relations. There are multitudes who think lightly of it, and therefore feel a good deal of compassion for those who suffer at the hands of society such a terrible punishment for it. There are others who can have mercy on it while they contemplate it, as it were, at a distance and do not realise how mortal to the very soul of womanhood is the habitual desecration of all the sacraments of love. Lastly, there are some who force themselves to have mercy on it out of reverence for the example of Christ. But of those who see it near, and whose moral sense is keen enough to judge of it, the greater number pronounce it incurable. We know the pitiless cruelty with which virtuous women commonly regard it. Why is it that in this one case the female sex is more hard-hearted than the male? Probably because in this one case it feels more strongly, as might be expected, the heinousness of the offence; and those men who criticise women for their cruelty to their fallen sisters do not really judge from the advanced stage of mercy but from the lower stage of insensibility. It is commonly by love itself that men learn the sacredness of love. Yet, though Christ never entered the realm of sexual love, this sacredness seems to have been felt by him far more deeply than by other men. We have already had an opportunity of observing this in the case of the woman taken in adultery. He exhibited on that occasion a profound delicacy of which there is no other example in the ancient world, and which anticipates and excels all that is noblest in chivalrous and

The Law of Mercy

finest in modern manners. In his treatment of the prostitute, then, how might we expect him to act? Not, surely, with the ready tolerance of men, which is but laxity; we might expect from him rather the severity of women, which is purity. Disgust will overpower him here, if anywhere. He will say, " Thy sin's not accidental, but a trade. . . . 'Tis best that thou diest quickly." There is no doubt that he was not wanting in severity; the gratitude that washed his feet in tears was not inspired by mere good-nature. But he found mercy too, where mercy commonly fails even in the tender hearts of women. And mercy triumphed, where it commonly dies of mere despair.

These two stories may serve as specimens of Christ's redeeming power. At the same time they exhibit to us, it is plain, the natural working of the Enthusiasm of Humanity, the essential spirit of Christianity. The latter story in particular has gone to the heart of Christendom. It has given origin and even a name to institutions which are found wherever the Christian Church is found, and the object of which is to redeem women that have fallen from virtue. It has given to Christian art the figure of the Magdalen, which, when contrasted with the Venus of Greek sculpture, represents in a very palpable manner the change which Christ has wrought in the moral feelings of mankind with respect to women. May we then lay it down as one of the duties of positive morality to attempt the restoration to virtue of the criminal and outcast classes?

The Christian Church has certainly always reckoned this among its duties; nevertheless there exists at the present day among practical men a strong repugnance to all schemes of the kind, a repugnance founded on observation and experience, and therefore not likely to be wholly unreasonable. It will be well worth while to state the world's case against the Christian doctrine of repentance.

In the first place, the world will admit what has been said concerning the imperfection of the legal system. It is impossible to deny that the habit of regarding criminals with unmixed hatred is a pernicious one. Law taken by itself benefits the good, and so far is most useful; but at the same time it makes the wavering bad and the bad worse, and vice hereditary, and so far it does frightful mischief. Mercy therefore must be called in to temper justice, and here Christianity is right. In the treatment of the criminal we must consider his interest as well as the interest of the injured party. We must anxiously study the best means of moderating punishment so as to leave the criminal a hope of recovering the public esteem, the best means of inflicting a disgrace which shall not be indelible. This is a just principle, and Christ's protest against the pitiless rigour which the Jews exercised against the publicans and sinners was right and memorable. If we follow the example he set we may save many who under the legal system are lost inevitably. We may arrest some at the beginning of a bad career whom the legal system would hurry forward. But the hope of recovering all, of melting the most hardened, is an error of enthusiasm. Men who look facts in the face, it is said, recognise that vice when it has once fairly laid hold of a man is an incurable disease, and, moreover, that it lays hold of men with a fatal rapidity. There is such a thing as repentance, and this fact should not be forgotten; but, on the other hand, it is a mistake to attach very great importance to it, for a practical and valuable repentance is very rare; the stage in the criminal's career in which it is possible is a short one, and it is only the less heinous forms of criminality which admit of it at all.

This is probably the view which the most temperate of so-called practical men take of repentance when they do not allow themselves to be overawed by the authority of Christianity. Clearly it is not the view of Christ. He is far more hopeful; he believes that the most inveterate and enormous criminality may be shaken off, and he is so sanguine of the possibility of restoring the lost that he avows himself ready to neglect for this enterprise his other task of strengthening and developing the virtue of the good. Let us endeavour to discover the ground of this difference of opinion.

The popular view, then, is that there are two kinds of

The Law of Mercy

vice. The one includes whatever we understand by infirmities, as faults of temper, or passion. Uncontrolled temper or unbridled passions may lead to grave crimes; still we regard these vices as venial, and are at all times ready to believe in the repentance and reformation of one addicted to them. The other class includes such vices as perfidy, brutality, and cowardice; and of these, for the most part, " the world will not believe a man repents," and when it finds the Church undertaking to convert such characters and boasting of its success, it, whether openly or secretly, accuses Christianity of encouraging hypocrisy. Now if we consider this classification of vices, or if we ask ourselves how the vicious characters we are disposed to forgive differ from those to whom we refuse forgiveness, we shall find that the one thing which we consider indispensable is good impulses. The man who has these may commit any of the crimes to which turbulent passions may prompt or feebleness of will leave the path open, and yet he will not forfeit our sympathy. We shall continue to hope for him, and, if he should declare himself repentant and reformed, we shall not suspect him of insincerity, for we shall regard him as one who all along had the root of the matter in him. But the cold-blooded, low-minded criminal, whose crimes have cost him no struggle and no remorse, without ardour in his pulses or blush upon his cheek—when such a man abandons evil courses we but suspect him of some deeper treachery than usual, for we see no soil out of which virtue could spring. This is the rough philosophy of common life, and in ordinary cases it serves us well enough. " This wise world of ours is mainly right." But the question arises, How do these indispensable good impulses arise in the mind? If those who have them had them from earliest childhood in the same strength, and those who want them have never possessed them in any degree, then indeed we must reconcile ourselves to the maxim, " Once a villain, always a villain." But it will be found that the same rule holds of these good impulses which holds of all other human endowments, namely, that though different men may by nature possess them in different degrees, yet all possess them in some degree; and also that they require development by external influences. Further, it is possible that in the absence of such influences they do not die but remain within the man undiscovered and dormant. Accordingly, though it is quite true that where virtuous impulses are not active virtue cannot live, yet it is by no means certain that where such impulses are not active they do not exist, and may not, by the application of some influence, be roused into activity.

But, answers the world, the better impulses do sooner or later die of this torpor. It is true that they do not die at once, and there is a considerable period during which repentance is possible. But it never lasts longer than youth: this is the flexible and elastic time. Upon the young try all your methods of conversion and regeneration; but when youth is over, in middle age, when physical growth has ceased, when life has been explored, when habit has become as powerful as nature, when no new idea is welcome and few new ideas are intelligible, when a man's character is understood by his neighbours, and any change in his conduct would excite their surprise and disturb their calculations, when all things concur to produce uniformity and to prescribe an unchangeable routine both of thought and action,—in this stage moral disease is incurable, repentance impossible.

Again, there is much truth in this. It is an easy thing to bring the tears of repentance to the eyes of a boy; we see the most striking changes pass upon the whole life and mode of thinking of young men; but the period of experiments, the noviciate, expires, and the vicious habits of middle life resist, for the most part, the contagion of virtue and of noble examples. The power of the ordinary agencies of moral restoration which are at work in the world is thus limited. But the world will surely admit exceptions. Agencies have at different times been brought to bear which have had a greater power than this, and which have roused good impulses in hearts that seemed dead. A Whitefield, a Bernard, a Paul—not to say a Christ—have certainly shown that the most confirmed vice is not beyond the reach of regenerating influences. Inspired men like these appearing at intervals have wrought what may be called moral miracles. Nor is it possible to set bounds to the restoring and converting power of virtue, when, as it were, it takes fire—when, instead of a rule teaching a man to do justice to his neighbours, and to benefit them when an occasion presents itself, it becomes a burning and consuming passion of benevolence, an energy of self-devotion, an aggressive ardour of love. Well! it is this aggressive, exceptional virtue that Christ assumes to be employed, and that the world leaves out of calculation. Christ is consistent here; we have remarked repeatedly that he demands an enthusiasm, and it is consistent therefore that he should impose tasks to which only an enthusiasm is equal.

Once more, however, the world may answer, Christ may be consistent in this, but is he wise? It may be true that he does demand an enthusiasm, and that such an enthusiasm may be capable of awakening the moral sense in hearts in which it seemed dead. But if, notwithstanding this demand, only a very few members of the Christian Church are capable of the enthusiasm, what use in imposing on the whole body a task which the vast majority are not qualified to perform? Would it not be well to recognise the fact which we cannot alter, and to abstain from demanding from frail human nature what human nature cannot render? Would it not be well for the Church to impose upon its ordinary members only ordinary duties? When the Bernard or the Whitefield appears, let her by all means find occupation for him. Let her in such cases boldly invade the enemy's country. But in ordinary times would it not be well for her to confine herself to more modest and practicable undertakings? There is much for her to do even though she should honestly confess herself unable to reclaim the lost. She may train the young, administer reproof to slight lapses, maintain a high standard of virtue, soften manners, diffuse enlightenment. Would it not be well for her to adapt her ends to her means?

No, it would not be well; it would be fatal to do so; and Christ meant what he said, and said what was true, when he pronounced the Enthusiasm of Humanity to be everything, and the absence of it to be the absence of everything. The world understands its own routine well enough; what it does not understand is the mode of changing that routine. It has no appreciation of the nature or measure of the power of enthusiasm, and on this matter it learns nothing from experience, but after every fresh proof of that power relapses from its brief astonishment into its old ignorance, and commits precisely the same miscalculation on the next occasion. The power of enthusiasm is, indeed, far from being unlimited; in some cases it is very small. History is full of instances in which it has foamed itself away in utter impotence against physical obstacles. Painful it is to read, and yet one reads again and again, of citizens who have united in close league against some proud invader; with enthusiastic dependence upon the justice of their cause, the invincible force of their patriotism, and the protection of Providence, when justice has been found weaker than power, and enthusiasm than numbers, and Providence has coldly taken the side of the stronger battalions. But one power enthusiasm has almost without limit—the power of propagating itself—and it was for this that Christ depended on it. He contemplated a Church in which the Enthusiasm of Humanity should not be felt by two or three only but widely. In whatever heart it might be kindled, he calculated that it would pass rapidly into other hearts, and that, as it can make its heat felt outside the Church, so it would preserve the Church itself from lukewarmness. For a lukewarm Church he would not condescend to legislate, nor did he regard it as at all inevitable that the Church should become lukewarm. He laid it as a duty upon the Church to reclaim the lost, because he did not think it utopian to suppose that the Church might be not in its best members only, but through its whole body, inspired by that ardour of humanity that can charm away the bad passions of the wildest heart, and open to the savage and the outlaw lurking in moral wildernesses an entrancing view of the holy and tranquil order that broods over the streets and palaces of the city of God.

Nevertheless the stubborn fact remains. Whatever may be theoretically possible to the Enthusiasm of Humanity, it does not at the present day often rise to this energy. We do not, as a matter of fact, often see these wonderful conversions take place; and when they do appear to take place, we have had so much experience of the hollowness of such appearances that we expect to find in the end the change transitory or else hypocritical; or, if it be genuine, that the convert was never a criminal of the deepest dye, but perhaps rather unfortunate than guilty. Must we not, then, still conclude that Christ has in this instance made a miscalculation and that if he has not overrated the power of Enthusiasm so long as Enthusiasm exists, he has at least overrated the probability of its continuing long, and underrated the power of the agencies which are always at work to damp and quench it? Instead of presuming that the Church would generally be under the influence of enthusiasm, ought he not rather to have foreseen that it would generally be lukewarm and enthusiastic only at rare intervals? The answer is, that Christ does not actually seem to have been thus sanguine, but he counted the Enthusiasm not merely an important but an absolutely essential thing, and therefore left no directions as to what should be done when it was absent. He did not disguise from himself the probability of great seasons of depression occurring in the Church, ebbs in the tide of the Enthusiasm of Humanity. He spoke of a time when the love of many should wax cold; he doubted whether on his return to the earth he should find faith in it. And the Apostles in like manner became sensible that their inspiration was liable to intermissions. They regard it as possible to *grieve* the Divinity who resided within them, and even to *quench* his influence. But neither they nor Christ even for a moment suppose that, if he should take his flight, it is possible to do without him, or that the sphere of Christian duty is to be narrowed to suit the lukewarmness of Christian feeling. Christianity is an enthusiasm or it is nothing; and if there sometimes appear in the history of the Church instances of a tone which is pure and high without being enthusiastic, of a mood of Christian feeling which is calmly favourable to virtue without being victorious against vice, it will probably be found that all that is respectable in such a mood is but the slowly-subsiding movement of an earlier enthusiasm, and all that is produced by the lukewarmness of the time itself is hypocrisy and corrupt conventionalism.

Christianity, then, would sacrifice its divinity if it abandoned its missionary character and became a mere educational institution. Surely this Article of Conversion is the true *articulus stantis aut cadentis ecclesiæ*. When the power of reclaiming the lost dies out of the Church, it ceases to be the Church. It may remain a useful institution, though it is most likely to become an immoral and mischievous one. Where the power remains, there, whatever is wanting, it may still be said that " the tabernacle of God is with men."

CHAPTER XXI

THE LAW OF RESENTMENT

It is not the fault of the divine virtue of Mercy that it is so readily counterfeited by the vice of insensibility. The difference is indeed vast, but it often does not express itself at all in outward deeds. The difference lies in that indignation at vice which in the merciful man may often be suppressed, while in the merely tolerant man it has no existence. Mercy has been defined above as a feeling of mixed indignation and pity; properly speaking, Mercy is present wherever such a feeling is entertained, whether the action dictated by the feeling be punishment or forgiveness. There are occasions when the wise man who entertains this compound feeling will see fit to indulge the pity and suppress the indignation; there are other occasions when he will gratify the indignation and resist the impulses of pity. But he is not merciful unless he feels both. Thus the man who cannot be angry cannot be merciful, and we shall be able to assure ourselves that that unbounded compassion for sinners which Christ showed was really Mercy and not mere tolerance, by enquiring whether on other occasions he showed himself capable of anger.

Of the two feelings which go to compose Mercy the indignation requires to be satisfied first. The first impulse roused by the sight of vice should be the impulse of opposition and hostility. To convict it, to detect it, to contend with it, to put it down, is the first and indispensable thing. It is indeed a fair object of pity even while it remains undetected and prosperous, but such pity must be passive and must not dare to express itself in deeds. It is not mercy but treason against justice to relent towards vice so long as it is triumphant and insolent. So long, if we may venture upon the expression, mercy will be even sterner and more unpitying than justice, as the poet felt when he wrote—

> And oh! if some strange trance
> The eyelids of thy sterner sister press,
> Seize, Mercy, thou, more terrible, the brand,
> And hurl her thunderbolts with fiercer hand.

But the moment that indignation begins to be in some measure satisfied, pity awakes; and when indignation is satiated then Pity occupies the whole mind of the merciful man. We have seen Christ when his feelings were in this latter condition, when he moved among that class of criminals upon whom justice had in some measure done its work. They were suffering the sentence of social excommunication. His indignation towards them was not dead but satisfied, and therefore in his demeanour few traces of it appear. But there must have been in Palestine another class of criminals, a class which is found in all countries, whose vices are not detected or pass for virtues, and who accordingly reap all the advantages and suffer none of the penalties of crime. In the presence of such a class true Mercy, as we have seen, makes her face as a flint, and hardens and stiffens into mere Justice.

We find, then, in Palestine a class of persons towards whom Christ's demeanour was precisely of this kind. It was a class not less influential and important than might be produced in England by fusing the bar, the clergy, and universities and the literary class into one vast intellectual order. It is to be remembered that with the Jews theology, law, science, and literature were but different aspects of one thing, the Divine Revelation which had been made to their fathers and which was contained for them in the Scriptures of the Old Testament supplemented, in the view of the most influential party, by a Tradition of equal antiquity and authority. As there was but one sort of learning, there was but one learned profession, consisting of the expounders of this ancient wisdom. At least these constituted the one learned profession which had much influence at this time, and which could be said to deserve the title. The old Aaronic priesthood still existed, but it bore the stamp of a ruder age and wanted

The Law of Resentment

the character and acquirements which conferred influence in an age of books and study. As in Greece the priesthood passed into insignificance and resigned the task of instructing the people, so far as they had ever undertaken it, to the philosophers, so in Judæa they were eclipsed first by the prophets and afterwards, when the faith in inspiration began to die out, by the commentators on the old Law. The order of Aaron gave place to the order which regarded Ezra as its founder; the priest gave place to the Scribe or Lawyer.

At the time when the national institutions of Judæa were threatened by the Greek kings of Syria, there sprang up a party composed of those who clung most fondly to ancient traditions, the object of which was to preserve the nation from losing its peculiarity through the infection of Greek manners and opinions. They bore the name of Pharisees. As the national party they found it easy to become popular, and, in spite of some opposition and persecution from the Asmonean kings, they continued in the time of Christ to exercise a commanding influence over the people. It is natural to suppose that this party included most of that great learned profession just described. A Scribe would naturally be a Pharisee, inasmuch as one who devoted his life to the study of the Law would naturally be zealous in defence of it. Accordingly in the New Testament, the Scribes, Lawyers, and Pharisees are commonly named together, being in fact partly identical and altogether congenial in views and interests. And they may be considered as composing practically one party.

With the main object which this party had in view none can have sympathised more than Christ. None, certainly, regarded the ancient revelation with more reverence than he; none can have been more unwilling to see the national institutions of the Jews supplanted and superseded by the customs of the surrounding nations. It might therefore have been expected that Christ would rather take the lead among the Scribes and lawyers than set himself in opposition to them. And, indeed, it is likely enough that, as Socrates passed with the world for a sophist, so Christ was regarded by the people in general as a leading Scribe or expounder of the Law. But if we examine the character of that great party more closely, we shall find that they not only differed from Christ but were radically opposed to him, and that they were not only in spirit unchristian but essentially anti-christian. The whole course of this investigation has shown that the substance of Christ's teaching was his doctrine of Enthusiasm, or of a present Spirit dictating the right course of action and superseding the necessity of particular rules. Now the doctrine of the Scribes, lawyers, and Pharisees may be briefly summed up by saying that it consisted in the denial of a present Spirit, and in the assertion of the paramount necessity of particular rules. They believed that the inspiring Power which had dwelt with their ancestors and made them virtuous was withdrawn, and they compiled out of the works of those ancestors an elaborate system of rules which might serve them for guidance in his absence. In other words, their doctrine and Christ's were precisely contrary to each other.

Both Christ and the legalist desired to preserve Judaism, but the legalist believed that in order to do this it was necessary to adopt a defensive attitude, to throw up walls of partition, and as much as possible to isolate the Jew from those dangerous influences which might otherwise have obliterated his nationality. This belief was a confession of the weakness of the Jewish principle, a confession that it had ceased to be a match for the influences in the midst of which it was placed, and it suggested a number of hateful and immoral contrivances for perpetuating the division between Jew and Gentile. The hatred which the Jews incurred from the surrounding nations, the fancy current among the Gentiles that Moses had forbidden them to show a traveller the way unless he professed their own belief, or to direct a thirsty man to the fountain unless he were circumcised, had its rise in this odious theory of isolation.

Christ, on the contrary, proposed to preserve Judaism by putting it upon the offensive, by making it universal. And this plan implied his belief in its invincible, heaven-inspired strength. He held that the same Divine Power

The Law of Resentment

which had originally legislated for the Jews was still present, completing his legislation and annulling whatever in it was outworn by the Enthusiasm of Humanity kindled in men's hearts and issuing decrees as authoritative as those of Moses. And in this Enthusiasm he confided as powerful enough to resist whatever was corrupting in Gentile influences and to assimilate what was good. Therefore, while the legalists provoked the Gentile world to that final attack upon the Jewish nation which deprived it of its temple and its country, Christ initiated that reconciliation of Jew and Gentile which was seen in the early Church.

Again, both Christ and the legalist devoted themselves to the promotion of moral virtue. They agreed in thinking everything unimportant in comparison with Duty. But the legalist believed that the old method by which their ancestors had arrived at a knowledge of the requirements of Duty, namely, divine inspiration, was no longer available, and that nothing therefore remained but carefully to collect the results at which their ancestors had arrived by this method, to adopt these results as rules, and to observe them punctiliously. Devoutly believing that in the most trifling matter where action was involved there was a right course and a wrong one, and at the same time entirely deserted by the instinct or inspiration which distinguishes the one from the other, they invented the most frivolous casuistry that has ever been known. They overburdened men's memories and perplexed their lives with an endless multitude of rules, which sometimes were simply trivial: e.g. " An egg laid on a festival day may be eaten according to the school of Shammai, but the school of Hillel says it must not be eaten," and at other times were immoral, as in the case of the Corban which Christ selected for censure.

Precisely in opposition to this school Christ proclaimed that the inspiration which had instructed the ancient Jews was not only not withdrawn, but was given to his own generation in far greater measure than to any previous one. John the Baptist, he said, was the greatest of the prophets, and the least of his own followers was greater than John. The inspiration of the prophets had revealed to them some of their duties, but had left them unenlightened about others; an inspiration was now given which should illuminate the whole province of moral obligation. Casuistry therefore, so far from being important, was less needed than ever, and it was so far from being necessary to supplement the written Scriptures by a traditional law that those written Scriptures themselves, though they retained their sacredness and value, yet ceased henceforth to be, in the strict sense, a binding law.

So direct was Christ's opposition to the legal party. The method of promoting moral virtue which he proposed was not regarded by him as merely better than the casuistry of his opponents, but as the only method. The other method, in his view, could not produce virtue, though it might sometimes procure the performance of a right deed; it could but destroy in men's minds the very conception of virtue. It could issue in nothing but a certain moral pedantry and in pride. Therefore he denounced without qualification the whole system and the teachers of it. Apologetic voices might perhaps have been raised, urging that these teachers, if their system was worthless and mischievous, nevertheless did, at least in some cases, the best they could, that they were serious and made others serious, and that at the worst any moral teaching was better than none. We do not know how Christ would have answered this plea, but we know that he suffered no such considerations to mitigate the sternness of his condemnation. He who could make allowance for the publican and the prostitute made no allowance at all for the Pharisee. If we examine the charges he makes against them we shall see that he accuses them in the first place of downright, undisguised vice. He calls them plunderers of the poor, and declares that the countless rules which they impose upon others they take no trouble to observe themselves. We have not the evidence before us which might enable us to verify these accusations. All that can be said is that those who are constantly endeavouring to avoid infinitesimal sins, such as that of eating an egg laid on a festival day, are particularly apt to fall into

The Law of Resentment

sins that are "gross as a mountain, open, palpable." In this sense it is true that "la petite morale est l'ennemi de la grande." But it is evident that Christ was not better pleased with their good deeds than with their bad ones. Their good deeds had the nature of imposture, that is, they did not proceed from the motives from which such deeds naturally spring and from which the public suppose them to spring. When these men tithed their property for the service of religion, did they do so from the ardent feelings which had suggested the oblations of David in old times? No doubt the people thought so, but in truth they paid tithes from a motive which might just as well have prompted them to take tithes—respect for a traditional rule. When they searched and sifted the Scriptures, fancying, as Christ said, that in them they had eternal life, did they do so because they felt deeply the wisdom of the old prophets and legislators? The people, no doubt, thought that these diligent students were possessed with the spirit of what they read, but the truth was that they only pored over the ancient scrolls because they understood that it was proper to read them. Therefore the more they read the less they understood, and they paid the same reverence to the languid futilities of some purblind commentator as to the inspirations of Isaiah. When they lauded the ancient prophets and built their sepulchres, was it because they were congenial spirits, formed in their school and bent upon following in their steps? The people thought so, but Christ pronounced with memorable point and truth—what is true of many other worshippers of antiquity besides the Pharisees—that they were the legitimate representatives of *those who killed the prophets*, and that they betrayed this by the very worship which they paid to their memory.

Let us linger on this for a moment. It is trite, that an original man is persecuted in his lifetime and idolised after his death, but it is a less familiar truth that the posthumous idolators are the legitimate successors and representatives of the contemporary persecutors. The glory of the original man is this, that he does not take his virtues and his views of things at second hand, but draws wisdom fresh from nature and from the inspiration within him. To the majority in every age, that is, to the superficial and the feeble, such originality is alarming, perplexing, fatiguing. They unite to crush the innovator. But it may be that by his own energy and by the assistance of his followers he proves too strong for them. Gradually, about the close of his career, or, it may be, after it, they are compelled to withdraw their opposition and to imitate the man whom they had denounced. They are compelled to do that which is most frightful to them, to abandon their routine. And then there occurs to them a thought which brings inexpressible relief. Out of the example of the original man they can make a new routine. They may imitate him in everything except his originality. For one routine is as easy to pace as another. What they dread is the necessity of originating, the fatigue of being really alive. And thus the second half of the original man's destiny is really worse than the first, and his failure is written more legibly in the blind veneration of succeeding ages than in the blind hostility of his own. He broke the chains by which men were bound; he threw open to them the doors leading into the boundless freedom of nature and truth. But in the next generation *he* is idolised and nature and truth as much forgotten as ever; if he could return to earth he would find that the crowbars and files with which he made his way out of the prison-house have been forged into the bolts and chains of a new prison called by his own name. And who are those who idolise his memory? Who are found building his sepulchre? Precisely the same party which resisted his reform; those who are born for routine and can accommodate themselves to everything but freedom; those who in clinging to the wisdom of the past suppose they love wisdom but in fact love only the past, and love the past only because they hate the living present; those, in a word, who set Abraham, Isaac, and Jacob in opposition to Christ, and appeal to the God of the dead against the God of the living.

Thus it was that the legal party were *actors* in everything, winning the reverence of the multitude by false

The Law of Resentment

pretences, imitating inspired men in everything except their inspiration, following motives which did not actuate them but which they supposed ought to actuate them. And as must most infallibly happen to men living in such conventionalism, destitute of convictions, the healthy play of life artificially suspended, over the whole inert stagnation of the soul there grew a scurf of feeble corruption; petty vices, littlenesses, meannesses, were rife within them. They grew conceited, pompous, childish. They liked to hear the sound of their titles, to exaggerate the distinctions of their dress, to reflect upon their superiority to other men, to find that superiority acknowledged, to be greeted reverentially in public places, to recline on the first couch at dinner parties. The virtues to the cultivation of which in themselves and others they had devoted their lives refused altogether to be cultivated by the methods they used, and in the void place of their hearts where morality and sanctity, justice and the love of God, should have been, there appeared at last nothing to mark the religious man, nothing, we may suppose, except a little ill-temper, a faint spite against those who held wrong opinions, a feeble self-important pleasure in detecting heresy.

Such was the party which Christ denounced with so much passion. It may strike us that however corrupt they may have been they could hardly deserve to be pronounced worse than publicans and harlots. But Christ never went so far as this. He did indeed in a parable contrast the prayer of a Pharisee unfavourably with the prayer of a publican, but it was a publican repenting, and the moral of the comparison is, " Better commit a great sin and be ashamed of it, than a smaller one and be proud of it." And when he said that the very harlots entered the Christian Church before the Pharisees, he again meant to charge them not with being worse but less corrigible than those whose vices were too gross to leave room for self-delusion. Still it is plain that he gave way to anger far more in addressing Pharisees than in addressing publicans and harlots.

In doing so he only followed the rule laid down above.

It is not to be supposed that, as a lover of men, he felt less pity for those whom he denounced when all the world admired them than for those whose part he took when all the world disowned them. Indeed his most passionate invective closes in that singular lamentation over Jerusalem in which the saddest feelings of a sensitive patriot are so inimitably blended with the regal sense of personal greatness which he continually and with so much unconsciousness betrayed. He felt pity as well as anger, but he thought the anger had a better right to be expressed. The impostors must be first unmasked; they might be forgiven afterwards, if they should abandon their conventionalities. The lover of men is angry to see harm done to men. Harm was done by the publican and the prostitute, but anger could do no more against these than it did already. Men were on their guard against them, their power for evil was circumscribed as far as it could be, and justice was satisfied by the punishment of infamy which had been inflicted upon them. But the lover of men, when he contemplated the vast and united phalanx of legalists, saw that which carried him out of himself with anger and pain. He saw the multitude sitting at their feet as learners and addressing them with titles of veneration. He saw those whose lot confined them to the narrow cares of subsistence, those whose limbs indeed were continually exercised in handicrafts and their shrewdness in trades, but whose higher faculties rusted in disuse, and those of higher station, upon whom fell larger tasks of administration and government but still secular tasks overwhelming the mind with details and concealing eternal principles from its view,—he saw all this miscellaneous crowd gathering round their revered teachers eager for the wisdom and the instruction which might save their souls in the all-engulphing vortex of earthly life. He saw that in the hands of these teachers was laid the life and salvation of the nation, and that from them was certain to pass readily into other minds whatever enthusiasm of goodness might dwell in their own. He looked for this enthusiasm; doubtless he was prepared to find it immature and not altogether that Enthusiasm of

The Law of Resentment

Humanity which dwelt in himself. He observed these teachers—and he found they were mountebanks. Their gestures, their costume, were theatrical; their whole life was an acted play; the wisdom that came from their lips was repeated with more or less fluency, but it had been learned by rote; sometimes it was good, the wisdom of Moses or Isaiah, sometimes it was the dotage of a Shammai; but, wise or foolish, it came with equal emphasis from those who, solely occupied with the fretting and the strutting they considered proper to the part, declaimed it in the dress of teachers to an admiring audience. And marking this, he considered that the power of these men to do mischief was equal to or greater than their power to do good. It would be better that the Jews should have no teachers of wisdom at all, than that they should have teachers who should give them folly under the name of wisdom. Better that in the routine of a laborious life they should hear of wisdom as a thing more costly than pearls but beyond their reach, than that it should seem to be brought within their reach and they should discover it to be paste. Acknowledged penury of wisdom might leave them rich in humility, reverence, and faith; abundance of false wisdom could but make them impostors or cynics. If a divine revelation be the first of blessings, then the imposture that counterfeits it must be by far the greatest of all evils. And if the unlucky malefactor who in mere brutality of ignorance or narrowness of nature or of culture has wronged his neighbour excite our anger, how much deeper should be our indignation when intellect and eloquence are abused to selfish purposes, when studious leisure and learning and thought turn traitors to the cause of human well-being, and the wells of a nation's moral life are poisoned?

This, then, was the class of persons with whom Christ was angry, and these were the reasons of his anger. But now let us enquire what was the character of his anger. We must remember that this is he who was called a lamb. He was distinguished from the other remarkable characters of antiquity by his gentleness. He introduced into human nature those blended and complex feelings which distinguish modern characters from ancient. Now the question may be raised whether this complexity of character is not purchased at some expense of strength. Ancient valour was well-nigh pitiless. Modern soldiers mix pity with their valour: have they lost any valour by doing so? In like manner, when we are angry with men in these days, we are commonly angry with discrimination. We make reserves; we give some credit for good intentions; we make some allowance for temptations; we are sorry to be angry, and do not, like the ancients, enjoy the passion as if it were wine. The question then arises, has the passion of anger grown at all feebler in us? Are we at all emasculated by the complexity of our emotions? To find an answer let us look at the great Exemplar of modern characters; let us enquire whether he was feeble in his anger; let us consider the wrath of the Lamb.

The faults of the legal party were such as it is very difficult to reprove, because they were of so refined and impalpable a character. These men had not been guilty for the most part of open crime; if they had done wrong, they had done so probably not without some good intention; if they had deluded others, they had deluded themselves first. Christ recognised the impalpable, insidious character of their corrupting influence when he charged his followers to beware of the leaven, that is, the infection, of the Pharisees. It is difficult to reprove a party like this, without either making so many qualifications as to deprive the reproof of most of its force, or, on the other hand, committing an apparent injustice. But Christ's anger was not to be restrained by such considerations. One invective has been preserved, probably on account of the concentrated passion of indignation which breathes through it, and perhaps also because, more than anything else, it determined the legalists to lay their plot against Christ's life. It makes no qualifications, it says not a word about good intentions nor about overwhelming temptations. Delivered in the presence of the multitude, on whose admiration the legalists lived, it denounces a succession of woes upon the whole all-powerful order, reiterating many times the charge of imposture, and coup-

The Law of Resentment

ling it with almost every other biting reproach that can be imagined. It charges them with childish pedantry, with vexatious and grinding oppression, and, what was especially severe as addressed to the learned class, with ignorance and with the hatred of knowledge. To the men who supposed that they monopolised the most infallible rules, the most exquisite methods of discovering truth, he says, " You have taken away the key of knowledge; you enter not in yourselves, and those that were entering in you hinder." Finally, he calls them children of hell, serpents, a brood of vipers, and asks how it is possible for them to escape damnation.

Here, then, we see Christ in his attitude of hostility. His language itself is not wanting in energy, and it derived double emphasis from his position. In his political appearance he may be compared to the Gracchi. As they assailed a close and selfish ruling order by marshalling the people against it, and assuming that peculiar position of authorised agitators which the Roman constitution offered in the tribunate, so did Christ assail the order of legalists. The old Jewish constitution recognised the claim of the *prophet* to a certain authority. One who, advancing pretensions to the prophetic character, succeeded in producing conviction, so that by a kind of informal but irresistible *plebiscitum* he was recognised to be that which he professed to be, was thenceforward regarded as a mouthpiece of the Invisible King, and held an indefinite but at the same time constitutional authority in the land. He was not a mere *influence*, but, as it were, a magistrate, and almost, if he pleased, a dictator. This singular institution had, it is true, lain dormant for many centuries, not that the Jews had ceased to believe in prophets, but that no person had succeeded in winning the *plebiscitum* which conferred the prophetic authority. The office was understood not to be abolished but simply to be in abeyance. It is recorded that Judas Maccabæus when he purified the temple reserved some matters until a prophet should appear to give directions about them. The reign of the prophets had now begun again. John the Baptist had received that universal testimony to his divine mission which the legalists themselves, with all their contempt for the " cursed " populace, found it impossible to resist. To his authority Christ had succeeded. When, therefore, he assailed the dominant order, he did so as a magistrate, and his act was a political one. His power was less defined, but it was not less real than that of a Roman tribune of the people, and in extent it was greater, because it was undefined, and because it was perpetual and personal, instead of being delegated for the term of a year. Acknowledged as a prophet, and making no concealment of the fact that he regarded himself as a king, he must have meant his denunciations of the legal party for a mortal defiance. They were the final brimming over of the cup of indignation. They made all reconciliation between him and them impossible.

Our biographies tell us that he early foresaw in what the quarrel would end. He saw that he was driving his opponents to that point that, with their love of power and position, they must murder him. His life had been tranquil; the times were tranquil. How easy it might have been to lead a useful life, teaching men everywhere, setting an example of high aims and thoughts, leavening gradually the nation with his morality and sanctity! How easy it might have been to procure for himself a long life, which would have been full of blessing to mankind, and up to the end to see that which was the great wish of the Hebrew patriot, " peace upon Israel! " What prevented this happy prospect from being realised? Surely, we may think, to avoid bloodshed and shocking crimes a Christian would sacrifice much. What prevented the prospect from being realised? We must answer, Christ himself prevented it, simply because he would not restrain his anger. He might have remained silent about the Pharisees; he might have avoided meeting with them or talking of them; he might at least have qualified the severity of his reproofs. None of these things would he do; he gave his anger way, and drove his opponents to that which such men call the " necessity " of destroying him.

His resentment did not indeed show itself in action.

The Law of Resentment

He did not arm his followers against them; he would not, probably, had he been placed in a condition to do so, have done to them what Elijah did to the prophets of Baal at the brook Kishon. Yet it appears that the anger he felt would of itself have carried him as far as this. Setting forth in a parable his own relation to the legalists, and describing himself, as usual, as a king, he concluded with representing the king as saying, " And as for those mine enemies which would not that I should reign over them, bring them hither and *slay them before me.*"

In this profound resentment he never wavered. It is the custom to say that Christ died forgiving his enemies. True, no doubt, it is that he held the forgiveness of private enemies to be among the first of duties; and he did forgive the personal insults and barbarities that were practised upon him. But the legalists, whose crime was against the kingdom of God, the nation, and mankind, it does not appear that he ever forgave. The words of forgiveness uttered on the Cross refer simply to the Roman soldiers, for whom pardon is asked expressly on the ground that they do not understand what they are doing. The words may even contain distinct allusion to that other class of criminals who *did* know what they were doing, and for whom therefore the same prayer was not offered. At least this interpretation suggests itself to one who endeavours to discover from the expressions which he dropped what was passing in Christ's mind during the period of his sufferings. For those expressions indicate that he was neither thinking of his murderers with pity and forgiveness nor yet turning his mind to other subjects, but that he was brooding over their conduct with bitter indignation. To the high priest he replied with a menace, " You shall see the Son of Man sitting on the right hand of power." To the women that followed weeping as he was led to execution, he said, " Weep not for me, but for yourselves and your children. For if they (the legalists) do these things in the green tree, what shall be done in the dry ? " And to Pilate he said (drawing precisely the same distinction between the conduct of the Romans and that of the Jews which we conjecture to be implied in the words, " Father, forgive them, for they know not what they do "), " You would have no authority at all against me, were it not given you from above: therefore he who delivers me to you has greater sin"; meaning, apparently, " I should not be amenable to Roman authority at all but for that providential appointment which has placed the country for the time in foreign hands; the greater is the treason of him, the chief priest, who hands his countryman over to a foreign magistrate." These passages seem to show that if no forgiveness of his real murderers was uttered by Christ, it was not by chance, but because he continued to the last to think of them with anger.

It seemed worth while to discuss this subject at some length, lest it should be supposed that Christianity is really the emasculate, sentimental thing it is sometimes represented to be. Because it has had a considerable effect in softening manners, because it has given a new prominence and dignity to the female sex, and because it has produced great examples of passive virtues, Christianity is sometimes represented as averse to strong passions, as making men excessively unwilling to inflict pain, as fostering a morbid or at least a feminine tenderness. War, for example, and capital punishment, are frequently denounced as *unchristian*, because they involve circumstances of horror; and when the ardent champions of some great cause have declared that they would persevere although it should be necessary to lay waste a continent and exterminate a nation, the resolution is stigmatised as shocking and *unchristian*. Shocking it may be, but not therefore unchristian. The Enthusiasm of Humanity does indeed destroy a great deal of hatred, but it creates as much more. Selfish hatred is indeed charmed away, but a not less fiery passion takes its place. Dull serpentine malice dies, but a new unselfish anger begins to live. The bitter feelings which so easily spring up against those who thwart us, those who compete with us, those who surpass us, are destroyed by the Enthusiasm of Humanity; but it creates a new bitterness, which displays itself on occasions where before the mind had reposed in a bene-

The Law of Resentment 223

volent calm. It creates an intolerant anger against all who do wrong to human beings, an impatience of selfish enjoyment, a vindictive enmity to tyrants and oppressors, a bitterness against sophistry, superstition, self-complacent heartless speculation, an irreconcilable hostility to every form of imposture, such as the uninspired, inhumane soul could never entertain. And though Christ so understood his own special mission as to refrain from all acts of hostility or severity towards human beings, yet in the Christian view, which connects acts so closely with instinctive impulses, an act must be right which is dictated by a right impulse, and there will be cases when the Christian will hold it his duty to inflict pain.

What is called the Middle Age may be described as the period of Christian barbarism; that is, it was the time when genuine Christian impulses were combined with the greatest intellectual rudeness. But as impulse is commonly strong where intellect is dormant, we may note the working of Christian feeling more easily in the Middle Age than in the Modern Time. Now it is in the Middle Age that we meet with wars of religion, and with capital punishments for speculative error. Intellectually considered both were frightful mistakes. The Enthusiasm of Humanity, enlightened by a complete view of the facts, would not have dictated either. But it was the want of enlightenment, not the want of Christian humanity, that made it possible for men to commit these mistakes. Those Syrian battle-fields where so many Crusaders committed " their pure souls unto their Captain, Christ "; the image of Christ's death turned into an ensign of battle; the chalice of the Last Supper giving its name to an army— these things may shock, more or less, our good sense, but they do not shock, they rather refresh and delight, our humanity. These warriors wanted Christ's wisdom, but they had his spirit, his divine anger, his zeal for the franchises of the soul. Our good sense may be shocked still more when we think of the *auto da fé*. We may well exclaim upon the folly of those who could dream of curing intellectual error by intellectual bondage. Our humanity itself may be shocked by the greater number of these deeds of faith. We may say of the perpetrators of them, These are they that kill the prophets; their zeal for truth is feigned; they are the slaves of spiritual pride. But if you could be sure that it was not the prophet but the pernicious sophist that burned in the fire, and if by reducing his too busy brain to safe and orthodox ashes you could destroy his sophistries and create in other minds a wholesome fear of sophistry, without creating at the same time an unwholesome dread of intellectual activity and freedom, then Christian humanity might look with some satisfaction even on an *auto da fé*. At any rate, the ostensible object of such horrors was Christian, and the indignation which professedly prompts them is also Christian, and the assumption they involve, that agonies of pain and blood shed in rivers are less evils than the soul spotted and bewildered with sin, is most Christian.

CHAPTER XXII

THE LAW OF FORGIVENESS

We have now considered the Christian character in many of its aspects. We have seen that the Christian is one whose steps are guided by an enthusiasm that never leaves him and that does not allow him to doubt what he ought to do. We have seen that this enthusiasm is that love of man in the ideal of man, which in a low degree is natural to all, made powerful and ardent by a clearer knowledge of the ideal in Christ and by a sense of personal relation to Christ. We have seen that the operation of this enthusiasm is to make morality positive instead of negative, a constant endeavour to serve mankind instead of an endeavour to avoid injuring them. We have considered some of the principal kinds of service to mankind which it dictates. Of these the first was philanthropy, or an attention to their physical wants and happiness. The second was edification, or attention to their moral improvement. And when engaged in this latter duty we found the enthusiasm assuming two special aspects in relation to two peculiar classes of men. In the presence of immorality disguised and prosperous it exhibited itself in prophetic indignation, intolerant aggressive zeal, vehement reproof. On the other hand, in dealing with immorality punished, repudiated, and outcast, it appeared as Mercy.

The picture of the Christian in his active relations to society is complete. So far as society is the passive object of his cares, it is in this way that he will deal with it. But cases arise in which the initiative is not in his hands. It is important to know not merely how he will treat others, but also how he will receive others' treatment of himself. So long as this treatment is good and benevolent, the

Enthusiasm of Humanity will but make natural gratitude more lively. But when it is injurious how will the Christian deal with it?

Now it was on the treatment of injuries that Christ delivered the third of those special commands of which mention has been made. The famous sentences of the Sermon on the Mount which refer to this subject will at once occur to the reader, but there is another precept which it is important to bear in mind at the same time. In the Sermon on the Mount he bids his followers bear with absolute passive tolerance the most contumelious injuries: " If a man smite thee on the one cheek, turn to him the other also," etc. But the other precept is different: " If thy brother trespass against thee, rebuke him, and if he repent forgive him." Now the difference between these two precepts is not slight but substantial. The first distinctly forbids resenting an injury, the second as distinctly commands it. The expression, " Turn to him the other also," in the first is evidently selected with care to convey an extreme degree of uncomplaining submission. It is the direct opposite of the phrase, " Rebuke him," which occurs in the other precept. And that by " Rebuke him," Christ did not mean a faint expostulation, appears from what follows. For he adds: " if your brother will not hear you, bring it before the church; and if he refuse to hear the church, let him be to you as a heathen man or a publican; " in other words, let him be expelled from the Christian society. The two precepts, therefore, differ essentially and cannot be obeyed together. If you adopt the course prescribed in the one you must deviate from that prescribed in the other.

Nevertheless the two precepts do not necessarily contradict each other. Christ may mean to distinguish two kinds of injuries, the one of which is to be resented and the other to be suffered passively. Or he may mean to distinguish two classes of men committing injuries. Whether either of these two suppositions be true, and, if so, which, will be considered further on. In the meanwhile it is to be noted that in one respect the two precepts agree; in other words, that from these two commands

The Law of Forgiveness

of Christ a general Christian law in reference to injuries may be gathered. For in both precepts it is implied that every injury that can be committed is to be forgiven on certain conditions. In the one case we are told that injuries are to excite in our minds no resentment at all, that curses are to be requited with blessings, and persecution with prayers; in the other case we are indeed commanded to resent the injury, but at the same time we are commanded to accept in all cases the repentance of the offender.

Now this law that all injuries whatever are to be forgiven on certain conditions divides itself, when we consider it, into two. For it is necessary to examine separately the maxim that we are to be prepared, as a general rule, to forgive injuries, and the maxim that there is no injury so deadly but that it comes under this general rule. Let us begin, therefore, by examining the maxim that injuries as a general rule are to be forgiven on certain conditions.

It has already been remarked as a characteristic of Christianity that, while it excites an intense disapprobation of wrong-doing, it nevertheless regards wrong-doing as venial. Criminals that had been regarded under much laxer systems with unmixed hatred became under Christianity objects of pity. But it does not immediately follow that the injured party himself would be required to regard his injurer in that light. The relation of the injured party to the criminal is peculiar; his feelings are different from those of the bystander who has suffered nothing by the crime; and the Enthusiasm, though it moves the bystander to mercy, may very possibly produce a different effect upon him. In order to discover whether it does so or not it is necessary to enquire in what respect the natural feeling of the injured party himself towards the criminal differs from that of the bystander. Now the feeling of the bystander or disinterested person towards crime was examined in an earlier part of this treatise. It was there shown that in uncivilised times the feeling was pure indifference, but that as men advanced in moral culture they acquired a *sympathy* with one another. This sympathy produced the effect that whenever a given person was disturbed by any emotions, the bystander who observed him became affected by similar emotions. Such sympathetic emotions were always less powerful than the original ones, but they were stronger in proportion to the strength of the sympathy out of which they grew. The resentment which a man feels at crime from which he does not personally suffer is of this sympathetic kind. It is a reflection from the resentment felt by the injured party himself. Now we have seen that this sympathetic resentment is modified and made less pitiless by Christianity, and the question is, could this happen and yet the same effect not be produced by the same agent upon the original resentment? Plainly there is one way and only one way in which this might be. If Christianity mitigates sympathetic resentment by diminishing the sympathy which is one of its factors, then the mitigation will not extend to that resentment which is independent of sympathy. But we know that, so far from this, sympathy is vastly increased by the Christian enthusiasm. It follows that sympathetic resentment would be vastly increased at the same time, if Christianity did not also operate, and in a still greater degree, to soften the resentment itself. But if it operates upon the resentment itself, it will do so in the injured party who is animated by that alone as well as in the bystander, and therefore Christianity which enjoins mercy to criminals must at the same time enjoin forgiveness of personal injuries.

But no such indirect argument is required to show that Christianity must needs tend to diminish the sense of personal injury. We know that it is easier to forgive injuries to those whom we love, whether the love we feel be that love which is grounded on admiration, or that which arises out of the sense of relationship. Now Christianity creates for all mankind a sentiment which, though not identical with either of these, yet bears a considerable resemblance to them, and can hardly fail to operate in the same way. We may be sure also that revenge diminishes in proportion as we gain the power of going out of ourselves and of conceiving and realising interests and rights

The Law of Forgiveness

not our own. Revenge is the monomania of the isolated and unsympathising heart which intensely grasps the notion of personal right and property but for itself alone, and for which there is but one being and one *self* in the universe. It cannot therefore but be diminished by an enthusiasm which creates a moral universe for the soul where before there was darkness, which forces it to relax its stiff and crabbed tenacity by enlarging its sphere, which gives it the softness which comes with warmth, which educates it in the wisdom of sympathy and the calmness of wisdom.

But now what is to be the limit of forgiveness? It would probably have been allowed by many of the ancients that an unforgiving temper was not to be commended. They would have said, We are not to exact a penalty for every nice offence; we are to overlook some things; we are to be blind sometimes. But they would have said at the same time, We must be careful to keep our self-respect, and to be on a level with the world. On the whole, they would have said, It is the part of a man fully to requite to his friends their benefits and to his enemies their injuries. Christ, no doubt, bids men be more generous than this, be less meanly solicitous about their personal rights; but where does he place the limit? what is the injury for which we are to take no apology?

Christ said, " If thy brother trespass against thee seven times a day, and seven times a day turn again to thee, saying, I repent, thou shalt forgive him." Probably no reader of this passage would doubt that it means absolutely to take away all limitations of forgiveness, and to proclaim that there is no injury, however deadly, or however frequently repeated, which the Christian is not to forgive upon submission made. But to make this doubly sure it is recorded that Peter put the question directly to him, whether the seventh time was literally to be taken as a limit. The enquiry, it is worth while to remark by the way, throws a strong light upon the character of the followers whom Christ had gathered round him. " Lord, how often shall *my* brother offend against *me* and I forgive him? Until seven times? " There breathes, in the first place, through this question a singular earnestness. The use of the first person seems to show that Peter was not considering the problem as part of the theory of morals. He does not speak in the tone of Socrates' disciples. But he seems to be intently considering how Christ's principle of forgiveness can practically be worked. He speaks as though he had himself suffered an injury and had succeeded more than once in forgiving it, and now came to his Master to know how long the trial was to last. But, on the other hand, the question shows a singular want of the power or habit of generalising. It is the question of one who has never been accustomed to think, but who guides himself by precepts or texts learned by rote. He thinks it presumption to try to understand his Master's teaching, and accordingly he inevitably misunderstands it. What was delivered as a principle he instantly degrades into a rule. He has no power of distinguishing the form of the precept from the substance; and therefore being commanded to forgive an offending brother even if he should commit seven injuries, he proceeds at once to enquire how he should deal with the eighth. No turn of expression could more nicely indicate the process by which those high moralities which are the life of the world are converted into the conventionalities which are its bane. It is also worthy of remark that Christ in his reply refuses to abandon the figurative mode of expression. He vindicates, as it were, his right to use these forms of language, and insists that his followers shall learn to understand them, but at the same time he alters the figure so far as to remove the particular misunderstanding into which Peter had fallen. He replied, " I solemnly declare to you, not until seven times, but until seventy times seven."

Here then is the prohibition of all mortal feuds. Irreconcilable enmities are henceforth forbidden to human beings. Mercy to a submissive foe is to be no longer an exceptional and admirable reach of human goodness, but a plain duty. There may be again contentions upon the earth, wars between state and state, feuds between family and family, quarrels between man and man, but the war

The Law of Forgiveness

" without treaty and without herald " is in the modern world, what it was not in the ancient, immoral. Human beings have henceforth in all cases a right to terms, a right to quarter. However they may trample upon the rights of others, they cannot trample upon their own; however they may repudiate all human obligations, they cannot cancel, though they may change and modify, the obligations of others to them.

This is Christ's most striking innovation in morality. It has produced so much impression upon mankind that it is commonly regarded as the whole or at least the fundamental part of the Christian moral system. When a Christian spirit is spoken of, it may be remarked that a forgiving spirit is usually meant. But there is much more in the Christian system than the doctrine of forgiveness, nor does its importance in that system consist in its being the fundamental part upon which the other parts depend, for it is not this in any sense. Its importance lies simply in its being the most *distinctive* feature in the system, and in its *characterising* Christian morality more than any other doctrine of it. The other laws which have been considered, the law of philanthropy, the law of edification, the law of mercy and of moral resentment, though Christianity gave a new importance to them, cannot be called peculiar to Christianity. They were all in some degree recognised in heathen moralities, and though the originality of Christianity in respect to them is very real, yet it does not at once strike the eye and is not easy to make clear. But in the law of forgiveness, and still more in the law of unlimited forgiveness, a startling shock was given to the prevailing beliefs and notions of mankind. And by this law an ineffaceable and palpable division has been made between ancient and modern morality. The other Christian virtues were in a degree familiar to the heathen world; that is to say, they had often been witnessed and when witnessed they had always excited admiration. As *duties* they had never been recognised, but they had been known as the exceptional characteristics of men of rare virtue. Now of forgiveness we cannot certainly say that it was unknown to the ancients;

under certain conditions, no doubt, it was very common among them. In domestic and family life, in which all the germs of Christian virtue are to be found, it was undoubtedly common. Undoubtedly friends fell out and were reconciled in antiquity as amongst ourselves. But where the only relation between the two parties was that of injurer and injured, and the only claim of the offender to forgiveness was that he was a human being, there forgiveness seems not only not to have been practised, but not to have been enjoined nor approved. People not only did not forgive their enemies, but did not wish to do so, nor think better of themselves for having done so. That man considered himself fortunate who on his deathbed could say, in reviewing his past life, that no one had done more good to his friends or more mischief to his enemies. This was the celebrated felicity of Sulla; this is the crown of Xenophon's panegyric on Cyrus the Younger. No one in antiquity was more capable of amiable feelings than Cicero. Yet so much could he gloat over the misfortunes of an enemy, that in the second year after the death of Clodius he dates a letter the 560th day after the Battle of Bovillæ—that is, the fray in which Clodius was killed. This is to be noted not merely as an indication of the feeling which Cicero could cherish, but of the state of public opinion which could permit him, without any sense of degradation, to display the feeling to a friend. Still more striking is an example which may be drawn from the life of Julius Cæsar. He is eminent in antiquity as one who knew how to forgive. It is much to his credit that his execution of Vercingetorix on the occasion of his fourfold triumph has always been considered a blemish upon his career. The execution of the conquered general was a regular and important part of the triumphal ceremony; there could be no reason, except Cæsar's extraordinary clemency, to expect that it would be omitted on this occasion. And yet the expectation was general.[1] Why did he disappoint it? There was everything to incline his mind to generosity. Six years had passed since Vercingetorix had been his enemy, six

[1] See Dio Cassius, xl. 41.

years full of success and glory. Vercingetorix had been a chivalrous enemy, and his surrender had been made in a manner specially calculated to affect the feelings of his conqueror. Cæsar had pardoned multitudes of those who had injured him, of those who hated him mortally; why could he not pardon one whose only crime was that he had defended the independence of his country against him? Cæsar had pardoned many whom it might have been expedient to destroy; why could he not pardon one by whose death he gained nothing, and by whose forgiveness he would have conciliated a nation? The answer seems to be that on those days of triumph Cæsar gave himself up to the enjoyment of his success, that he was determined to drain to the dregs the whole intoxicating cup, and that even he could not conceive of happiness as perfect unless it were flavoured with revenge, or victory as complete while his enemy breathed. The one man who knew something of the pleasures of generosity was yet carried away by the universal opinion about the sweetness of vengeance, and could imagine no triumph but such as those we see represented in Egyptian bas-reliefs, where the victor's foot is planted on the necks of his captives, or that we read of in the life of the pupil of Aristotle, who actually dragged the living body of one of the most heroic of his enemies at the tail of his chariot.

The Roman Triumph with its naked ostentation of revenge fairly represents the common feeling of the ancients. Nevertheless, forgiveness even of an enemy was not unknown to them. They could conceive it, and they could feel that there was a divine beauty in it, but it seemed to them not merely, like the other Christian virtues, more than could be expected of ordinary men, but almost more than could be expected of human nature itself, almost superhuman. A passage near the close of the Ajax of Sophocles will illustrate this. As there was nothing of the antiquarian spirit about Greek tragedy, as it probably never occurred to Sophocles that the ancient heroes he depicts belonged to a less civilised age than his own, but, on the contrary, as he conceived them to be better and nobler than his contemporaries, we may fairly suppose the feelings described in this passage to be of the highest standard of the poet's own age, the age of Pericles. Ulysses, after the death of his enemy Ajax, is described as relenting towards him so far as to intercede with Agamemnon that his body may be decently buried, and not be exposed to the beasts and birds. This may seem to be no great stretch of generosity. But the request is received by Agamemnon with the utmost bewilderment and annoyance. "What can you mean?" he says, "*do you feel pity for a dead enemy?*" On the other hand, the friends of Ajax are not less astonished, and break out into rapturous applause, "but," says Teucer, "I hesitate to allow you to touch the grave, lest it should be disagreeable to the dead man."

The impression of strangeness which these words, *Do you feel pity for a dead enemy?* produce upon us is a proof of the change which Christianity has wrought in manners. A modern dramatist might have written the words, if he had been delineating an extremely savage character, but Sophocles is doing no such thing. He is expressing the natural sentiment of an average man. A modern poet, endeavouring to do the same thing, hits upon a precisely opposite sentiment:—

>Sirs, pass we on,
>And let the bodies follow us on biers.
>Wolf of the weald and yellow-footed kite,
>Enough is spread for you of meaner prey.

And that the change of feeling indicated by this difference of language has really taken place is not to be disproved by special instances of atrocious malignity, however numerous, which may be quoted from modern history, nor yet by the fact that the duel is a peculiarly modern institution. That there have been and are revengeful men proves nothing, but it proves much that such characters are now remarked as exceptions and excite always dislike, in extreme cases horror and disgust. In antiquity they were, as a rule, not disapproved, but in the extreme case they incurred censure of the same gentle kind as we pass on those who push any good or natural feeling to extravagance. The duel is, no doubt, at first

The Law of Forgiveness

sight a startling phenomenon. It seems bold to assert that the moderns are more forgiving than the ancients, when it is certain that in antiquity the grossest personal insults were constantly overlooked, and that we find a Cicero holding amicable intercourse with men whom he had assailed in public with venomous personal abuse, whereas fifty years ago a man was held disgraced who did not wash out an insult in blood. When we remember this it may seem more correct to say that the modern spirit has consecrated revenge and made it into a duty, than to say that it has adopted Christ's law of forgiveness.

And, indeed, it is impossible to deny that the duel is an example of the failure of Christianity. It is a barbaric usage, which may be traced distinctly to a barbaric origin, and which is entirely opposed to Christ's law. Assuredly if a Paul or a John could have witnessed two Christians facing each other with loaded pistols to avenge a hasty word, they would have called for the crack of doom to end all. And yet it is a usage which prevailed through all Christian countries at a very recent period. Barbarism in this instance prevailed signally over Christian influences. Further, it is not to be denied that the spirit of revenge entered into this usage. Nevertheless if we compare in our imaginations the duellist of modern times with the Agamemnon of Sophocles insulting the corpse of his dead enemy, or with the Ajax of the same play torturing in his tent the ram he supposes to be Ulysses, we shall perceive a vast difference between the two, and shall remain convinced, in spite of all adverse appearances, that the spirit of revenge, if not expelled from human life, has been at least dethroned and fettered by Christ. The revenge described by Sophocles is unmixed hatred and spite. It delights in mischief as mischief; it is intent upon its prey as a vulture upon a carcase; it feasts upon the misery of its object as upon delicious food. The feelings of the duellist may in exceptional cases have been similar, but in ordinary cases they were totally different. And it was only because they were assumed to be totally different that the usage was approved by society. Into these feelings revenge scarcely entered at all. Often, instead of wishing the destruction of his enemy, he rather desired him to escape. Even if the enmity was mortal, at least he *only* wished for his destruction, not that he might suffer as much misery as possible. What he desired principally was first to show that he possessed the courage to expose himself to danger, next, to show that he possessed that sense of personal dignity which could not put up with insult, and that resolution which might save him from the risk of insult in future. And it was for the sense of personal honour which it was supposed to keep alive in men, and for the value which it gave to courage, that the duel was long maintained and defended by society. The usage, then, was not a consecration of revenge, but of the principle of self-respect. Doubtless public opinion approved also of a moderate gratification of revenge, but assuredly a remorseless spirit was no more approved or admired by those who approved of duels than by others, and was only even excused in the case of an extreme and intolerable injury.

We may therefore maintain that the general principle of the forgiveness of injuries, as announced by Christ, has been accepted by the world, has become part of morality, and has made a great and perceptible difference in the average of human characters. The principle of *unlimited* forgiveness, even on condition of repentance, remains, no doubt, to a certain extent a stumblingblock. Few of us even profess that there are no injuries which we are not prepared to forgive; probably few of us wish to have the forgiving spirit in this perfection. It is not merely that such unlimited forgiveness is almost impossible to practise; men do not merely regard it as an unattainable virtue, but they deny it to be a virtue at all. Not under the influence of strong passion, but deliberately, they regard it as a mark of servility and suspect it of being inseparable from creeping vices. Modern literature is full of the evidences of this feeling. Shakspeare says,—

> Swear priests, and cowards, and men cautelous,
> Old feeble carrions, and such suffering souls
> That welcome wrongs; unto bad causes swear
> Such creatures as men doubt;

and a modern novelist makes one of his characters say, "There are some wrongs that no one ought to forgive, and I shall be a villain on the day I shake that man's hand." It is therefore a plausible opinion that mankind have accepted half of the Christian doctrine of forgiveness and rejected the other half, that they have consented to forgive, but not all injuries, not until seventy times seven.

Nevertheless this opinion will not bear examination. It will be found that men do approve and admire unlimited forgiveness provided it be certainly sincere, and that they would themselves think it right to accept repentance of the most extreme injury, provided the penitence were certainly sincere. But in most practical cases that arise both repentance and forgiveness lie under the suspicion of being spurious. There is a manifest temptation on the part of the offender to feign repentance; it is his natural expedient for averting punishment. Repentance therefore is very extensively counterfeited, and there has arisen a prejudice against the name which is easily confounded with a prejudice against the thing. The thing repentance all would agree is good, but then it is rare; for the name repentance people generally have slight respect because it seldom represents the thing. And the suspicion attaching to professions of repentance increases with the heinousness of the injury. It is a common belief that a person capable of committing atrocious wrong must be incapable of repenting of it, and such a person's professions are accordingly contemptuously disregarded. When therefore people deliberately consider it mean to forgive extreme injuries they are really setting a limit not to the duty of forgiveness but to the possibility of genuine repentance. The words, "I shall be a villain on the day that I shake that man's hand," do not mean that the wrong done has been too great to be forgiven with honour, but that it implies a criminality inconsistent with penitence. The words, "There are some injuries that no one ought to forgive," mean really, There are some injuries of which it is impossible to repent. In the same way, the contempt with which we often regard those who forgive injuries does not really imply any dislike of the principle of forgiveness itself, but only a suspicion that in the particular case the forgiveness was not genuine. For forgiveness is a thing not less liable to be counterfeited than repentance. When we were considering the virtue of Mercy we remarked that the acts which it dictates are often precisely those which would be suggested by mere laxity or indifference to wrong. Just so forgiveness acts in the same way as mere servility. The bystander therefore may easily have a difficulty in distinguishing them, and, as forgiveness, like all high virtues, is rare, and servility, like all low vices, common, the chances are in any given case that the act which might have been dictated by either was actually dictated by the latter. When the wrong forgiven is exceptionally heinous this probability becomes still greater, and so men form a habit of regarding the forgiveness of extreme injuries as a contemptible thing except in those cases where their previous knowledge of the person who forgives makes it impossible to suspect him of servility. In such cases they betray their genuine approbation of the principle of unlimited forgiveness by enthusiastic admiration.

A few cases of forgiveness will yet remain which we can scarcely help regarding with repugnance even though we have no antecedent reason to suspect servility. Othello is certainly not wanting in manly spirit, yet we should despise and almost detest him if he forgave Iago. But this, again, does not prove that forgiveness itself is in any circumstances shocking to us. What it proves is that circumstances may be imagined of injury so extreme and malignant that the difficulty of forgiveness becomes incalculable, and that any other way of accounting for the injured man's abstinence from revenge, however improbable and almost impossible in itself, becomes easier to conceive than that he could be capable of sincere forgiveness. But every virtue, and not forgiveness only, becomes in certain cases impossible to human infirmity. Every virtue in the extreme limit becomes confounded with some vice, and the only peculiarity in the case of this virtue is that the vice which counterfeits it is peculiarly contemptible.

The Law of Forgiveness

To sum up: the forgiveness of injuries, which was regarded in the ancient world as a virtue indeed but an almost impossible one, appears to the moderns in ordinary cases a plain duty; and whereas the ancients regarded with admiration the man who practised it, the moderns regard with dislike the man who does not. Where the injury forgiven is extreme the moderns regard the man who forgives as the ancients regarded the man who forgave an ordinary injury, that is, with extreme admiration, provided they are convinced of the genuineness of the forgiveness. On the whole, therefore, it appears that a new virtue has been introduced into human life. Not only has it been inculcated, but it has passed so completely into the number of recognised and indispensable virtues, that every one in some degree practises it, and that by not practising it men incur odium and loss of character. To the other great changes wrought in men's minds by Christ this is now to be added, the most signal and beneficent, if not the greatest, of all. It is here especially that Christianity coincides with civilisation. Revenge is the badge of barbarism; civil society imposes conditions and limitations upon it, demands that not more than an eye shall be exacted for an eye, not more than a tooth for a tooth, then takes revenge out of the hand of the injured party and gives it to authorised public avengers, called kings or judges. A gentler spirit springs up, and the perpetual bandying of insult and wrong, the web[1] of murderous feuds at which the barbarian sits all his life weaving and which he bequeaths to his children, gives place to more tranquil pursuits. Revenge begins to be only one out of many occupations of life, not its main business. In this stage it becomes for the first time conceivable that there may be a certain dignity and beauty in refraining from revenge. So far could ordinary influences advance men. They were carried forward another long stage by a sudden divine impulse followed by a powerful word. Not the Enthusiasm of Humanity alone, not the great sentences

[1]. . . . οὐδ' ἡμῖν ἀνάσσεμεν, οἷσιν ἄρα Ζεὺς
ἐκ νεότητος ἔδωκε καὶ εἰς γῆρας τολυπεύειν
ἀργαλέους πολέμους.

of the Sermon on the Mount alone, but both together, the creative meeting of the Spirit and the Word, brought to life the new virtue of forgiveness. To paraphrase the ancient Hebrew language, the Spirit of Christ brooded upon the face of the waters, and Christ said, Let there be forgiveness and there was forgiveness.

CHAPTER XXIII

THE LAW OF FORGIVENESS—*continued*

But up to this point in considering Christ's principle of forgiveness we have disregarded entirely the words in which he proclaims it. That we should be prepared to forgive all injuries upon condition of repentance is involved in those words, but they contain much more. It has been remarked that the two texts which refer to the subject of injuries coincide to this extent, but that from this point they differ irreconcilably. Having considered that in which they agree, it is time for us to discuss that in which they differ.

The one text commands the Christian, if a brother trespass against him, to rebuke the offender. The other gives a directly contrary precept, " If a man smite thee on the one cheek, turn to him the other also." This apparent contradiction will be removed if it can be shown that Christ was not contemplating the same class of injurers in the two cases. Now if we examine the first passage we immediately discover that the injurer referred to is a Christian. In the first place, he is called a brother, which we know to have been the term adopted by the first Christians in speaking of each other. In the second place, the text goes on to direct that if the offender do not listen to the rebuke, the matter be brought before the Church, and that if he continue contumacious he be treated for the future as a heathen, in which it is of course implied that at the beginning he had been a Christian. So much then being certain, it is natural to conclude that the other text which gives us different direction refers to injuries received from heathens. Let us examine whether this conjecture is confirmed by the expressions used in the passage itself.

That passage (Matt. v. 38-48) divides itself into two

parts—one which tells us what feelings we ought to entertain towards those who injure us, the other which tells us what we ought to do to them. Now in the first part [1] there is nothing which, after what has been said above, requires any explanation. It forbids us to *hate* the injurer. It directs us to continue well-disposed to him and to follow the example of Almighty God, who does not at once interdict the sinner *aquâ et igni* and leave him to perish, but continues to him and to the land he tills the blessings of sunlight and rain. As a matter of course, Christianity must speak in this strain. The Christian is a man not indifferent to his fellow-men, but regarding them as such with an enthusiastic kindliness. If he were indifferent to them originally, his feelings towards each individual would be determined entirely by the behaviour of the individual to him. He would love those who benefited him and hate those who did him hurt. But as he starts from love, it is not to be supposed that injury would excite hatred in him. It might indeed diminish his love, but Christ expresses the intense and ideal character of the love he enjoins and inspires by declaring that it must not have even this effect.

But because we are not to hate an enemy, it does not immediately follow that we are not to take vengeance upon him. The infliction of pain and damage is quite consistent with love, as we all acknowledge in the instance of a parent punishing a child. In fact, if Christ had said no more than this we should rather have gathered that he approved of the requital of injuries. For he bids us imitate Almighty God, who though He does not withdraw from sinners the rain and sunlight, yet most assuredly, as Christ held, punishes them. If we are to imitate Him in our treatment of injuries, then we ought to remember not only that His tender mercies are over all His works, but also that " God is jealous, and the Lord revengeth; the Lord revengeth and is furious."

So far, then, this passage is in no way inconsistent with that other in which we are directed to *rebuke* one who wrongs us, nor is there anything in it which strongly suggests that Christ was thinking of one particular class of

[1] Which, however, stands second in St. Matthew (v. 43-48).

The Law of Forgiveness

offenders more than another. The rule that we are to love those who injure us is no doubt absolutely universal, whatever course of action we adopt in reference to the injury. But when the same passage tells us how we are to *act*—when it directs us to endure the most outrageous insults without a murmur of complaint or expostulation, to offer the left cheek to him who smites us on the right, to offer the cloak to him who takes away the coat—is this rule equally universal, or is there anything to indicate that the oppressor is to be understood to be a heathen?

It may seem impossible to limit one part of the passage without at the same time limiting the other. But if Christ's thoughts were intent upon the question in what way his followers were to conduct themselves towards the heathen world in the midst of which they lived, so that the other question, how they were to conduct themselves towards each other, did not at the time occur to his mind, nothing is more natural than that he should in the same breath have delivered rules applicable only to the case in hand and other rules equally applicable to it, but applicable to other cases as well. Now if we read the first chapter of the Sermon on the Mount connectedly, we shall see that he actually was occupied with this question, and that, though heathen are not expressly mentioned, the Christian is always supposed to be dealing with them. Christ, in short, has given here a manual of the behaviour he requires from his followers towards those who are not his followers. For example, they are to consider themselves happy when men (i.e. *heathen* men) revile and persecute them. They are to consider themselves as lights in the world, that is, as illuminating the darkness of *heathenism ;* they are to be the salt of the earth, that is, their Christian enthusiasm is to give a tone to the languid and lifeless *heathen* society. And in the passage itself with which we are dealing, it is sufficiently apparent that the injuries supposed are not those to which in the intercourse of life every one alike is liable; the blow on the cheek, the spiteful treatment, the persecution, point to the insults and cruelties which a hated and despised sect had to expect from the outer world.

Add to this the word *enemy*. It may not strike us at first in reading the passage that this cannot possibly apply to a fellow-Christian. That there are enmities and hatreds between Christians is to us a familiar fact; we find nothing very strange in the thought of one Christian striking another on the cheek. But we must be careful not to antedate this sad knowledge. It is inconceivable that in the very act of founding a society of brothers sworn to mutual love, in the very freshness of Christian feeling, Christ should have supposed the existence of savage enmities in the very bosom of the Church, and should have commanded them to be tolerated. Such gloomy foresight is not characteristic of the Sermon on the Mount. On the contrary, there breathes through it more of that ardour which realises a distant ideal, and overlooks intermediate difficulties, than appears in any other discourse of Christ. It is the first, the simplest, the largest utterance of the new Law, the most inspired expression of the civilisation of the modern world, the fundamental document of ripe morality. It inaugurated a golden age of reconciliation and union. It is the earliest and softest note of that heavenly Dove which has built its nest among men, and which, though often scared away for a time, has still returned. True indeed it is, that the actual reconciliation of mankind was further off than might at that time have seemed. True that Christ on other occasions recognised this with a strange sagacity and certainty. Still, nothing is so incredible as that he should have countenanced or tolerated in thought so complete an obliteration of the distinction between the Church and the surrounding world as might make it possible to apply to the same person the terms "enemy" and "fellow-Christian."

If, then, we take it for proved that the directions contained in this passage refer only to the case of injuries inflicted by heathens, we arrive at this remarkable conclusion, that Christ held such injuries to stand on a materially different footing from those committed by Christians. We have seen that in all cases whatever he commanded his followers to be ready to forgive on condition of re-

The Law of Forgiveness

pentance. But he commands them, when dealing with a brother Christian, firmly to exact that repentance, not to pass the injury by, not even to rest content with a rebuke, unless the rebuke accomplish its purpose, but to bring the matter before the Church and prosecute it until the offender make submission. On the other hand, when they are dealing with a heathen, they are to bear themselves quite differently. They are to compose themselves to an absolute passive tolerance, and to bear in silence whatever may be inflicted. And this is no mere political contrivance for carrying a helpless sect through times of persecution. Christians are not to tolerate injuries simply because, in the presence of superior force, nothing would be gained by resenting them. Their tolerance is not to be reluctant or sullen, nor is it to be a stoical indifference. They are to think of their oppressors with positive goodwill; they are to requite curses not with silence, much less with silent contempt, but with blessings, and malice not with indifference but with acts of kindness.

Now what is the ground of this distinction? What so great difference is there between the Christian and the heathen that they should be treated so differently? Several times in this treatise we have had occasion to mark the essential difference between a Christian and a heathen. We have found it to depend upon that universal relation of every man to every other man beyond the special relation of kindred which Christians recognise and heathens do not. It is on this universal relation of human beings to each other that the Church is founded. And it must be understood that they conceived this relation to be antecedent to the foundation of the Church and altogether independent of it. Christians did not regard each other as brothers because they were alike members of the Church, but they became members of the Church because they regarded each other as brothers. Therefore they cherished the same feeling towards those who were not members of the Church and who did not reciprocate the feeling. On the other hand, the heathen, as such, recognised only special obligations towards particular classes of men, his relations or fellow-citizens. If he recognised any wider obligations, they were formal obligations created by positive legal enactment and resting, in his view, on no essential justice. In the heathen theory the relation of men towards each other, where no tie of nature or of treaty had bound them together, was that of enemies. They were rival claimants of the earth's wealth; their interests were supposed to be conflicting; and therefore their natural condition was hostility.

This being so, an injury committed by a heathen must have been essentially different from an injury committed by a Christian. Both alike were violations of obligation, but the latter was a conscious, the former an unconscious violation. They differed as much as homicide committed in war upon an enemy differs from homicide committed in peace upon a fellow-citizen. The heathen injured one whom he conceived to be his enemy by a law of nature and to be prepared at any moment to perpetrate a similar injury upon himself. But an injury committed by a Christian was like one of those breaches of the right of hospitality or of the right of a suppliant from which even barbarians shrank; it was the violation of a solemn compact. It was reasonable, therefore, that the two classes of injuries should be dealt with in a very different way. The injurious Christian was a proper subject of resentment. But it was unreasonable to be angry with the injurious heathen. Anger, where it is healthy and justifiable, is the feeling excited in us by wrong, by laws broken, covenants disregarded. The heathen as such broke no law and disregarded no covenant, for he knew of none. He might be noxious and mischievous, but he could not, in the strict sense of the word, be injurious. It might be most necessary to inform him of the obligation he neglected, but it was impossible to be angry with him for neglecting it.

This description of the heathen would be justly charged with exaggeration if it professed to describe the ordinary or average heathen. But what it professes to describe is the ideal heathen, or the heathen as he would have been had he lived consistently with his theory. Doubtless this is as much an abstraction as a mathematical point or line. No person perfectly heathen probably ever existed.

The Law of Forgiveness 247

The individual heathen excelled his own moral system as much as the individual Christian falls short of his. Natural kindness was in every one a kind of substitute for Christianity. Still it is not easy to overestimate the hardening effect of an antisocial theory of life which, besides seconding all selfish instincts, did not appear to those who held it a theory but a truth too obvious, too universally held, consecrated too much by usage, to admit of being questioned. We may imagine the almost irresistible force of this universal prejudice upon minds which had never heard it called in question, if we remark the difficulty which most men feel at the present day in viewing otherwise than as the wildest of paradoxes the proposition that the happiness of the brute creation deserves a moment's consideration when compared with the convenience or profit of human beings. If a similar insensibility to *human* sufferings compared with *personal* convenience reigned with equal dominion in the minds of the ancients, if their virtues extended no farther than the family and the state, if they " loved their brethren only," it was quite reasonable that the Christians should take account of the fact in their dealings with them, and instead of rebuking them for a hardness which violated no principle which they acknowledged, should endeavour to teach them better by forbearance and by unexpected retaliations of kindness.

It will be worth while here to raise the question, If injuries committed by heathens were thus sharply distinguished from injuries committed by Christians, how would it be proper for a Christian to deal with an injury received from a Jew? Judaism stands midway between heathenism and Christianity. It rose out of heathenism as twilight out of night, and melted into Christianity as twilight into morning. In its earlier period it had many peculiarities in common with heathenism, but its later form closely resembled Christianity. It did not, indeed, clearly announce the great Christian law of humanity, and it had points which led those who embraced it in a perverse spirit into an inhumanity almost worse, though less brutal, than the inhumanity of heathenism. But it contained the germs of the Christian humanity in its doctrine of the unity of God and of the creation of man in God's image. It would therefore have been unreasonable for a Christian to treat a Jew as one utterly untaught in humanity. The Jew was the possessor of a certain crude Christianity, and even if he had not been, yet an injury done by him to a Christian would generally be the trespass of a *brother* and not the attack of an enemy, since, though the Jews were not Christians, the earliest Christians, at any rate, were for the most part Jews.

Christians could claim at the hands of Jews the rights of countrymen and the rights of fellow-citizenship in the ancient theocracy. Abraham and Moses belonged to both, the Psalms of David and the prophecies of Isaiah. An injury done by a Jew was therefore a thing to be resented by a Christian, and not a thing to be passively tolerated. This being understood, it is instructive to observe how exactly Christ, when he became the object of insult and injury, observed his own law. In his murder both Jews and Romans were concerned. It has been pointed out in a former chapter, in how different a spirit he bore the cruelties of his accusers and those of his executioners. Towards the Jews he cherishes throughout a bitter feeling of resentment, which breaks out before the high-priest into threatening words. But before Pilate he bears himself gently; he exhibits no sign of anger, and declares his Roman judge to be comparatively guiltless of his unjust condemnation. He prays that his Roman executioners may be forgiven, although they did not merely obey orders but heaped wanton insults upon him; and his reason is, " they know not what they do." This litter of Roman wolves, to whom and to whose ancestors no prophet had ever preached, whose only morality in dealing with foreigners was to subdue and crush them, what wonder if they revelled in brutal insult of a Jew who had called himself a king? The burning anger he had felt before Caiaphas subsided at once in the presence of Roman brutality. He rebuked the *brother* that trespassed against him, but when the *enemy* smote him on the one cheek he turned to him the other.

Another point now requires notice. By Christ's law the Christian is commanded in some cases of injury to go

The Law of Forgiveness 249

without redress altogether, in others to apply for it to the Christian assembly. But the Christian assembly had no power of compulsion, and therefore if the offender proved contumacious, redress was denied to the injured man in this case also. It appears, then, that in no case whatever does Christ countenance any appeal to the secular courts. Are we then to suppose that all that machinery for checking and punishing crime, which has been established in every human society alike, is rejected and repudiated by Christ? Since he forbade his followers to avail themselves of this machinery, are we to suppose that he disapproved of it, and that he intended, when society should be remodelled in accordance with his morality, that it should be abolished, and that men should depend in future for their protection against violence upon the power of forgiveness to charm away the lawlessness of the robber and the plunderer?

It is certainly evident that if Christ's law were universally practised in a Christian land the administration of justice would be suspended. Where all alike contented themselves with first rebuking and in case of contumacy renouncing the society of those who injured them, there would be no trials, for there would be no prosecutions. Government would be obliged to abdicate its function of maintaining tranquillity and good order in the kingdom. Is this, then, what Christ intended, and did he believe that the influence of the Enthusiasm of Humanity would be such as to render law and police superfluous? Of Christ's views on civil government we know very little. Still it is not conceivable that he should have rejected altogether the notion of punishment, since we see that in describing the Divine government he introduces it freely. In various parables he has represented himself as a ruler, and his conception of the functions of a ruler appears not to differ from that commonly received. It most distinctly includes criminal jurisdiction and punishment. We may be sure that one who habitually considered governors as charged with the duty of inflicting punishment, cannot have considered it the duty of subjects to prevent punishment from being inflicted.

It is in the circumstances of the Church at its foundation that we shall find the explanation of the difficulty. Christ forbids his followers to appeal to the secular courts, not because he disapproved of criminal law in the abstract, but for the same reason for which he systematically passed over everything relating to politics and government. It was because the Church was established in the midst of a heathen society which it was in no way to countenance and yet in no way to resist. Of this society the Church was in one sense a mortal enemy; that is, she did not acknowledge its right to exist, and she looked forward to a time when it should be reconstructed on the basis of an acknowledgment of Christ and of the law of Humanity. On the other hand, it was Christ's fixed resolution to enter into no contest with the civil power. Therefore he enjoins upon his followers an absolutely passive behaviour towards it, and in every rule that he lays down, while he recognises the fact that the Church itself has no power of compulsion, he makes no use whatever of that power residing in the state.

It appears, then, that the law we have been considering was dictated by special circumstances. It was given to men who had practically no country. The paramount duty to humanity had for a time suspended their obligations to the government under which they lived. Or rather they were men who, while bearing all the burdens laid upon them by the government, declined for special reasons all the advantages they might have derived from government. It was for a society thus deprived by circumstances of all political interests that Christ legislated, for a society which was directed to act as good citizens do under a usurping but still a settled government,—that is, to become political quietists, disturbing as little as possible the public tranquillity, but at the same time countenancing as little as possible the unrighteous power. Accordingly, in laying down a law for the treatment of injuries, Christ entirely disregards the political bearings of the question. He considers no interests but those of the parties immediately concerned. To raise the question whether his law of abstinence from prosecution is consistent with social order is therefore to misunderstand it. Owing to special circumstances this element was eliminated

The Law of Forgiveness

from the problem. Like the First Law of Motion, this law postulates the absence of external forces. What it affirms is that, supposing a wrong committed in redressing which only the injured party is interested, he should endeavour to bring the offender to submission by patience if it be an offence of ignorance, by rebuke if he knew better, but in no case by force.

The special circumstances have long passed away, and it is now impossible to eliminate from the problem all that bears upon public order. Society, and not the injured party only, has now to be considered in the treatment of an injury. Christ's law therefore ceases in many cases to be serviceable as a rule of life. But if this were so in *all* cases, it would not therefore lose its value. The First Law of Motion is still the foundation of mechanics, although no body in the universe was ever actually in the condition that law supposes. Christ's law may be no longer an invariable law for action, but it is an invariable law for feeling and for motive. Instead of abstaining from prosecution it may now be a positive duty to prosecute, but it must no longer be a *pleasure* to prosecute. The prosecution that duty dictates is externally the same act as the prosecution prompted by selfish revenge, but essentially it is a totally different act. That this essential difference is now clear, and that it is applicable to practice, is one abiding effect of Christ's law. Nor is prosecution inconsistent with kindness. Punishments may once more, since the Church became reconciled to the State, have become Christian acts and may have their use, and discharge in some cases the same functions that Christ intended to be discharged by passive tolerance. The sense of a rule higher than self-interest may be roused sometimes by severity, sometimes by unexpected gentleness, sometimes by the mixture of both. But though the prohibition of severity must now be considered as taken off, yet the emphatic recommendation of gentleness remains. It remains a duty in all cases where such a course is likely to succeed to endeavour by every act of kindness consistent with duty to the public to point out to the rude and heathenish heart " the more excellent way of charity."

CHAPTER XXIV

CONCLUSION

The outline of Christian morality is now completely drawn, and it only remains to take a parting glance at the picture from some point where we can see it all in one view.

Let us endeavour, then, once more to answer the question, What is the Christian Church?

First, it is a commonwealth. In other words, it is a society of men who meet together for common objects, and it differs from the minor clubs or unions under which men avail themselves of the principle of association, and resembles those greater societies which we call states, in this respect that it claims unlimited self-sacrifice on the part of its members, and demands that the interest and safety of the whole shall be set by each member above his own interest and above all private interests whatever.

Secondly, as all commonwealths are originally based upon some common quality, and for the most part on a blood-relationship, real or supposed, of the members, so is the Christian Church based upon a blood-relationship, but the most comprehensive of all, the kindred of every human being to every other.

It is therefore absolutely open to all human beings who choose to become members of it.

But the objects for which this commonwealth exists are much less obvious and intelligible than those for which the local commonwealths of the earth exist. Accordingly it is demanded of every member of the Christian Commonwealth that he be introduced into it with a prescribed form and in a public manner, that he be instructed in the objects for which it exists, and that he testify his membership from time to time by a common meal taken

Conclusion

in conjunction with other members also according to a prescribed form.

The effect of this system and of the absence of local boundaries is that the objects of the Christian commonwealth, though less obvious, are far better defined than those of other commonwealths, and that it approaches far nearer to the theoretical perfection of a state. Other states are but accidental aggregates, whose attraction of cohesion was originally a clannish instinct or a common terror of some near enemy or the external pressure of physical barriers; such states, though when once formed they may conveniently be used for definite objects, yet cannot properly be said to have any definite object at all. But the Christian Commonwealth has the same object now which it had at the beginning, and what that object is it is and always has been easy to discover.

The Christian has, as such, a definite relation to every other human being, to every Christian as a fellow-citizen, and to every person who is not Christian as possessing that humanity which is the ground of Christianity.

In ordinary states there arises out of the union, the relationships, the intercourse, the common interests of the citizens, a sense of duties towards each other and of justice. This sense expresses itself in laws, which, at first few and but half-just, have a reacting effect upon the sense of justice which produced them, developing it and causing it gradually to produce more and juster laws. By this system of laws the citizens are taught to abstain from doing serious injuries to each other, and a spirit of sympathy is fostered which disposes them to help each other in difficulties. The morality which thus springs up does not at the beginning influence the citizens in their dealings with foreigners, but is supposed to be inseparable from the civic relation. In a time of general intercourse between nations the obligations of justice become in a certain degree recognised even between foreigners, but grudgingly, and active sympathy between them scarcely exists at all.

A similar process goes forward in the Christian Commonwealth, and, as it includes all mankind, the sense of duty which springs up in it is a sense of duty to man as man, and whatever kindness it fosters is also not exclusive but truly cosmopolitan or humane. In the Christian Commonwealth also the sense of duty gives birth to laws; and whatever laws are common to all secular states are transferred to it, while some new ones are suggested by its peculiar conditions. But whereas in other states the greatest importance is attached to these laws and the greatest trouble taken to make them as just, as numerous, and as exact as possible, in the Christian Commonwealth a different view is taken. The laws themselves are not considered as very important; no pains are bestowed upon forming them precisely; and they exist rather as rules generally understood in the minds of the citizens than as written statutes. On the other hand, that sense of obligation in which all laws have their origin is regarded as inexpressibly important. Every expedient is used to increase the keenness of this sense to such a point that it shall instantly and instinctively suggest the proper course of action in any given case.

This increased and intense moral sensitiveness has an effect upon the objective morality of the Christian Commonwealth, and it also gives a peculiar tone to the character of individual Christians. Its effect upon objective morality is to create a number of new duties which the duller moral sense of secular states does not apprehend. These new duties, as has been said, are not carefully formulated, but they are apprehended very plainly and universally recognised. Of these new duties some do not differ in kind from these which secular morality prescribes. They are but new applications of principles which under other systems are admitted but applied imperfectly. But besides these a whole class of new duties arise in the Christian Commonwealth which are different in kind from those acknowledged in secular commonwealths. These are positive or active duties—duties, that is, not of refraining from injuries but of promoting actively the welfare of others. In secular states, though men had frequently appeared who had performed these duties, they had not performed them *as duties* but rather as works of supererogation, and for performing them they had received from their fellow-citizens not simple approbation but such admiration as we bestow on those who do something extraordinary. These extraordinary services to humanity become ordinary and imperative in the Christian Commonwealth. They fall naturally into two classes—services to the bodies of men and services to their characters and moral development; and to perform either class of duties well, truly to serve men's bodies or their souls, requires the most assiduous study, calls for comprehensive knowledge and perpetual earnest endeavour.

But the fact that in the Christian Commonwealth so much importance is attached to a strong moral sense, the fact that this is used as a substitute for strict laws, modifies individual character even more than objective morality. As this moral sense is expected to discover the right course of action in any given case without the help of a law, so, *vice versâ,* it is not considered satisfactory that the right act should be done, unless the moral sense be active in dictating it. Merely for the purpose of discovering the right act the moral sense would often be unnecessary; in most cases the right act is determined for us by the customs of society, or by our own previous experience of similar cases. But the rule of the Christian Commonwealth is, that though the feeling be not necessary to discover the right act, yet the act must always be accompanied by the feeling. Therefore to perform an act of kindness coldly, an act of self-denial reluctantly, an act of forgiveness with suppressed ill-will, or any right act whatever from interested motives, whether to escape punishment or to win applause, or mechanically from a habit of following fixed maxims, or from any other motive except the moral sense, is to break the fundamental law of the Christian Commonwealth. The Christian therefore must, it appears, cherish a peculiar temperament, such that every combination of circumstances involving moral considerations may instantaneously affect him in a peculiar way and excite peculiar feelings in him. He must not arrive at the right practical conclusion after a calculation or a struggle, but by an instantaneous impulse. Rightly to appreciate what the circumstances are may indeed cost him thought and study, but when once the position is made clear to his mind, the moral sense should speak as promptly as the note sounds when the string of a musical instrument is struck.

This moral sensitiveness, this absolute harmony of inward desire with outward obligation, was called by Christ and his Apostles by a name of which *holiness* is the recognised English equivalent, and it is attributed to the presence of a Divine Spirit within the soul. It is the absolute and ultimate test of true membership in the Christian Commonwealth. He who has it not cannot be a true member whatever he may have, and he who has it is a member whatever he may lack. But how is this moral sensitiveness produced? It is the effect of a single ardent feeling excited in the soul. A single conception enthusiastically grasped is found powerful enough to destroy the very root of all immorality within the heart. As every enthusiasm that a man can conceive makes a certain class of sins impossible to him, and raises him not only above the commission of them, but beyond the very temptation to commit them, so there exists an enthusiasm which makes all sin whatever impossible. This enthusiasm is emphatically the presence of the Holy Spirit. It is called here the Enthusiasm of Humanity, because it is that respect for human beings which no one altogether wants raised to the point of enthusiasm. Being a reverence for human beings *as such*, and not for the good qualities they may exhibit, it embraces the bad as well as the good, and as it contemplates human beings in their ideal—that is, in what they might be—it desires not the apparent, but the real and highest welfare of each; lastly, it includes the person himself who feels it, and, loving self too only in the ideal, differs as much as possible from selfishness, being associated with self-respect, humility and independence, as selfishness is allied with self-contempt, with arrogance, and with vanity.

Conclusion

Once more, how is this enthusiasm kindled? All virtues perpetuate themselves in a manner. When the pattern is once given it will be printed in a thousand copies. This enthusiasm, then, was shown to men in its most consummate form in Jesus Christ. From him it flows as from a fountain. How it was kindled in him who knows? "The abysmal deeps of personality" hide this secret. It was the will of God to beget no second son like him. But since Christ showed it to men, it has been found possible for them to imitate it, and every new imitation, by bringing the marvel visibly before us, revives the power of the original. As a matter of fact the Enthusiasm is kindled constantly in new hearts, and though in few it burns brightly, yet perhaps there are not very many in which it altogether goes out. At least the conception of morality which Christ gave has now become the universal one, and no man is thought good who does not in some measure satisfy it.

Living examples are, as a general rule, more potent than those of which we read in books. And it is true that the sight of very humble degrees of Christian humanity in action will do more to kindle the Enthusiasm, in most cases, than reading the most impressive scenes in the life of Christ. It cannot, therefore, be said that Christ is the direct source of all humanity. It is handed on like the torch from runner to runner in the race of life. Still it not only existed in Christ in a pre-eminent degree, but the circumstances of his life and death gave him pre-eminent opportunities of displaying it. The story of his life will always remain the one record in which the moral perfection of man stands revealed in its root and its unity, the hidden spring made palpably manifest by which the whole machine is moved. And as, in the will of God, this unique man was elected to a unique sorrow, and holds as undisputed a sovereignty in suffering as in self-devotion, all lesser examples and lives will for ever hold a subordinate place, and serve chiefly to reflect light on the central and original Example. In his wounds all human sorrows will hide themselves, and all human self-denials support themselves against his cross.—But we are travelling into questions which we are not yet in a condition to discuss.

Our subject has hitherto been Christian morality. We have considered the scheme by which Christ united men together, cured them of their natural antipathy, cured them of their selfishness. But man has other enemies beside himself, and has need of protections and supports which morality cannot give. He is at enmity with Nature as well as with his brother-man. He is beset by two great enemies with whom he knows not how to cope. The first is Physical Evil; the second is Death. The harm which is done to us by our fellow-men we can at least understand. We understand either that they are angry with us for some reason, or that they have personal objects to gratify which involve suffering to us. What we can understand we can sometimes guard against, we can generally foresee. But when the forces of Nature become hostile to us, we know neither why it is so nor what to do. Most of these enemies attack us capriciously, but one of them is certain to attack us sooner or later, and certain to prevail. He may not be the worst among them; he may not be an enemy at all; but he is more dreaded than any, because he is more mysterious. And though we know little of Death, we cannot help thinking it a comfortless torpor, that deprives the hero of his heroism, the face of its smile, the eye of its expression, that first strikes the human form with a dull, unsocial stiffness, and then peels the beauty from it like a rind and exposes the skeleton. In different degrees men learn and always have learnt to overcome this terror, and to meet death with contentment, and even in some cases with joy. But death remains the fatal bar to all complete satisfaction, the disturber of all great plans, the Nemesis of all great happiness, the standing dire discouragement of human nature.

What comfort Christ gave men under these evils, how he reconciled them to nature as well as to each other by offering to them new views of the Power by which the world is governed, by his own triumph over death, and by his revelation of eternity, will be the subject of another treatise.

Conclusion 259

In closing the subject for the present, let us reflect for a moment upon the magnitude of the work which Christ accomplished, and the nature of which we have been investigating. We may consider it in two very different aspects. It was, in the first place, a work of speculation, which we may compare with the endeavours of several ancient philosophers to picture to themselves a commonwealth founded on juster and clearer principles than the states they saw around them. Plato made such an attempt, and a later philosopher was on the point of realising his conception in an actual, palpable, Platonopolis. The Kingdom of God, the New Jerusalem, which Christ founded, was similar to this speculative state. He seized upon the substantial principles which lie at the foundation of every civil society, and without waiting for favourable circumstances or for permission of kings, and not only dispensing with but utterly repudiating a local habitation, he conceived a commonwealth developed, as it were, from within. It was one of those daring imaginations, in which, as a general rule, we allow philosophers to indulge in their studies, not because we imagine for a moment that they can ever be realised, but because they are useful educational exercises for youth, and because in filling up the paper design suggestions may be thrown out which a practical man may be able gradually to work into the constitution of some existing state. To make any more practical use of such schemes almost all the practical statesmen that ever lived would at once pronounce impossible. They know better, of course, than all other men with how little wisdom the world is governed. They regard the whole framework of all institutions as determined by the plain, universal, animal, propensities of men and the irresistible constraint of external conditions. They believe that for the most part nothing can be done by the wisdom of individuals but to watch the operation of these causes, to take advantage of each passion as it rises, and sometimes to procure the adoption of a measure which is solidly good, when it happens to be momentarily popular. But any comprehensive scheme, appealing to first principles and at the same time demanding sacrifices from men, they consider in the nature of things impracticable. Such, then, was Christ's scheme regarded as a speculation.

We do not compare Plato's Republic with the republics of Athens or Rome, because, however interesting the former may be on paper, it has never been realised. It may be very perfect, but Athens and Rome were more; they *existed*. But the speculative commonwealth of Christ may be compared to the commonwealths of the world as well as to those of philosophers. For, however impossible it may seem, this speculation of a commonwealth developed from first principles *has* been realised on a grand scale. It stands in history among other states; it subsists in the midst of other states, connected with them and yet distinct. Though so refined and philosophic in its constitution, it has not less vigour than the states which are founded on the relations of family, or language, or the convenience of self-defence and trade. Not less vigour, and certainly far more vitality. It has already long outlasted all the states which were existing at the time of its foundation; it numbers far more citizens than any of the states which it has seen spring up near it. It subsists without the help of costly armaments; resting on no accidental aid or physical support, but on an inherent immortality, it defied the enmity of ancient civilisation, the brutality of mediæval barbarism, and under the present universal empire of public opinion, it is so secure that even those parts of it seem indestructible which deserve to die. It has added a new chapter to the science of politics; it has passed through almost every change of form which a state can know; it has been democratical, aristocratical; it has even made some essays towards constitutional monarchy; and it has furnished the most majestic and scientific tyranny of which history makes mention.

For the New Jerusalem, as we witness it, is no more exempt from corruption than was the Old. That early Christian poet who saw it descending in incorruptible purity " out of heaven from God," saw, as poets use, an deal. He saw that which perhaps for a point of time was

Conclusion

almost realised, that which may be realised again. But what we see in history behind us and in the world about us is, it must be confessed, not like " a bride adorned for her husband." We see something that is admirable and much that is great and wonderful, but not this splendour of maiden purity. The bridal dress is worn out, and the orange-flower is faded. First the rottenness of dying superstitions, then barbaric manners, then intellectualism preferring system and debate to brotherhood, strangling Christianity with theories and framing out of it a charlatan's philosophy which madly strives to stop the progress of science—all these corruptions have in the successive ages of its long life infected the Church, and many new and monstrous perversions of individual character have disgraced it. The creed which makes human nature richer and larger, makes men at the same time capable of profounder sins; admitted into a holier sanctuary, they are exposed to the temptation of a greater sacrilege; awakened to the sense of new obligations, they sometimes lose their simple respect for the old ones; saints that have resisted the subtlest temptations sometimes begin again, as it were, by yielding without a struggle to the coarsest; hypocrisy has become tenfold more ingenious and better supplied with disguises; in short, human nature has inevitably developed downwards as well as upwards, and if the Christian ages be compared with those of heathenism they are found worse as well as better, and it is possible to make it a question whether mankind has gained on the whole.

To be sure, the question is a frivolous one. What good for the grown man to regret his childhood, and to think his intelligence and experience a poor compensation for the careless happiness that accompanied his childish ignorance? It was by Nature's law that he grew to manhood, and if infancy can be happy without wisdom, a foolish and superstitious man cannot hope for the same happiness. Those who saw " old Proteus rising from the sea " may or may not have been happier than we are; we, at any rate, should be none the happier for seeing him. But the triumph of the Christian Church is that it is *there*,—that the most daring of all speculative dreams, instead of being found impracticable, has been carried into effect, and, when carried into effect, instead of being confined to a few select spirits, has spread itself over a vast space of the earth's surface, and, when thus diffused instead of giving place after an age or two to something more adapted to a later time, has endured for two thousand years, and, at the end of two thousand years, instead of lingering as a mere wreck spared by the tolerance of the lovers of the past, still displays vigour and a capacity of adjusting itself to new conditions, and lastly, in all the transformations it undergoes, remains visibly the same thing and inspired by its Founder's universal and unquenchable spirit.

It is in this and not in any freedom from abuses that the divine power of Christianity appears. Again, it is in this, and not in any completeness or all-sufficiency. It is a common mistake of Christians to represent their faith as alone valuable and as, by itself, containing all that man can want or can desire. But it is only one of many revelations, and is very insufficient by itself for man's happiness. Some of the men in whom the Christian spirit has been strongest have been among the most miserable of the race; some nations have imbibed it deeply and have not been led by it to happiness and power, but have only been consoled by it in degradation. Happiness wants besides some physical conditions, animal health and energy; it wants also much prudence, knowledge of physical facts, and resource. To assist us in arranging the physical conditions of our well-being another mighty revelation has been made to us, for the most part in these latter ages. We live under the blessed light of science, a light yet far from its meridian and dispersing every day some noxious superstition, some cowardice of the human spirit. These two revelations stand side by side. The points in which they have been supposed to come into collision do not belong to our present subject; they concern the theology and not the morality of the Christian Church. The moral revelation which we have been considering has never been supposed to jar with science. Both are true and both are essential to human happiness. It may be that since the methods of science were reformed and its steady progress began, it has been less exposed to error and perversion than Christianity, and, as it is peculiarly the treasure belonging to the present age, it becomes us to guard it with peculiar jealousy, to press its claims, and to treat those who, content with Christianity, disregard science as Christ treated the enemies of light, " those that took away the keys of knowledge," in his day. Assuredly they are graceless zealots who quote Moses against the expounders of a wisdom which Moses desired in vain, because it was reserved for a far later generation, for these modern men, to whom we may with accurate truth apply Christ's words and say that the least among them is greater than Moses. On the other hand, the Christian morality, if somewhat less safe and exempt from perversion than science, is more directly and vitally beneficial to mankind. The scientific life is less noble than the Christian; it is better, so to speak, to be a citizen in the New Jerusalem than in the New Athens; it is better, surely, to find everywhere a brother and friend, like the Christian, than, like the philosopher, to " disregard your relative and friend so completely as to be ignorant not only how he gets on, but almost whether he is a human being or some other sort of creature." [1]

But the achievement of Christ, in founding by his single will and power a structure so durable and so universal, is like no other achievement which history records. The masterpieces of the men of action are coarse and common in comparison with it, and the masterpieces of speculation flimsy and insubstantial. When we speak of it the commonplaces of admiration fail us altogether. Shall we speak of the originality of the design, of the skill displayed in the execution? All such terms are inadequate. Originality and contriving skill operated indeed, but, as it were, implicitly. The creative effort which produced that against which, it is said, the gates of hell shall not prevail, cannot be analysed. No architects' designs were furnished for the New Jerusalem, no committee drew up rules for the Universal Commonwealth. If in the works of Nature we can trace the indications of calculation, of a struggle

[1] Plato, Theaet. p. 80.

with difficulties, of precaution, of ingenuity, then in Christ's work it may be that the same indications occur. But these inferior and secondary powers were not consciously exercised; they were implicitly present in the manifold yet single creative act. The inconceivable work was done in calmness; before the eyes of men it was noiselessly accomplished, attracting little attention. Who can describe that which unites men? Who has entered into the formation of speech which is the symbol of their union? Who can describe exhaustively the origin of civil society? He who can do these things can explain the origin of the Christian Church. For others it must be enough to say, " the Holy Ghost fell on those that believed." No man saw the building of the New Jerusalem, the workmen crowded together, the unfinished walls and unpaved streets; no man heard the clink of trowel and pickaxe; it descended *out of heaven from God.*

EVERYMAN'S LIBRARY: A Selected List

BIOGRAPHY

Brontë, Charlotte (1816–55). LIFE, 1857. By *Mrs Gaskell*. 318
Byron, Lord (1788–1824). LETTERS. Edited by *R. G. Howarth*, B.LITT. 931
Dickens, Charles (1812–70). LIFE, 1874. By *John Forster* (1812–76). 2 vols. 781–2
Hudson, William Henry (1841–1922). FAR AWAY AND LONG AGO, 1918. 956
Johnson, Samuel (1709–84). LIVES OF THE ENGLISH POETS, 1781. 2 vols. 770–1.
   BOSWELL'S LIFE OF JOHNSON, 1791. 2 vols. 1–2
Keats, John (1795–1821). LIFE AND LETTERS, 1848, by *Lord Houghton* (1809–85). 801
Napoleon Buonaparte (1769–1821). LETTERS. Some 300 letters. 995
Pepys, Samuel (1633–1703). DIARY. Newly edited (1953), with modernized spelling.
   3 vols. 53–5
Scott, Sir Walter (1771–1832). LOCKHART'S LIFE OF SCOTT. An abridgment from the
   seven-volume work by *J. G. Lockhart* himself. 39
Sévigné, Marie de Rabutin-Chantal, Marquise de (1626–96). SELECTED LETTERS. 98

ESSAYS AND CRITICISM

Bacon, Francis, Lord Verulam (1561–1626). ESSAYS, 1597–1626. 10
Bagehot, Walter (1826–77). LITERARY STUDIES, 1879. 2 vols. 520–1
Belloc, Hilaire (1870–1953). STORIES, ESSAYS AND POEMS. 948
Chesterton, Gilbert Keith (1874–1936). STORIES, ESSAYS AND POEMS. 913
Coleridge, Samuel Taylor (1772–1834). BIOGRAPHIA LITERARIA, 1817. 11. SHAKE-
   SPEAREAN CRITICISM, 1849. Edited by *Prof. T. M. Raysor* (1960), 2 vols. 162, 183
De la Mare, Walter (1873–1956), STORIES, ESSAYS AND POEMS. 940
De Quincey, Thomas (1785–1859). CONFESSIONS OF AN ENGLISH OPIUM-EATER, 1822.
   Edited by *Prof. J. E. Jordan* (1960). 223. ENGLISH MAIL-COACH AND OTHER
   WRITINGS. 609
Hazlitt, William (1778–1830). LECTURES ON THE ENGLISH COMIC WRITERS, 1819; and
   MISCELLANEOUS ESSAYS. 411. LECTURES ON THE ENGLISH POETS, 1818, etc., 1825.
   459. THE ROUND TABLE and CHARACTERS OF SHAKESPEAR'S PLAYS, 1817–18. 65.
   TABLE TALK, 1821–2. 321
Huxley, Aldous Leonard (*b*. 1894). STORIES, ESSAYS AND POEMS. 935
Johnson, Samuel (1709–84). THE RAMBLER. 994
Lawrence, David Herbert (1885–1930). STORIES, ESSAYS AND POEMS. 958
Locke, John (1632–1704). AN ESSAY CONCERNING HUMAN UNDERSTANDNIG, 1690.
   2 vols. 332, 984
Lynd, Robert (1879–1949). ESSAYS ON LIFE AND LITERATURE. 990
Macaulay, Thomas Babington, Lord (1800–59). CRITICAL AND HISTORICAL ESSAYS,
   1843. 2 vols. 225–6. MISCELLANEOUS ESSAYS, 1823–59; LAYS OF ANCIENT ROME,
   1842; and MISCELLANEOUS POEMS, 1812–47. 439
Milton, John (1608–74). PROSE WRITINGS. 795
Newman, John Henry (1801–90). ON THE SCOPE AND NATURE OF UNIVERSITY EDUCA-
   TION; and CHRISTIANITY AND SCIENTIFIC INVESTIGATION, 1852. 723
Quiller-Couch, Sir Arthur (1863–1944). CAMBRIDGE LECTURES. 974
Steele, Sir Richard (1672–1729). THE TATLER, 1709–11. 993
Swinnerton, Frank (*b*. 1884). THE GEORGIAN LITERARY SCENE. Revised 1951. 943

FICTION

American Short Stories of the 19th Century. 840
Austen, Jane (1775–1817). EMMA, 1816. 24. MANSFIELD PARK, 1814. 23. PRIDE
   AND PREJUDICE, 1823. 22. SENSE AND SENSIBILITY, 1811. 21. NORTHANGER
   ABBEY, 1818; and PERSUASION, 1818. 25
Balzac, Honoré de (1799–1850). AT THE SIGN OF THE CAT AND RACKET, 1830; and
   OTHER STORIES. Translated by *Clara Bell*. 349. THE COUNTRY DOCTOR, 1833. Trans-
   lated by *Ellen Marriage*, 530. EUGÉNIE GRANDET, 1834. Translated by *Ellen
   Marriage*. 169. OLD GORIOT, 1835. Translated by *Ellen Marriage*. 170. THE WILD
   ASS'S SKIN, 1831. 26
Bennett, Arnold (1867–1931). THE OLD WIVES' TALE, 1908. 919
Boccaccio, Giovanni (1313–75). DECAMERON, 1471. The unabridged *Rigg* Translation.
   2 vols. 845–6
Borrow, George (1803–81). THE ROMANY RYE, 1857. Practically a sequel to *Lavengro*.
   120

Brontë, Anne (1820–49). THE TENANT OF WILDFELL HALL and AGNES GREY. 68
Brontë, Charlotte (1816–55). For Mrs Gaskell's 'Life' *see* Biography. JANE EYRE 1847. 287. THE PROFESSOR, 1857. 417. SHIRLEY, 1849. 288. VILLETTE, 1853. 3.
Brontë, Emily (1818–48). WUTHERING HEIGHTS, 1848; and POEMS. 24
Butler, Samuel (1835–1902). EREWHON, 1872 (revised 1901); and EREWHON REVISITED 1901. 881. THE WAY OF ALL FLESH, 1903. 895
Cervantes Saavedra, Miguel de (1547–1616). DON QUIXOTE DE LA MANCHA. Translated by *P. A. Motteux*. 2 vols. 385-
Collins, Wilkie (1824–89). THE MOONSTONE, 1868. 979. THE WOMAN IN WHITE, 1860 46
Conrad, Joseph (1857–1924). LORD JIM, 1900. Typically set in the East Indies. 92
THE NIGGER OF THE 'MARCISSUS'; TYPHOON; and THE SHADOW LINE. 980. NOSTROMO, 1904. New edition of Conrad's greatest novel. 38. THE SECRET AGENT, 28
Defoe, Daniel (1661?–1731). THE FORTUNES AND MISFORTUNES OF MOLL FLANDERS 1722. 837. JOURNAL OF THE PLAGUE YEAR, 1722. 289. LIFE, ADVENTURES O THE FAMOUS CAPTAIN SINGLETON, 1720. 74. ROBINSON CRUSOE, 1719. Parts 1 an 2 complete. 59
Dickens, Charles (1812–70). WORKS. (*See also* Biography.)
Dostoyevsky, Fyodor (1821–81). THE BROTHERS KARAMAZOV, 1879–80. Translated b *Constance Garnett*. 2 vols. 802–3. CRIME AND PUNISHMENT, 1866. *Constance Garnett* Translation. 501. THE IDIOT, 1873. Translated by *Eva M. Martin*. 682. LETTERS FROM THE UNDERWORLD, 1864; and OTHER TALES. 654. POOR FOLK, 1845; and THE GAMBLER, 1867. 711. THE POSSESSED, 1871. Translated by *Constance Garnett* 2 vols. 861–2
Dumas, Alexandre (1802–70). THE BLACK TULIP, 1850. The brothers De Witt in Holland, 1672–5. 174. COUNT OF MONTE CRISTO, 1844. 2 vols. Napoleon's later phase 393–4. MARGUERITE DE VALOIS, 1845. The Eve of St Bartholomew. 326. THE THREE MUSKETEERS, 1844. The France of Cardinal Richelieu. 81
Eliot, George. ADAM BEDE, 1859. 27. DANIEL DERONDA, 1876. 2 vols. 539–40. MIDDLE MARCH, 1872. 2 vols. 854–5. THE MILL ON THE FLOSS, 1860. 325. ROMOLA, 1863 The Florence of Savonarola. 231. SILAS MARNER, THE WEAVER OF RAVELOE, 1861. 12
Fielding, Henry (1707–54). AMELIA, 1751. 2 vols. Amelia is drawn from Fielding's firs wife. 852–3. JONATHAN WILD, 1743; and JOURNAL OF A VOYAGE TO LISBON, 1755 877. JOSEPH ANDREWS, 1742. A skit on Richardson's *Pamela*. 467. TOM JONES 1749. 2 vols. The first great English novel of humour. 355–6
Flaubert, Gustave (1821–80). MADAME BOVARY, 1857. Translated by *Eleanor Marx Aveling*. 808. SALAMMBO, 1862. Translated by *J. C. Chartres*. 869. SENTIMENTAL EDUCATION, 1869. Translated by *Anthony Goldsmith*. 969
Forster, Edward Morgan (b. 1879). A PASSAGE TO INDIA. 1924. 972
Galsworthy, John (1867–1933). THE COUNTRY HOUSE. 917
Gaskell, Mrs Elizabeth (1810–65). CRANFORD, 1853. 83
Gogol, Nikolay (1809–52). DEAD SOULS, 1842. 726
Goldsmith, Oliver (1728–74). THE VICAR OF WAKEFIELD, 1766. 295
Gorky, Maxim (1868–1936). THROUGH RUSSIA. 741
Hugo, Victor Marie (1802–85). LES MISÉRABLES, 1862. 2 vols. 363–4. NOTRE DAME DE PARIS, 1831. 422. TOILERS OF THE SEA, 1866. 509
James, Henry (1843–1916). THE AMBASSADORS, 1903. 987. THE TURN OF THE SCREW, 1898; and THE ASPERN PAPERS, 1888. 912
Jerome, Jerome K. (1859–1927). THREE MEN IN A BOAT and THREE MEN ON THE BUMMEL. 118
Kingsley, Charles (1819–75). HEREWARD THE WAKE, 1866. 296. WESTWARD HO! 1855. 20
Lytton, Edward Bulwer, Baron (1803–73). THE LAST DAYS OF POMPEII, 1834. 80
Maugham, W. Somerset (b. 1874). CAKES AND ALE, 1930. 932
Maupassant, Guy de (1850–93). SHORT STORIES. Translated by *Marjorie Laurie*. 907
Melville, Herman (1819–91). MOBY DICK, 1851. 179. TYPEE, 1846; and BILLY BUDD (*published*) 1924). South Seas adventures. 180
Meredith, George (1828–1909). THE ORDEAL OF RICHARD FEVEREL, 1859. 916
Modern Short Stories. Selected by *John Hadfield*. Twenty stories. 954
Moore, George (1852–1933). ESTHER WATERS, 1894. 933
Priestley, J. B. (b. 1894). ANGEL PAVEMENT, 1931. A finely conceived London novel. 938
Rabelais, François (1494?–1553). THE HEROIC DEEDS OF GARGANTUA AND PANTAGRUEL, 1532–5. 2 vols. *Urquhart and Motteux's* unabridged Translation, 1653–94. 826–2
Russian Short Stories. Translated by *Rochelle S. Townsend*. 758
Scott, Sir Walter (1771–1832). WORKS.
Shelley, Mary Wollstonecraft (1797–1851). FRANKENSTEIN, 1818. 616
Smollett, Tobias (1721–71). THE EXPEDITION OF HUMPHRY CLINKER, 1771. 975. PEREGRINE PICKLE, 1751. 2 vols. 838–9. RODERICK RANDOM, 1742. 790
Stendhal (pseudonym of Henri Beyle, 1783–1842). SCARLET AND BLACK, 1831. Translated by *C. K. Scott Moncrieff*. 2 vols. 945–6
Stevenson, Robert Louis (1850–94). DR JEKYLL AND MR HYDE, 1886; THE MERRY MEN, 1887; WILL O' THE MILL, 1878; MARKHEIM, 1886; THRAWN JANET, 1881; OLALLA, 1885; THE TREASURE OF FRANCHARD. 767. THE MASTER OF BALLANTRAE,

2

1869; WEIR OF HERMISTON, 1896. 764. ST IVES, 1898. Completed by Sir Arthur Quiller-Couch. 904.   TREASURE ISLAND, 1883; and NEW ARABIAN NIGHTS, 1886. 763
les of Detection. Nineteen stories. 928
Thackeray, William Makepeace (1811–63). HENRY ESMOND, 1852. 73. THE NEWCOMES, 1853–5. 2 vols. 465–6. PENDENNIS, 1848–50. 2 vols. 425–6. VANITY FAIR, 1847–8. 298. THE VIRGINIANS, 1857–9. 2 vols. 507–8
Tolstoy, Count Leo (1828–1910). ANNA KARENINA, 1873–7. Translated by *Rochelle S. Townsend*. 2 vols. 612–13.   MASTER AND MAN, 1895; and OTHER PARABLES AND TALES. 469.   WAR AND PEACE, 1864–9. 3 vols. 525–7
Trollope, Anthony (1815–82). THE WARDEN, 1855. 182. BARCHESTER TOWERS, 1857. 30. DOCTOR THORNE, 1858. 360. FRAMLEY PARSONAGE, 1861. 181. THE SMALL HOUSE AT ALLINGTON, 1864, 361. THE LAST CHRONICLE OF BARSET, 1867. 2 vols. 391–2
Twain, Mark (pseudonym of Samuel Langhorne Clemens, 1835–1910). TOM SAWYER, 1876; and HUCKLEBERRY FINN, 1884. 976
Verne, Jules (1828–1905). FIVE WEEKS IN A BALLOON, 1862, translated by *Arthur Chambers*; and AROUND THE WORLD IN EIGHTY DAYS, translated by *P. Desages*. 779. TWENTY THOUSAND LEAGUES UNDER THE SEA, 1869. 319
Wells, Herbert George (1866–1946). ANN VERONICA, 1909. 977.   THE WHEELS OF CHANCE, 1896; and THE TIME MACHINE, 1895. 915
Woolf, Virginia (1882–1941). TO THE LIGHTHOUSE, 1927. 949

HISTORY

Creasy, Sir Edward (1812–78). FIFTEEN DECISIVE BATTLES OF THE WORLD, 1852. 300
Gibbon, Edward (1737–94). THE DECLINE AND FALL OF THE ROMAN EMPIRE, 1776–88. Complete text. 6 vols. 434–6, 474–6
Macaulay, Thomas Babington, Baron (1800–59). THE HISTORY OF ENGLAND. 4 vols. 34–7
Voltaire, François Marie Arouet de (1694–1778). THE AGE OF LOUIS XIV, 1751. Translated by *Martyn P. Pollack*. 780

LEGENDS AND SAGAS

Chrétien de Troyes (fl. 12th cent.). ARTHURIAN ROMANCES. 698
Kalevala, or The Land of Heroes. Translated by *W. F. Kirby*. 2 vols. 259–60
Njal's Saga. THE STORY OF BURNT NJAL (written about 1280–90). Translated from the Icelandic by *Sir G. W. Dasent* (1861). 558

POETRY AND DRAMA

Anglo-Saxon Poetry. A.D. 650 to 1000. Translated by *Prof. R. K. Gordon*, M.A. 794
Ballads, A Book of British. 572
Beaumont, Francis (1584–1616), and **Fletcher, John** (1579–1625). SELECT PLAYS. 506
Blake, William (1757–1827). POEMS AND PROPHECIES. Edited by *Max Plowman*. 792
Browning, Robert (1812–89). POEMS AND PLAYS, 1833–64. 2 vols. 41–2. THE RING AND THE BOOK, 1868–9. 502. POEMS, 1871–90. 2 vols. 964, 966
Century. A CENTURY OF HUMOROUS VERSE, 1850–1950. 813
Chaucer, Geoffrey (c. 1343–1400). CANTERBURY TALES. New standard text edited by *A. C. Cawley*, M.A., PH.D. 307.   TROILUS AND CRISEYDE. 992
Cowper, William (1731–1800). POEMS. 872
Dryden, John (1631–1700). POEMS. Edited by *Bonamy Dobrée*, O.B.E., M.A. 910
Goethe, Johann Wolfgang von (1749–1832). FAUST. Both parts of the tragedy, in the re-edited translation of *Sir Theodore Martin*. 335
Goldsmith, Oliver (1728–74). POEMS AND PLAYS. Edited by *Austin Dobson*. 415
Homer (? ninth century B.C.). ILIAD. New verse translation by *S. O. Andrew* and *Michael Oakley*. 453.   ODYSSEY. The new verse translation (first published 1953) by *S. O. Andrew*. 454
Ibsen, Henrik (1828–1906). BRAND, a poetic drama. 1866. Translated by *F. E. Garrett*. 716. A DOLL'S HOUSE, 1879; THE WILD DUCK, 1884; and THE LADY FROM THE SEA, 1888. Translated by *R. Farquharson Sharp* and *Eleanor Marx-Aveling*. 494.   GHOSTS, 1881; THE WARRIORS AT HELGELAND, 1857; and AN ENEMY OF THE PEOPLE, 1882. Translated by *R. Farquharson Sharp*. 552.   PEER GYNT, 1867. Translated by *R. Farquharson Sharp*. 747.   THE PRETENDERS, 1864; PILLARS OF SOCIETY, 1877; and ROSMERSHOLM, 1887. Translated by *R. Farquharson Sharp*. 659
Ingoldsby Legends. Edited by *D. C. Browning*, M.A., B.LITT. 185
International Modern Plays. 989
Marlowe, Christopher (1564–93). PLAYS AND POEMS. New edition by *M. R. Ridley*, M.A. 383
Milton, John (1608–74). POEMS. New edition by *Prof. B. A. Wright*, M.A. 384
Molière, Jean Baptiste de (1622–73). COMEDIES. 2 vols. 830–1
Poems of our Time. An Anthology edited by *Richard Church*, C.B.E., *M. M. Bozman* and *Edith Sitwell*, D.LITT., D.B.E. Nearly 400 poems by about 130 poets. 981

Rossetti, Dante Gabriel (1828–82). POEMS. 6
Shakespeare, William (1564–1616). A Complete Edition. Cambridge Text. Glossar
    3 vols. Comedies. 153; Histories. Poems and Sonnets, 154; Tragedies, 155
Spenser, Edmund (1552–99). THE FAERIE QUEENE. Glossary. 2 vols. 443–4.   Tl
    SHEPHERD'S CALENDAR, 1579; and OTHER POEMS. 879
Synge, J. M. (1871–1909). PLAYS, POEMS AND PROSE. 9
Tchekhov, Anton (1860–1904). PLAYS AND STORIES. 9
Twenty-four One-Act Plays. 9
Webster, John (1580 ?–1625 ?), and **Ford, John** (1586–1639). SELECTED PLAYS. 8
Wilde, Oscar (1854–1900). PLAYS, PROSE WRITINGS AND POEMS. 8
Wordsworth, William (1770–1850). POEMS. Ed. *Philip Wayne*, M.A. 3 vols. 203, 311, 99

RELIGION AND PHILOSOPHY

Aristotle (384–322 B.C.). POLITICS, etc. Edited and translated by *John Warringto*
    605. METAPHYSICS. Edited and translated by *John Warrington*. 1000
Berkeley, George (1685–1753). A NEW THEORY OF VISION, 1709. 48
Browne, Sir Thomas (1605–82). RELIGIO MEDICI, 1642. 9
Bunyan, John (1628–88). GRACE ABOUNDING 1666; and THE LIFE AND DEATH OF M
    BADMAN, 1658. 81
Burton, Robert (1577–1640). THE ANATOMY OF MELANCHOLY. 1621. 3 vols. 886–
Chinese Philosophy in Classical Times. Covering the period 1500 B.C.–A.D. 100. 97
Descartes, René (1596–1650). A DISCOURSE ON METHOD, 1637; MEDITATIONS ON TH
    FIRST PHILOSOPHY, 1641; and PRINCIPLES OF PHILOSOPHY, 1644. Translated b
    Prof. J. Veitch. 57
Hobbes, Thomas (1588–1679). LEVIATHAN, 1651. 69
Hooker, Richard (1554–1600). OF THE LAWS OF ECCLESIASTICAL POLITY, 1597. 2 vols
    201
Koran, The. *Rodwell's* Translation, 1861. 38
Law, William (1686–1761). A SERIOUS CALL TO A DEVOUT AND HOLY LIFE, 1728. 9
Leibniz, Gottfried Wilhelm (1646–1716). PHILOSOPHICAL WRITINGS. Selected and trans
    lated by *Mary Morris.* 90
Locke, John (1632–1704). TWO TREATISES OF CIVIL GOVERNMENT, 1690. 75
Marcus Aurelius (121–80). MEDITATIONS. *A. S. L. Farquharson* Translation.
Mill, John Stuart (1806–73). UTILITARIANISM, 1863; LIBERTY, 1859; and REPRE
    SENTATIVE GOVERNMENT, 1861. 48
Paine, Thomas (1737–1809). RIGHTS OF MAN, 1792. 71
Plato (427–347 B.C.). THE LAWS. *A. E. Taylor* (1869–1945) Translation. 275. TH
    REPUBLIC. Translated by *A. D. Lindsay* C.B.E., LL.D. 64. THE TRIAL AND DEATH
    OF SOCRATES. 457
Saint Augustine (353–430). CONFESSIONS. *Dr Pusey's* Translation, 1838. 200. THE
    CITY OF GOD. Complete text. 2 vols. 982–3
Saint Francis (1182–1226). THE LITTLE FLOWERS; THE MIRROR OF PERFECTION (by
    Leo of Assisi); and THE LIFE OF ST FRANCIS (by St Bonaventura). 48
Spinoza, Benedictus de (1632–77). ETHICS, 1677, etc. Translated by *Andrew Boyle*. 48

SCIENCE

Darwin, Charles (1809–82). THE ORIGIN OF SPECIES, 1859. Embodies Darwin's fina
    additions. 811
Eddington, Arthur Stanley (1882–1944). THE NATURE OF THE PHYSICAL WORLD, 1928.
    922
Marx, Karl (1818–83). CAPITAL, 1867. Translated by *Eden* and *Cedar Paul*. 2 vols.
    848–9
Owen, Robert (1771–1858). A NEW VIEW OF SOCIETY, 1813; and OTHER WRITINGS. 799
Smith, Adam (1723–90). THE WEALTH OF NATIONS, 1766. 2 vols. 412–13
Wollstonecraft, Mary (1759–97), THE RIGHTS OF WOMAN, 1792; and **Mill, John Stuart**
    (1806–73), THE SUBJECTION OF WOMEN, 1869. 825

TRAVEL AND TOPOGRAPHY

Borrow, George (1803–81). THE BIBLE IN SPAIN, 1842. 151. WILD WALES, 1862. 49
Boswell, James (1740–95). JOURNAL OF A TOUR TO THE HEBRIDES WITH SAMUEL
    JOHNSON, 1786. 387
Calderón de la Barca, Mme (1804–82). LIFE IN MEXICO, 1843. 664
Cobbett, William (1762–1835). RURAL RIDES, 1830. 2 vols. 638–9
Darwin, Charles (1809–82). THE VOYAGE OF THE 'BEAGLE', 1839. 104
Kinglake, Alexander (1809–91). EOTHEN, 1844. 337
Polo, Marco (1254–1324). TRAVELS. 306
Portuguese Voyages, 1498–1663. Edited by *Charles David Ley*. 986
Stow, John (1525 ?–1605). THE SURVEY OF LONDON. Elizabethan London. 589